Vanilla Vocabulary

A Visualized/Verbalized Vocabulary Book

Level II

featuring

Gunny and Ivan

by

Nanci Bell and Phyllis Lindamood

Illustrations
Phyllis Lindamood

Design Consultant & Typesetter
Patrick Misner

Acknowledgements
Vicki and Nels Hanson for creativity with the visualization sentences.
Kirk Lindamood for final editing and rare humor.

ISBN 0-945-856-03-2

Dedication

To our Patty, the Queen of Vocabulary.
Try to find a word she doesn't know. Go ahead.

Preface

The Purpose of the book

This is a workbook to develop vocabulary through imagery—visualizing and verbalizing. And it works.

In our clinical practice with children and adults, including speakers of English as a Second Language (ESL), we struggled to locate a specific methodology to develop vocabulary. Why? Because oral vocabulary is a critical factor in language comprehension and expression. Without well developed vocabulary, accurate and confident decoding can be useless. Without well developed vocabulary, vivid and connected concept imagery for language comprehension can also be useless.

As we looked at vocabulary development, the questions for us were numerous. How do we store meanings of words in our brain? What is the cognitive function(s) we use? How can we stimulate vocabulary effectively and efficiently, and speed-up the acquisition of it?

So we thought and talked and read about vocabulary. And the answer we came up with can be easily experienced by you. Try it. Ask yourself what works in your brain when you think of a concrete word. Try the word "recital." What happened in your brain? Try an easier word—"horse." Try "cat." Try "tiger." Are you noticing that you image—visualize? For "recital" did you see a girl playing a piano or a boy the violin or an adult the cello?

We attach meaning to language through images. Now try "pusillanimous." Many of you won't have meaning for that word because you won't have images for it. The same is true for foreign languages. Try *megiza*, a word in the Ojibway language. No meaning? No images. But *megiza* means *eagle*. Now do you have meaning? Images. You can see and hear the gestalt of a word, perceiving all the phonemes in it, but without an image for meaning the oral and written symbol is meaningless.

So, from our own experience we can know the link between imagery and vocabulary. If we need verification, much is written on the subject. In 1930, John Dewey made this interesting observation: "Symbols are a necessity in mental development, but they have their place as tools for economizing effort; presented by themselves they are a mass of meaningless and arbitrary ideas imposed from without. **The image is the great instrument of instruction.** What a child gets out of any subject presented to him is simply the images which he himself forms with regard to it. If nine-tenths of the energy at present directed towards making the child learn certain things were spent in seeing to it that the child was forming proper images, the work of instruction would be indefinitely facilitated."

Allan Paivio, a prominent cognitive psychologist, theorizes that imagery and language are the two halves of our dual coding system—*for all our cognition.* Paivio (1986) said, **"The dual coding interpretation is straightforward. The concrete descriptive tasks require a high degree of referential exchange between the verbal and imagery systems."**

It is clear that images store meaning for concrete words, but what about abstract words, things that can't be "seen"? Paul Worthington in his forthcoming book *The Journey to Know* continues to provide some interesting analysis. "The anthropological perspective is that there are three levels of perception: 1) the real thing; 2) the mental representation—image—that is the next level away and as close as you can get to the real thing; and finally 3) the oral and written representation. For example, the ability to comprehend words moves from the concrete to the abstract. A concrete word's beginning is grounded in the real world with the object, the "thing" that exists. There is a real pen that I am writing with. It has shape, substance, etc. If I put this pen down and leave the room, the pen does not cease to exist, it is just *once removed* in my brain from the real thing. It now becomes my mental representation of the pen. The image. Finally there is the word **pen** *twice removed* from the real thing. The written or spoken word "pen" is only a symbolically pre-agreed-upon orthographic or speech code used by my brain—our brains—to create a representation to get to the real thing. And, as we move from the more concrete to the more abstract, the essential coding functions do not change. Acquiring an abstract vocabulary word requires utilizing some form of concrete imagery."

Think about it. Our concrete images interact in relationships to represent abstraction. For example, to have meaning for *freedom*, we can image animals free in the countryside. In addition, we can use other senses of imagery, besides visual imagery. We may imagine a sound, a sensation, an emotion. The richer and stronger our images, the more solid our grasp of meaning. Thus, the need for rich, vivid images for the words in this book.

As Albert Einstein said, "If I can't picture it, I can't understand it."

How to Use the Book

To stimulate vocabulary through imagery we knew we had to be sure each word was imaged and "languaged"—dual coded. Thus each word had to be 1) **visualized and verbalized,** then 2) **experienced in context.** In order to accommodate the above steps, this book has two specific parts: The Dictionary and The Vignettes.

Each individual should have his own book (we'll refer to the individual as "he" to save time and space, and stimulate your imagery). This will enable him to visualize and verbalize, create his own sentences, and enjoy the vignettes that further stimulate imagery. Here's how to use it:

The Vanilla Vocabulary Dictionary

1. Each word has a definition and high imagery sentences for the individual to **visualize**. Question for imagery, don't assume it. He must **verbalize** and gesture what he visualizes. See the book *Visualizing/Verbalizing for Language Comprehension and Thinking.* (A great book.)

2. After that he **verbalizes** his *own sentence* and, if possible, writes the sentence on the lines provided for "Verbalizing." The goal is for his sentence to be 1) personal, using the word in a context familiar to him, 2) descriptive by comparison, and 3) humorous or vivid or exaggerated. For example, here is a *bad* sentence for the word immense: "The tree was immense." The sentence can so easily be modified to a *good* sentence: "The immense redwood tree was as large as the tall skyscraper." *And, this sentence will further stimulate vivid imagery, and better storage and retrieval!*

The Gunny and Ivan Vignettes

1. The Gunny/Ivan Vignettes, besides adding humor and fun to the task of learning, have a very specific purpose. They allow the individual to **experience** the words in context—a very important means of garnering vocabulary. Individuals learn vocabulary by being around people who use higher level vocabulary—the exposure method. The Gunny and Ivan Vignettes offer exposure and experience with the words previously visualized and verbalized.

Some Additional Stimulation

1. "Vanilla Vocabulary Cards" can be created for trouble words. Simply created on 3X5 cards, the vocab word is on one side and the definition and personal sentence, with a blank for the word, on the other. The blank allows him to hypothesize, and visualize from context, the word being learned. Thus, he can practice from both sides of the card. The cards can then be grouped in piles of "fast, medium, slow, " and practiced.

2. In order for expressive vocabulary to be developed, individuals must begin to use the words in conversation. He can be encouraged to use new words by playing the "Vanilla Vocabulary Challenge." Here's how: He and a partner agree on the five words for the week or day, then the challenge is to use those words in front of his partner in conversation. Whenever he uses one of the words he nudges her, winks, makes meaningful eye contact, or clicks his tongue! Something that calls attention to his success. He and she can even keep points.

Summary

This book develops vocabulary through imagery. It is for teachers, parents, or individuals for self-teaching. A dictionary of approximately 4th through 6th grade words, it is to be **visualized and verbalized** and then **experienced** through the Gunny and Ivan Vignettes.

There will be (perhaps *is* by the time you read this) a series of Vanilla Vocabulary books: Level I (approximately 1st through 3rd grade), Level III (approximately 7th through 9th grade), and Level IV (approximately 10th through Adult). We are also creating additional Gunny/Ivan story books of Level II vocabulary in order to offer further exposure, experience, and imagery with the words in context. But, we are most excited about the audio tapes of Gunny and Ivan that will *stimulate concept imagery* as well as develop vocabulary.

We hope that individuals of all ages, from all backgrounds, will be assisted in increasing their oral vocabulary. Most importantly, we hope they will learn a tool—conscious use of imagery—to acquire new vocabulary *beyond* the pages of the *Vanilla Vocabulary Books*.

Nanci Bell and Phyllis Lindamood

Table of Contents

Chapter 1

The A's

ability: the power to do something

Visualize...

1. A monkey has the *ability* to peel a banana with its hands.
2. Superman has the *ability* to fly and to leap tall buildings with a single bound.
3. Greg has more *ability* in football than I do. He can run faster and tackle harder.
4. "You have the *ability* to do much better," Bill's mother said when she saw his report card.

and Verbalize...

_____

_____

_____

abundant: a lot; more than enough

Visualize...

1. Long ago wild game was *abundant* and the Indians had plenty of fresh meat.
2. Dan and Della walked hand in hand among the *abundant* flowers and blooming trees.
3. The pond has *abundant* water for all the cows in the pasture.
4. There was an *abundant* amount of money—enough to build new classrooms and a new library too.

and Verbalize...

_____

_____

_____

A

access: the ability or right to enter or use

Visualize...

1. The open gate gave Bob *access* to the playground and he ran across the grass to the swings.
2. Jerome's summer home has *access* to the beach. His back door is 20 feet from the waves!
3. The banker didn't have *access* to Mr. Wong's money because the safe was locked until morning.
4. "I don't have *access* to my father's car," Tim said. "He won't let me drive it until I'm 17."

and Verbalize...

_____

_____

_____

accompany: to go along with

Visualize...

1. Mary's parents always *accompany* her when she goes trick-or-treating on Halloween.
2. No one wanted to *accompany* Bob, so he went to the movies alone.
3. Fred *accompanied* June when she went to the dentist so she wouldn't be nervous.
4. Mary's dog always tries to *accompany* her when she walks to school.

and Verbalize...

_____

_____

_____

accomplish: to do or complete

Visualize...

1. Pam did all of her yard work in one hour. She *accomplished* it very quickly.
2. Dan saved all his money for a year and finally *accomplished* his goal of buying a bike.
3. All the kids helped paint the class mural in order to *accomplish* the work before Christmas.
4. "I can't *accomplish* anything with all this noise," Tom said. "I'll have to go to the library to study."

and Verbalize...

_____

_____

_____

accumulate: to gather or pile up

Visualize...

1. As the autumn wind blew, fallen leaves began to *accumulate* on the lawn.
2. Spider webs began to *accumulate* across the windows of the empty house.
3. José put money in the bank every week and it *accumulated* until he had $100.
4. "Those dirty plates are going to *accumulate* in the sink if you don't wash them soon," Tim's mother warned him.

and Verbalize...

_____

_____

_____

accurate: correct

Visualize...

1. Mr. Green pointed to the math problems on the blackboard. "Are these numbers all *accurate*, or are some of them wrong?" he asked.
2. Dr. Gray's thermometer is very precise and always shows an *accurate* temperature.
3. Jane checks her facts carefully to make sure her reports are *accurate*.
4. "Oh no," Phil groaned. "If this gas gauge is *accurate*, our car will run out of gas before we get to the next corner!"

and Verbalize...

_____

_____

_____

ache: a dull or constant pain (n)

Visualize...

1. Harry gets an *ache* in his teeth every time he drinks something cold.
2. Rod got a bad *ache* in his lower back when he tried to lift the sofa by himself.
3. When Tim eats ice cream too fast, he begins to get an *ache* across the back of his head.
4. The doctor asked the injured football player, "When I touch your knee like this, do you feel a sharp pain or a dull *ache*?"

and Verbalize...

_____

_____

_____

A

ache: to hurt with a dull or constant pain (v)

Visualize...

1. Ruby slipped and hurt her knee and now it *aches* all night long.
2. Does your ear still *ache* or did those ear drops stop the pain?
3. Lucy's sore foot stopped *aching* when she soaked it in a pan of hot water.
4. "My heart *aches* now that we're apart," the prince wrote to the princess.

and Verbalize...

_____

_____

_____

achieve: to gain through effort or work

Visualize...

1. On his birthday the 120-year-old man *achieved* his goal of being the oldest man alive.
2. Mary hopes to *achieve* her dream of becoming a movie star.
3. "After *achieving* so much, this is a terrible thing," said the ice skater when she broke her leg.
4. Magic Johnson *achieved* world fame with his great skills in basketball.

and Verbalize...

_____

_____

_____

achievement: something that has been gained or accomplished through great effort

Visualize...

1. Jeff's *achievement* was to finish four years of high school in three years.
2. Raising three children and sending them to college was my father's proudest *achievement*.
3. Painting the fence was only a small *achievement*, but Ted felt proud of it anyway.
4. What's your greatest *achievement*—hitting 50 home runs or stealing 80 bases?

and Verbalize...

_____

_____

_____

acrobat: a person who can do hard tricks like tumbling and balancing

Visualize...

1. The *acrobat* ran across the rubber mat and turned two somersaults in the air.
2. Bill learned to be a good *acrobat* in gym class last year.
3. The circus *acrobat* stood on his hands while he rode a big white horse around the ring.
4. The little dog jumped into the air like an *acrobat*, catching the frisbee in his teeth.

and Verbalize...

_____

_____

_____

active: moving around or doing something a lot; lively, full of energy

Visualize...

1. My grandfather is still very *active*. He swims, runs, and goes bowling.
2. At night our cat is *active*, roaming the neighborhood, but in the daytime all he does is sleep.
3. The *active* child began to make his mother tired. "How about a little nap?" she said.
4. "Is that as *active* as your dog gets?" Ruby asked, pointing at Spot as he walked slowly toward his bowl of food.

and Verbalize...

_____

_____

_____

adore: to love very much

Visualize...

1. Rex *adores* country music—it's the only music he listens to.
2. Della used to *adore* Tom, but now she doesn't even like him because he threw an orange at her dog.
3. Mr. Finch still *adores* his wife, even after 40 years.
4. "I love and *adore* and cherish you," Max wrote in his love letter to Susan.

and Verbalize...

_____

_____

_____

A

advantage: a better position from which to get something

Visualize...

1. In basketball, a taller player usually has an *advantage* over a shorter player.
2. In a race, it's not an *advantage* to be a slow runner.
3. One *advantage* of being a kid is that you can play outside all summer.
4. "My big muscles gave me an *advantage* over the other wrestlers," Greg bragged.

and Verbalize...

_____

_____

_____

adventure: an exciting or unusual experience

Visualize...

1. Mr. Wong had quite an *adventure* when his car broke down on the freeway.
2. Fred likes to read about the *adventures* of Robin Hood.
3. Since José broke his arm, just putting on his socks is an *adventure*.
4. "I never have any *adventures*," Mary complained. "Every day I just get up, eat, go to school, come home, watch T.V., and go to bed."

and Verbalize...

_____

_____

_____

advertise: to call attention to a product with the intention of selling it

Visualize...

1. Stores always *advertise* big sales in the Sunday newspaper.
2. Jerome decided to go see the new movie after he saw it *advertised* on T.V.
3. The highway billboard showing a woman diving into a swimming pool *advertised* a hotel in the next town.
4. Mr. Jones *advertises* his hot dog stand by giving away free french fries.

and Verbalize...

_____

_____

_____

advice: an idea you give someone about how to act or how to solve a problem

Visualize...

1. Jan needed *advice* about what to wear to the party, so she called Pam.
2. The carpenter gave Bob's father some good *advice* about fixing the leaky roof.
3. Ron followed his doctor's *advice* and stopped eating greasy hamburgers.
4. "My *advice* to everyone is to take a raincoat with you this morning," the T.V. weatherman said.

and Verbalize...

_____

_____

_____

aerial: of or in the air

Visualize...

1. The camera on the blimp gave an *aerial* view of the football stadium.
2. Ground and *aerial* photos of the big fire were printed in today's paper.
3. Monkeys who live in trees are *aerial* acrobats.
4. We took *aerial* pictures of our town as we drifted over it in a hot-air balloon.

and Verbalize...

_____

_____

_____

agile: able to move and react quickly and easily

Visualize...

1. The *agile* halfback dodged one tackler, stepped around another, and then dived through the air to make a touchdown.
2. My grandfather broke his hip last summer. He's better now, but he's still not *agile* enough to climb stairs.
3. If you want to be a professional dancer, it helps to be strong and *agile*.
4. A deer is much more *agile* than an elephant.

and Verbalize...

_____

_____

_____

A

agriculture: the science of growing food and raising animals

Visualize...

1. A farmer is someone who is an expert in *agriculture*.
2. All the fresh food at the grocery store—big red apples, sweet cherries, crisp green lettuce, fat orange pumpkins—are products of *agriculture*.
3. Rex wants to study *agriculture* because he plans to own a ranch and raise cattle.
4. "I think I'll go to college and major in *agriculture* so I can study farm animals," said June.

and Verbalize...

_____

_____

_____

aide: a helper

Visualize...

1. Dr. Gray's *aides* are her nurses, Wanda and Phil.
2. The teacher's *aide* helps me with my reading when Mrs. Smith is busy.
3. Can you tell me how many *aides* there are on General Grant's staff?
4. "I'm so busy at work I've got to hire at least two more *aides*," Mr. Wong told his wife.

and Verbalize...

_____

_____

_____

airborne: off the ground; carried by the air

Visualize...

1. The worried pilot was happy when his overloaded plane became *airborne*.
2. The strange, huge bird left its perch and was *airborne*, gliding over the city.
3. Can you catch a cold from *airborne* germs or do you have to touch something?
4. In the spring, *airborne* pollen makes Wanda sneeze.

and Verbalize...

_____

_____

_____

album: a book with blank pages for photos or stamps; a record or a set of songs

Visualize...

1. Ruby gave Mr. Martinez a stamp from Mexico to paste in his stamp *album.*
2. On rainy days we pull out our family *album*s and look at the old photos.
3. You can get M.C. Hammer's new *album* on a record, a tape, or a CD.
4. The needle jumped up and down because the record *album* was badly scratched.

and Verbalize...

_____

_____

_____

algae: tiny water plants

Visualize...

1. "Yuck!" Mary said when she saw the green scum on the pond. "This water is full of *algae!*"
2. Green and brown *algae* floated on the surface of the dirty water in the barrel.
3. Mark helped his father clean the swimming pool to get rid of the *algae.*
4. I hate it when my feet slip in the *algae* at the bottom of the pond.

and Verbalize...

_____

_____

_____

alien: someone who isn't a citizen of the country he or she lives in; a being from outer space

Visualize...

1. Beth's uncle is an *alien*—he is a citizen of France who lives in New York.
2. An American citizen would be an *alien* if he lived in Mexico.
3. "I saw *aliens!*" the little boy screamed, running into the house. "They landed in a big spaceship and they have blue arms and three eyes!"
4. "Sometimes I wonder if you're from Earth, or if you're an *alien* from some other planet," my brother said to me.

and Verbalize...

_____

_____

_____

A

aloft: up in the air

Visualize...

1. The pilot had enough fuel to keep his plane *aloft* for six hours.
2. The bird with the hurt wing tried to fly but it couldn't stay *aloft.*
3. The hawk grabbed a fish with his claws and carried it *aloft.*
4. The boy threw a shell at the sea gulls and suddenly they were all *aloft,* beating their wings and screeching.

and Verbalize...

_____

_____

_____

alternative: a choice between two or more things

Visualize...

1. When she fell into the lake, Lucy's only *alternatives* were to sink or swim.
2. The doctor told Fred to try fruit juice as an *alternative* to soft drinks.
3. One *alternative* to watching T.V. is listening to music.
4. "I don't want to go to school today," Ruby told her mother. "Don't I have any other *alternative?*"

and Verbalize...

_____

_____

_____

altitude: how high something is

Visualize...

1. A jet plane can fly at an *altitude* of 50,000 feet.
2. The *altitude* of Denver, Colorado is one mile above sea level.
3. My ears pop when we drive up a mountain road and the *altitude* changes.
4. "At what *altitude* does the Earth stop looking flat and begin to look round?" Lars asked the astronaut.

and Verbalize...

_____

_____

_____

A

ambitious: having a strong desire to achieve something

Visualize...

1. Hortense is *ambitious* to become the first woman president of the United States.
2. Don really wants to be an artist, so he isn't very *ambitious* about math.
3. Ed is such an *ambitious* man that some day he might own every store in town.
4. "Mark is a good actor but he's not very *ambitious*," the director of the school play said. "He doesn't care if he plays the king or the horse."

and Verbalize...

_____

_____

_____

ancestor: a family member who lived a long time ago

Visualize...

1. Lucy says that her *ancestors* were Pilgrims who ate at the first Thanksgiving.
2. Most scientists believe that apes are man's *ancestors*.
3. Mr. Wong says that *ancestors* are very important in China. People pray to them and put silk ribbons around their pictures.
4. My great-great-grandfather is my favorite *ancestor*.

and Verbalize...

_____

_____

_____

anticipate: to look forward to; to expect

Visualize...

1. Jerome and Bob were *anticipating* summer vacation. "In two weeks we'll be FREE!" they told each other.
2. Pam *anticipated* the trip to the beach so much that when she lay in bed at night she could almost hear the waves.
3. "Even though it's cloudy, we don't *anticipate* any rain today," the weatherman said.
4. The ranchers began to *anticipate* a good year for their cattle when the grass grew green and tall.

and Verbalize...

_____

_____

_____

A

appeal: to ask strongly for something; to be attractive or interesting

Visualize...

1. When his car stalled on the highway, Mr. Wong *appealed* for help by waving a red flag at people driving by.
2. "On behalf of hungry children in our city, I *appeal* to you for donations of food and money," Mr. Morris told the audience of rich men and women.
3. I like that new car with the glass roof and the shiny fins. It really *appeals* to me.
4. "Does this new dress *appeal* to you?" my mother asked my father as she walked across the living room.

and Verbalize...

_____

_____

_____

appetite: the wish for food

Visualize...

1. Frank was sick and didn't have much of an *appetite*. He even said no to ice cream.
2. You need a pretty big *appetite* to eat five cheeseburgers.
3. All June ate for breakfast was an apple, and by lunchtime her *appetite* was huge.
4. I lose my *appetite* when I'm nervous or worried.

and Verbalize...

_____

_____

_____

applause: the clapping of hands to show approval

Visualize...

1. There was a long round of *applause* from the audience when Madonna finished her song.
2. The loud *applause* came from 50,000 people clapping their hands.
3. After Jerome finished his speech, he blushed at the *applause* from the class.
4. "Please," said the clown, "no *applause*—just throw money."

and Verbalize...

_____

_____

_____

approach: to come near

Visualize...

1. Mary tried to *approach* the hungry cat but it ran away when she got too close.
2. Lars *approached* the ticket seller and asked her how much the movie cost.
3. When the leaves begin to fall and the days get shorter, you can feel winter *approaching*.
4. Toward sundown I saw a fleet of small white fishing boats *approaching* the harbor.

and Verbalize...

_____

_____

_____

arch: a curved shape, usually in a building or at the top of a door

Visualize...

1. An *arch* is shaped like a horseshoe.
2. We have a wide round *arch* between our living room and kitchen instead of a regular doorway.
3. The bridge across the river was held up by four stone *arches*.
4. Yellow roses grow across the wooden *arch* over my grandmother's gate.

and Verbalize...

_____

_____

_____

archeology: the study of people and things from long ago, especially through the discovery of buried ruins

Visualize...

1. Doug studied *archeology* because he wanted to dig for ancient cities buried in the desert..
2. In *archeology*, most of the digging is done with spoon-sized tools and tiny brushes, not with shovels.
3. The discovery of King Tut's tomb ranks as one of the great finds in the history of *archeology*.
4. Professor Lopez showed his *archeology* class part of a golden cup from a site in Africa.

and Verbalize...

_____

_____

_____

A

architecture: the art of designing buildings; a special building style or method

Visualize...

1. That skyscraper is a masterpiece of *architecture*—it is 100 stories tall!
2. If you want to design buildings, you have to study *architecture*.
3. New office buildings in California have the kind of *architecture* which keeps them safe during earthquakes.
4. Roman *architecture* used lots of columns and arches.

and Verbalize...

_____

_____

_____

arrange: to put something in a certain position or order; to plan

Visualize...

1. The students *arranged* their chairs in a circle so that they could see each other when they talked.
2. Flo *arranged* the flowers in the glass vase so the blue ones were in front and the yellow ones were in back.
3. Please *arrange* to take that sick dog to the veterinarian tomorrow.
4. If you *arrange* your time carefully, you should have time to work and play.

and Verbalize...

_____

_____

_____

artifact: something made by people long ago

Visualize...

1. Stone knife blades were among the many Indian *artifacts* in the museum.
2. The archeologists found silver plates and other *artifacts* when they excavated the Greek ruins.
3. Professor Lopez's collection of Aztec *artifacts* includes a stone sun dial.
4. "Don't drop that!" Agnes warned Lars. "That old brown bowl is a real *artifact!*"

and Verbalize...

_____

_____

_____

artificial: not real or natural

Visualize...

1. The *artificial* roses we make in art class are pretty, but I like real ones better.
2. Lucy's kitchen table is *artificial* wood made from a special kind of plastic.
3. The engineers built a dam to create an *artificial* lake in the valley.
4. My uncle lost his arm in an accident and now he wears an *artificial* one.

and Verbalize...

_____

_____

_____

artistic: showing skill and a sense of beauty

Visualize...

1. My mother's *artistic* use of soft colors and plants makes this room feel peaceful.
2. Mr. Wong was *artistic* in planning his yard, especially in choosing the beautiful palm trees.
3. Della knows how to cut raw carrots into *artistic* shapes like stars and flowers.
4. "Gus, your finger painting is sloppy and not very *artistic*," said the grumpy teacher.

and Verbalize...

_____

_____

_____

ascend: to climb or go up, to rise

Visualize...

1. Jerome *ascended* the stairs of the tower slowly, stopping to rest on the way.
2. The climbers were *ascending* the mountain when the thunderstorm began.
3. Bob dropped the string of his yellow balloon and watched it *ascend* into the sky.
4. "Five—4—3—2—1—LIFT OFF!" the voice on the loudspeaker said. With a roar, the rocket began to *ascend* into the blue sky.

and Verbalize...

_____

_____

_____

A

assemble: to put together; to gather or meet

Visualize...

1. It took José over 10 hours to *assemble* the model airplane because it had 200 parts.
2. Greg's new red wagon came in pieces, so his father used a screwdriver to *assemble* it for him.
3. A big crowd *assembled* in the park after dinner to hear the town band play.
4. "Let's all *assemble* in front of the school at 8:00 a.m.," Professor Lopez told his students. "The bus will be waiting for us."

and Verbalize...

_____

_____

_____

assignment: a job to do

Visualize...

1. Your father gave you a hard *assignment* when he asked you to rake all those leaves today.
2. Bill called Stan after school to ask him what the math *assignment* was.
3. Tim's father received a new *assignment* from his boss and will be traveling to L.A. next week.
4. Wanda's *assignment* is to help Dr. Gray do blood tests.

and Verbalize...

_____

_____

_____

assist: to help

Visualize...

1. Phil *assisted* Dr. Gray in setting Dan's broken arm.
2. Gus ran to *assist* his grandmother when she fell down.
3. I took Aunt Mary's arm and *assisted* her across the street when I saw she was getting tired.
4. Ruby *assisted* her father by holding his ladder as he climbed down from the roof.

and Verbalize...

_____

_____

_____

athlete: a person trained in a sport, exercise, or other physical skill

Visualize...

1. Pro football players are *athletes* who get paid for playing football.
2. Ron will be a good *athlete* because he's quick, agile, and strong.
3. When Ted hit the ball over the fence, the coach realized Ted was a great *athlete*.
4. I would be a better *athlete* if I could run a little faster.

and Verbalize...

_____

_____

_____

attain: to get by hard work, to earn

Visualize...

1. After hours of struggling up the mountain, the climbers at last *attained* the peak.
2. You have to go to college for five years to *attain* your teaching degree.
3. José's father was proud when José *attained* the rank of Eagle Scout.
4. "Nothing was given to me—I had to *attain* it all myself," Tim's brother said, then showed us his big house and his three new cars in the garage.

and Verbalize...

_____

_____

_____

attempt: to try

Visualize...

1. The swimmer *attempted* to swim across the river, but the current was too strong.
2. The four men *attempted* to climb the world's highest mountain but they had to turn back when the heavy snowstorm began.
3. The children *attempted* to fly by waving their arms like wings.
4. "Don't *attempt* to bake a cake without a recipe," my mother warned me, "or you might end up with a pancake!"

and Verbalize...

_____

_____

_____

A

attendance: the act of being present; the number of people present at an event

Visualize...

1. Mark's school *attendance* was perfect—he didn't miss a day all year.
2. I have to go to the meeting because my boss insists upon my *attendance*.
3. The *attendance* at the big game was over 5,000, and all the bleachers were filled.
4. The ticket taker counted the ticket stubs to figure the *attendance* at the masked ball.

and Verbalize...

_____

_____

_____

attentive: paying careful attention to

Visualize...

1. When the senator spoke, the audience was *attentive*. Everyone listened and no one went to sleep.
2. Mr. Finch isn't a very *attentive* driver—he often runs red lights and hits curbs.
3. The *attentive* bookkeeper found the mistake halfway down the column of numbers.
4. "You can't be *attentive* to my lesson and talk to each other at the same time," Professor Lopez told his class.

and Verbalize...

_____

_____

_____

attitude: a way of feeling toward something or someone

Visualize...

1. When Lars was in bed with a broken leg, he kept a good *attitude*. He didn't complain or feel sorry for himself.
2. Ruby's *attitude* toward June improved when she realized June always tells the truth.
3. The *attitude* of the players changed for the worse when they saw they were about to lose the game.
4. Someone with a good *attitude* is nice and positive. Someone with a bad *attitude* is grumpy and negative.

and Verbalize...

_____

_____

_____

attract: to bring near; to get the attention or admiration of

Visualize...

1. The sandwich Frank left on the patio table *attracted* a lot of flies.
2. A yellow porch light doesn't *attract* as many moths as a white light does.
3. Whenever Mickey Mouse walks down the sidewalk, he *attracts* a large crowd of fans.
4. Is it Lucy's beautiful black hair or her cheerful attitude that *attracts* so many admirers?

and Verbalize...

_____

_____

_____

attractive: pleasing, charming, pretty

Visualize...

1. Martha thought the blue silk dress with the pink butterflies was *attractive*, so she tried it on.
2. "What an *attractive* yard you have!" Mary told Mr. Wong as she admired the palm trees and the green, well-kept lawn.
3. When a man says a woman is pretty, he means that she is physically *attractive*.
4. The flower's perfume was *attractive* to the bees who buzzed and buzzed around the yellow petals.

and Verbalize...

_____

_____

_____

auditorium: a large room where people watch plays and concerts or hear lectures

Visualize...

1. Gus and Ted helped set up chairs in the *auditorium* for the school play.
2. Everyone in the *auditorium* was silent as the famous scientist began to speak.
3. Over 5,000 people attended the concert in the *auditorium* downtown.
4. The man at the door took our tickets as we entered the lobby of the *auditorium*.

and Verbalize...

_____

_____

_____

A

authority: the power to make decisions, to command, to act, or to control; a person or group having this power

Visualize...

1. A policeman has the *authority* to arrest you if he has evidence that you've broken the law.
2. A mother and father have the *authority* to decide when their children go to bed.
3. The judge is the *authority* in the courtroom, and everyone must abide by his decisions.
4. When I found the bag of dangerous drugs in my driveway, I phoned the *authorities*.

and Verbalize...

_____

_____

_____

automatic: able to operate by itself; done without thought or attention

Visualize...

1. Do you have to open the garage yourself, or do you have an *automatic* garage door opener?
2. I don't like to shift every time I change gears, so I bought a car with an *automatic* transmission.
3. Your heartbeat is *automatic*—you don't need to think about making your heart work.
4. When I smell hot buttered popcorn, I have an *automatic* reaction. I get hungry.

and Verbalize...

_____

_____

_____

average: the usual amount or kind; the number you get by adding two or more numbers together and then dividing the answer by how many numbers you've added

Visualize...

1. Nothing unusual happens on an *average* day: I ride the bus to school, walk home, eat supper, and go to bed by nine o'clock.
2. We've received 10 inches of rain this spring, which is twice the *average* rainfall for this time of year.
3. Ted had the highest *average* on the baseball team because he got a hit every time he went to bat.
4. To find the "*average*" of 2, 6, and 7, I add them together and then divide by 3. The *average* is 5.

and Verbalize...

_____

_____

_____

aviation: the science of flying aircraft

Visualize...

1. Fred studied *aviation* because he was interested in airplanes and wanted to learn to fly them.
2. The Wright brothers were important pioneers in the field of *aviation* because they were the first men to fly an airplane.
3. After I read the book on *aviation*, I knew about flaps and rudders, air speed and elevation, altitude and maximum ceiling.
4. Lindbergh's solo flight across the Atlantic in 1927 was a landmark in the history of *aviation*.

and Verbalize...

_____

_____

_____

avoid: to keep away from

Visualize...

1. Joan tries to *avoid* Ed because he always pulls her long hair.
2. Dr. Gray told Agnes she could eat vegetables and fruit but she had to *avoid* cookies and cake.
3. I *avoid* walking alone at night because the city streets are dangerous.
4. Dan's father hit the brakes and jerked the wheel to *avoid* hitting the dog that ran across the street.

and Verbalize...

_____

_____

_____

awesome: causing wonder, fear, or amazement

Visualize...

1. All scientists are impressed by the sun's *awesome* power.
2. The burning factory was an *awesome* sight. I shivered and my heart beat fast as I watched 100 windows blow out one by one.
3. The bomb's *awesome* blast knocked down every tree for a mile.
4. When Jim and José visited the naval dock, they were amazed by the aircraft carrier's *awesome* size.

and Verbalize...

_____

_____

_____

Chapter 2

The B's

bail: to dip water out of a boat with a pail or other container

Visualize...

1. Stan and Lars grabbed two buckets and began *bailing* water out of the sinking rowboat.
2. June's mother asked her to help *bail* the water from the flooded cellar.
3. Della *bailed* the water from the floor of the motorboat with a coffee can.
4. "*Bail! Bail!*" the captain shouted to his men as their ship took on more and more water from the storm.

and Verbalize...

_____

_____

_____

barricade: a temporary wall or fence used for protection, defense, or as a means of preventing entry

Visualize...

1. The police erected a *barricade* across the road to stop the bank robbers from getting away.
2. The soldiers built a *barricade* of stones, pieces of wood, and barbed wire to keep the enemy troops from crossing the border.
3. When the shooting started, all the soldiers put on their helmets and ducked down behind the *barricade*.
4. Fred made a *barricade* of sand bags so the rising river wouldn't flood his house.

and Verbalize...

_____

_____

_____

B

barrier: something that blocks the way

Visualize...

1. The concrete *barrier* down the middle of the highway keeps cars from crossing over onto the wrong side.
2. A coral reef forms a *barrier* that protects an island from the open sea.
3. Not reading well is a serious *barrier* to getting a good job.
4. "This hard homework is no *barrier* to me!" Bob said. "I'm going to ask my sister for help!"

and Verbalize...

_____

_____

_____

beetle: a kind of insect with hard, shiny front wings and thin back wings

Visualize...

1. A ladybug is a little red *beetle* with black spots on its wings.
2. "Yow!" Hortense yelled. "The black beetle in the sink is the size of a bus!"
3. The big *beetle* on the sidewalk was trying to turn over—it lay on its back and waved its legs in the air.
4. All *beetles* are insects because they have six legs and their bodies are divided into three parts: the head, thorax, and abdomen.

and Verbalize...

_____

_____

_____

benefit: to be helped by; to help make better

Visualize...

1. When I swam across the bay, I realized how much I'd *benefited* from swimming 100 laps in the pool every day.
2. When Mr. Wells was sick, he *benefited* from having a son who was a doctor.
3. The polio vaccine *benefits* everyone by freeing us from a terrible disease.
4. It doesn't *benefit* my waistline to eat 15 cookies. But who cares!

and Verbalize...

_____

_____

_____

bifocal: a glass lens for seeing close up and far away

Visualize...

1. Ruby's mother traded in her pair of reading glasses and her pair of driving glasses for a single pair of *bifocals*.
2. Some *bifocals* have a little "window" in each lens.
3. "Can you get contact lenses that are *bifocals*?" Mary asked the eye doctor.
4. Glasses with three lenses wouldn't be *bifocals* but "trifocals."

and Verbalize...

_____

_____

_____

bind: to fasten or tie

Visualize...

1. June wrapped the gift with paper, *bound* it with string, then mailed it to her sister.
2. Mr. Wong captured the robber and *bound* his hands and feet with rope so he wouldn't escape.
3. Dr. Gray used splints and tape to *bind* Fred's broken arm.
4. The pet bear was *bound* to the tree with a heavy chain.

and Verbalize...

_____

_____

_____

bound: a limiting line or area (n)

Visualize...

1. This fence marks the *bounds* of Agnes' farm. The land on the other side belongs to her neighbor, Mr. Finch.
2. Tim thought the ball was "fair," but the umpire said it was "out of *bounds*" because it landed outside the foul line.
3. Mrs. Smith told the children to stay within the *bounds* of the school yard and not go wandering into the surrounding fields.
4. Della's hopes knew no *bounds*—she was sure that someday she'd be the most famous movie star in the world.

and Verbalize...

_____

_____

_____

B

bound: to move in a jumping run (v)

Visualize...

1. Two white-tailed deer *bounded* across the creek and began running up the hill.
2. The kangaroo escaped from the pen by *bounding* over the five-foot fence.
3. The children *bounded* onto the bus that was headed for Disneyland.
4. Dr. Gray *bounded* from her car and rushed to aid the accident victim.

and Verbalize...

_____

_____

_____

bracelet: jewelry worn around the arm or wrist

Visualize...

1. The dancer wore rings on her fingers and *bracelets* on her arms.
2. Some watches for women are made as part of a necklace or *bracelet*.
3. Rod's uncle wears a copper *bracelet* on his wrist because he says it helps his arthritis.
4. "Oooh," Pam said, slipping the gold *bracelet* over her hand. "This is a wonderful gift!"

and Verbalize...

_____

_____

_____

breakthrough: an important discovery that helps solve a problem

Visualize...

1. Learning to tie his own shoes was a real *breakthrough* for Flo's little brother.
2. The splitting of the atom was a scientific *breakthrough* that changed the world.
3. The plant scientist made a *breakthrough* in his research on giant tomatoes.
4. "The discovery of penicillin was a big *breakthrough*," Dr. Gray said. "Before we had it, people used to die from strep throat."

and Verbalize...

_____

_____

_____

brilliant: very bright or sparkling; very, very intelligent

Visualize...

1. The queen's *brilliant* diamond necklace flashed in the sun.
2. The moonlight was so *brilliant* that I could see my shadow on the ground behind me.
3. Albert Einstein was one of the most *brilliant* scientists who ever lived.
4. Dan gets good grades because he studies every night, not because he's *brilliant*.

and Verbalize...

_____

_____

_____

brink: the edge at the top of a steep place; the moment just before something happens

Visualize...

1. Jerome stood at the *brink* of the cliff and looked down at the valley below.
2. The empty boat floated to the *brink* of the waterfall and then plunged to the lake below.
3. Agnes was just on the *brink* of eating some chocolate cake when Dr. Gray called and asked her how her dieting was going.
4. Mark and June were on the *brink* of an argument when the recess bell rang.

and Verbalize...

_____

_____

_____

broadcast: to send out over television or radio; to spread information widely

Visualize...

1. Is our local T.V. station going to *broadcast* the game tonight?
2. The concert was *broadcast* live on Sunday and on tape today.
3. Is KRBL *broadcasting* tonight, or is their transmission tower still not working?
4. "Don't *broadcast* this," Lucy whispered to Della, "but I think José likes me a lot."

and Verbalize...

_____

_____

_____

B

burial: the placing of a dead body in a grave

Visualize...

1. The grave-diggers dug a hole six feet deep for the *burial* of the coffin.
2. A week after the *burial* of the old man, the grass began to grow back across the grave.
3. Some cultures place their dead on towers or raised platforms instead of having ground *burials*.
4. In a *burial* at sea, the coffin is dropped into the water.

and Verbalize...

_____

_____

_____

bury: to put something under the ground; to cover completely

Visualize...

1. The pirates *buried* their treasure chest on the desert island.
2. Spot *buried* his soup bone near some flowers in the backyard.
3. The thick layer of fallen leaves *buried* the rake Tim left on the front lawn.
4. The blizzard *buried* the city streets under two feet of snow.

and Verbalize...

_____

_____

_____

business: the buying and selling of things; an agency which buys or sells things

Visualize...

1. Fred's father is in the used car *business*. He buys and sells used cars and trucks.
2. Ted wants to go into *business* instead of becoming a teacher.
3. Mr. Finch's brother owns a shoe repair *business* downtown called "Happy Feet."
4. The *businesses* in the mall stay open until 9 p.m. every night.

and Verbalize...

_____

_____

_____

bust: a woman's breasts; a statue of a person's head and shoulders

Visualize...

1. Agnes stood in front of the mirror with a scowl on her face. "This new blouse is too tight in the *bust*," she complained.
2. The average woman gains weight in her hips, not in her *bust*.
3. The Romans always made marble *busts* of their great generals and rulers.
4. "Do you want a full-body statue, or only a *bust*?" the sculptor asked the famous general.

and Verbalize...

_____

_____

_____

bustle: to move with a lot of energy

Visualize...

1. Della's grandmother *bustled* around the living room, fluffing pillows and rearranging chairs, then hurried into the kitchen to make dinner.
2. The waiter *bustled* from one table to another as he quickly took everyone's order.
3. Everything in the store was on sale and the eager shoppers *bustled* up and down the aisles looking for bargains.
4. Busy nurses *bustled* up and down the halls of the hospital.

and Verbalize...

_____

_____

_____

Chapter 3

The C's

calculate: to find out by using arithmetic; to plan

Visualize...

1. To *calculate* the answer to the hard math problem, June had to subtract, multiply, and divide.
2 "If I've *calculated* correctly," sighed Rex, "I owe my father $45.42."
3. Gus didn't *calculate* on having a test, so he flunked the surprise quiz.
4. Beth *calculated* on meeting Mrs. Smith downtown at the coffee shop.

and Verbalize...

_____

_____

_____

candidate: a person who runs for or is considered for an office or award

Visualize...

1. The two *candidates* for president debated each other on T.V.
2. How many *candidates* are running in the school board election?
3. Jane won the nomination, became her party's *candidate*, then won the race for governor.
4. The poet's latest book made him a *candidate* for the Nobel Prize in literature.

and Verbalize...

_____

_____

_____

C

capable: skillful; able to

Visualize...

1. Woody is a very *capable* mechanic. When he fixes a car it stays fixed.
2. Five days a week, the *capable* father got his children dressed, fed, and to school on time.
3. Are you *capable* of eating two popsicles at once?
4. "My dog is very smart," Ruby said. "No matter where I hide his bone, he's always *capable* of finding it."

and Verbalize...

_____

_____

_____

capacity: the amount that can be held in a space; the ability to do or be something; a position or role

Visualize...

1. The town auditorium has a *capacity* of 5,000 people.
2. This machine has the *capacity* to put the lids on 1,000 jars of olives every hour.
3. My sister is very kind and generous and has a great *capacity* for friendship.
4. In what *capacity* do you work for the city? Are you a fireman or a policeman?

and Verbalize...

_____

_____

_____

capsule: a small, thin case that encloses powdered medicine; part of a spacecraft

Visualize...

1. You can buy cold medicine in tablets, *capsules*, or liquid.
2. Ruby's little brother grabbed the vitamin *capsule*, broke it in half, and watched the vitamin powder spill out on the rug.
3. The *capsule* where the astronauts ride forms the nose of the rocket.
4. Using its parachute, the space *capsule* floated down gently toward the sea.

and Verbalize...

_____

_____

_____

captive: a prisoner or anyone held by force

Visualize...

1. The enemy tribe took four *captives*—two men and two women—when they raided our camp.
2. The six *captives* walked along blindfolded with their hands tied behind them.
3. The *captive* in the zoo cage was a tiger.
4. The young princess was a *captive* in the evil king's castle.

and Verbalize...

_____

_____

_____

caravan: a group of people traveling together, especially in the desert; a number of vehicles traveling together

Visualize...

1. The great traveler Marco Polo joined a camel *caravan* on his way to China.
2. When the desert sand began to blow, our *caravan* stopped and set up camp.
3. The school children from Germany arrived in a *caravan* of buses.
4. The friends drove their cars in a line, forming one long *caravan.*

and Verbalize...

_____

_____

_____

career: a person's long-term work

Visualize...

1. Tim's father had a long, successful *career* as a trial lawyer.
2. How many home runs did Hank Aaron hit in his *career*?
3. When Mark's uncle retired from the Navy, he began a new *career* as a high school math teacher.
4. "Have you thought about a *career* in the circus?" June asked her bratty brother.

and Verbalize...

_____

_____

_____

C

cargo: goods carried by a ship, airplane, truck, or other vehicle

Visualize...

1. The ship tied up at the pier and began unloading its *cargo* of bananas from South America.
2. The backs of the army trucks were covered with canvas tarps so no one could see what *cargo* they carried.
3. The DC-3 carried a *cargo* of medicine, blankets, and food to the earthquake victims.
4. The customs inspector checked the truck's *cargo* for drugs before he allowed the driver to cross the border.

and Verbalize...

_____

_____

_____

carnival: a fair or festival that has games, rides, and other amusements

Visualize...

1. At the *carnival* we ate cotton candy, rode on the Ferris wheel, and bought balloons.
2. Lars and Frank got scared at the *carnival* when they walked through the House of Mirrors.
3. Fred's cousin ran the merry-go-round and traveled from town to town with the *carnival*.
4. Our family reunions often look like a *carnival*!

and Verbalize...

_____

_____

_____

cartilage: the body tissue that connects bones

Visualize...

1. Ears are made of *cartilage* and skin.
2. *Cartilage* is more flexible than bone and not as hard.
3. The football player had to have an operation because the *cartilage* in his knee was torn.
4. Mr. Finch has trouble throwing a ball because he damaged the *cartilage* in his shoulder.

and Verbalize...

_____

_____

_____

carve: to cut something into a shape; to cut meat into slices or pieces

Visualize...

1. The sculptor *carved* a great stone head out of the block of marble.
2. Some experts know how to *carve* beautiful swans out of ice.
3. Susan knows how to *carve* little animals out of soft wood.
4. "Find your place at the table!" Bob's father called. "We're ready to *carve* the turkey!"

and Verbalize...

_____

_____

_____

cascade: to tumble down like a waterfall

Visualize...

1. Greg thought he was inside a waterfall when he looked out the window and saw the heavy rain *cascading* from the roof.
2. Root beer *cascaded* down the stairs when the delivery man dropped and broke the wooden barrel.
3. The river flowed over the falls and *cascaded* to the lake 100 feet below.
4. The molten steel *cascaded* from the vat when the foreman of the foundry threw the switch.

and Verbalize...

_____

_____

_____

category: a group or class of things

Visualize...

1. Lars arranged the tools in piles, one pile for each *category*: new tools, old tools, broken tools.
2. The books in my library are arranged by *category*: history, science, literature.
3. To find a book in the library, you need to know what *category* it belongs to.
4. "These bills are divided by *category*," Phil told Dr. Gray. "Car bills, utility bills, doctors' bills."

and Verbalize...

_____

_____

_____

caution: great care

Visualize...

1. Della uses *caution* when she crosses a street: she stops at the corner and looks both ways to make sure no cars are coming.
2. If Martin had been less careless and shown more *caution*, he wouldn't have gotten into that accident with the cow.
3. The warning label on the bottle said, "*CAUTION!* Keep out of the reach of children."
4. When it rains, the streets are slick and Mr. Wong slows down and drives with extra *caution*.

and Verbalize...

_____

_____

_____

cavern: a large cave, especially one underground

Visualize...

1. The men turned on their flashlights and slowly entered the huge *cavern*.
2. Carlsbad *Caverns* are large underground caves in New Mexico.
3. Tom's voice echoed and re-echoed when he shouted his name inside the *cavern*.
4. The explorer held up his torch and suddenly saw that the walls of the *cavern* were covered with sleeping bats.

and Verbalize...

_____

_____

_____

ceremony: an act or set of acts for special events

Visualize...

1. An important moment in every marriage *ceremony* is when the bride and groom exchange rings.
2. The president of the college handed out the diplomas at the graduation *ceremony*.
3. Rod's father received a gold watch at his retirement *ceremony*.
4. "If you want to be in our club, you have to go through our secret *ceremony*," the other boys told Gus. "It has to be after dark—we walk to the park holding candles and chanting our special song."

and Verbalize...

_____

_____

_____

challenge: a call to take part in a contest or fight; something that is hard to do (n)

Visualize...

1. I heard his *challenge*, accepted it, then lifted my fists to hit him as he tried to hit me.
2. Tim turned down Rod's *challenge* because he didn't have time to play a game of chess.
3. Carrying a pack for 10 miles was a real *challenge* for the new hiker.
4. It's not a *challenge* for me to eat cookies, but it is a *challenge* for me to eat broccoli.

and Verbalize...

_____

_____

_____

challenge: to ask to take part in a contest or fight (v)

Visualize...

1. Bob *challenged* Tom to a wrestling match.
2. Stan beat Rex in the 100-yard dash after Rex *challenged* him to a race.
3. The teacher *challenged* Jerome to read two books a week, and Jerome accepted her challenge.
4. In previous times, men used to *challenge* each other to duels with guns or swords in order to defend their honor.

and Verbalize...

_____

_____

_____

chamber: a room in a house or other building; a hall where lawmakers meet; an enclosed space in the body of an animal or plant

Visualize...

1. The detective followed the muddy footprints from room to room until he reached the pantry, a small *chamber* next to the kitchen.
2. Wanda visited both *chambers* of Congress—first the House of Representatives and then the Senate.
3. There are four *chambers* in the human heart: the right ventricle, the left ventricle, the right atrium, and the left atrium.
4. A chambered nautilus is a sea animal that has a spiral shell with many *chambers*.

and Verbalize...

_____

_____

_____

champion: the first-place winner

Visualize...

1. Muhammad Ali was heavyweight boxing *champion* of the world.
2. Greg was the pizza-eating *champion* of his school.
3. The *champion* was awarded a gold trophy, and the second- and third-place winners received wristwatches.
4. "Silver Bells has the legs of a *champion*," the jockey said. "I'm sure he'll win the race today."

and Verbalize...

_____

_____

_____

channel: the water between two land masses; the deepest part of a river, harbor, or other waterway; a canal; the special set of electrical waves used to send out programs from a T.V. or radio station

Visualize...

1. A part of the Atlantic Ocean called the "English *Channel*" separates England and France.
2. Boats stay out in the middle of a river *channel* so they won't run aground in the shallow places close to shore.
3. The Panama Canal is a man-made *channel* across the Isthmus of Panama. It allows ships to pass between the Pacific and the Caribbean.
4. Mr. Smith has cable T.V. and can get 25 *channels*.

and Verbalize...

_____

_____

_____

chant: to sing, say, or shout a short phrase over and over

Visualize...

1. "We're Number One, We're Number One!" the football fans *chanted* over and over.
2. The Indians painted their faces red and yellow and began to *chant* their war songs.
3. The monks *chanted* their prayers and held sticks of incense as they entered the temple.
4. "Up, down, up, down, up, down," the coach *chanted* as we did our exercises.

and Verbalize...

_____

_____

_____

character: the way a person thinks, feels, or acts; the qualities or features of something; a person or animal in a book, play, or movie

Visualize...

1. Della's *character* is a fine one: she's loyal, kind, trustworthy, and brave.
2. I like the special *character* of cedar wood—its strength, red color, and its sweet scent.
3. Mickey Mouse is my favorite cartoon *character*.
4. Scarlet O'Hara is Nanci's favorite *character* in the book <u>Gone</u> <u>with</u> <u>the</u> <u>Wind</u>.

and Verbalize...

_____

_____

_____

chasm: a deep canyon, crack, or opening in the Earth's surface

Visualize...

1. The Grand Canyon is the deepest and widest natural *chasm* in the United States.
2. Using ropes, we climbed down 1,000 feet to the bottom of the *chasm.*
3. "Is that a deep gorge?" Frank asked. "Yes," his father said, "that *chasm* is half a mile deep!"
4. The earth began to quake and then a great *chasm* opened up at our feet.

and Verbalize...

_____

_____

_____

circular: round

Visualize...

1. A wheel is *circular* but a railroad boxcar is rectangular.
2. Is the moon square or *circular*?
3. The hands of a clock turn in a *circular* direction around its round face.
4. The moon's orbit of the Earth is not perfectly *circular*.

and Verbalize...

_____

_____

_____

C

civilization: the society and culture of a people

Visualize...

1. Democracy was an invention of ancient Greek *civilization*.
2. I'm going to study the history of Mexico because I'm interested in the Mayan and Aztec *civilizations*.
3. There is no real *civilization* at the South Pole because no one lives there all the time.
4. Archeologists learn about an ancient *civilization* by studying its physical remains.

and Verbalize...

_____

_____

_____

clash: to fight or be in conflict

Visualize...

1. The children *clashed* over who would get the last ice cream bar.
2. The angry crowd *clashed* with police when the officers tried to take Superman to jail.
3. Fred and Tim *clash* every time they get together.
4. June's clothes *clashed* when she wore the purple hat, the red sweater, the orange blouse, and the bright green pants.

and Verbalize...

_____

_____

_____

cleft: a deep crack or opening

Visualize...

1. The strong earthquake left a series of *clefts* in the rock.
2. The artillery shell hit the fort and made a *cleft* in the wall.
3. There was a *cleft* in the old road, so we had to build a bridge of boards to get across.
4. Through the *cleft* in the mountain we could see the green valley beyond.

and Verbalize...

_____

_____

_____

climate: the main weather patterns of a place

Visualize...

1. I am enjoying the desert's dry *climate* after living in the rain forest of Brazil for three years.
2. Which has a colder *climate*, the North Pole or the South Pole?
3. Phil likes the tropical *climate* of Tahiti because there are bananas and coconuts to eat all year round.
4. The world's *climate* changed when the Ice Age began.

and Verbalize...

_____

_____

_____

clumsy: awkward

Visualize...

1. The *clumsy* boy knocked the fish bowl off the table as he walked across the room.
2. June didn't like to dance with Gus because he was *clumsy* and always stepped on her toes.
3. Babies who are learning to walk are *clumsy* in a sweet way.
4. "It's one thing to be *clumsy*, it's another to be careless," my mother said when I broke her favorite cup.

and Verbalize...

_____

_____

_____

coax: to urge gently

Visualize...

1. Mark held out a bone and tried to *coax* his puppy back inside the open gate.
2. Bill licked the spoon himself and then made a happy face, but he couldn't *coax* the baby to eat.
3. "I'll make some cookies if you'll mow the lawn," June said, trying to *coax* her brother to get up from the sofa.
4. "Come on," Della *coaxed* Stan. "Let's walk home together and I'll help you with your homework."

and Verbalize...

_____

_____

_____

C

collapse: to fall in or fall down

Visualize...

1. The old bridge *collapsed* and fell into the river when the heavy truck was half way across it.
2. Dan kicked the tent pole by accident and the tent *collapsed.*
3. My uncle had a heart attack and *collapsed* in his driveway.
4. Sometimes Mark's father is so tired when he gets home that he just *collapses* on the sofa and goes to sleep.

and Verbalize...

_____

_____

_____

comic: funny

Visualize...

1. The clown had a *comic* face and all the children laughed at him.
2. The movie was supposed to be a comedy, but it wasn't *comic* at all—it made everyone in the audience start to cry.
3. "Ted is a *comic* guy," José said, "especially when he talks like Daffy Duck."
4. Tom Hanks is a wonderful *comic* actor.

and Verbalize...

_____

_____

_____

command: an order to do something; having the authority to control

Visualize...

1. The soldiers received the general's *command* and marched into battle.
2. Fred gave the computer an incorrect *command* and the screen went blank.
3. The officer in *command* of the army base gave the soldiers orders to clean their guns.
4. "I want you to clean your room up right now!" Bob's mother said. "In this house, I'm the one in *command.*"

and Verbalize...

_____

_____

_____

communicate: to exchange or pass along feelings, thoughts, or information

Visualize...

1. I want to *communicate* my thanks to you for all the help you've given me.
2. Mary's baby brother doesn't *communicate* very well because he is just learning to talk.
3. Stan and Frank were talking, but they weren't *communicating*, and soon they were arguing and then shouting at each other.
4. The teacher *communicated* to the class that there would be a party on Valentine's Day.

and Verbalize...

_____

_____

_____

compact: firmly or tightly packed or pressed together; small in size

Visualize...

1. The large tent collapses and folds up into a *compact* bundle you can store in a dresser drawer.
2. A collapsed star can be the size of a basketball, but it is very *compact* and weighs more than the Earth.
3. This new T.V. set is so *compact* you can hold it in the palm of your hand.
4. *Compact* cars get better gas mileage than big cars do.

and Verbalize...

_____

_____

_____

companion: someone who is with you, a friend

Visualize...

1. Agnes doesn't get lonely because her dog King is her constant *companion.*
2. Ruby had no *companions* when she left the house. She went to the movies alone.
3. Mark and two *companions* went hiking last weekend.
4. My grandmother's favorite *companion* is her friend Martha.

and Verbalize...

_____

_____

_____

compare: to see how two things are alike or different

Visualize...

1. Fred felt sad when he *compared* his old bicycle to Jeff's brand new one.
2. Lucy *compared* the two dresses and asked her mother for the blue-and-white one.
3. My little sister *compared* her hand to her dog's paw. "Rover has five toes and I have five fingers," she said.
4. "You can't *compare* my dog to your cat," Della said. "It's like comparing apples and oranges."

and Verbalize...

_____

_____

_____

compete: to take part in a contest; to try to outdo someone else

Visualize...

1. How many horses are *competing* in the big race?
2. All the students in the school *competed* in the spelling contest.
3. I tried to *compete* with José, but he was too good a swimmer and left me far behind.
4. The twin boys *competed* with each other for their mother's attention.

and Verbalize...

_____

_____

_____

competition: a contest; the act of competing

Visualize...

1. How many runners have entered the long-distance *competition?*
2. Hortense won the chess *competition* and was awarded a silver trophy.
3. Della wants to be on the basketball team, but she doesn't know if she'll be chosen because there's a lot of *competition.*
4. The two shoe salesmen are in *competition* for customers. They both rush up to any new person who walks through the door.

and Verbalize...

_____

_____

_____

comprehend: to understand

Visualize...

1. Did you *comprehend* my instructions, or do you want me to give them to you again?
2. Greg's Spanish is poor, so he only *comprehended* half of what Mrs. Mendoza was telling him.
3. Rex read the newspaper over and over but he still couldn't *comprehend* its meaning.
4. You'll *comprehend* everything you read if you visualize it!

and Verbalize...

_____

_____

_____

compress: to squeeze together into less space

Visualize...

1. Ted *compressed* the mud into a tight, hard ball and threw it across the yard.
2. Jerome pushed a button and watched the machine *compress* a roomful of aluminum cans into a square the size of a small T.V. set.
3. "You need to *compress* this report a little," Mrs. Smith told Stan. "Fifteen pages is too much about earthworms!"
4. The mayor had to *compress* his speech when the funnel cloud approached the park.

and Verbalize...

_____

_____

_____

conceal: to hide

Visualize...

1. Fred *concealed* his money in a secret box under his bed.
2. The greedy boy *concealed* the candy bar inside his coat so he wouldn't have to share it with his friends.
3. Mrs. Thomas sewed a patch on Bob's jeans to *conceal* a hole.
4. "You should *conceal* your diamond ring in case there's a thief in the crowd," Mr. Finch warned Agnes.

and Verbalize...

_____

_____

_____

concentrate: to pay close attention to; to focus efforts on

Visualize...

1. "*Concentrate, concentrate,*" the hypnotist said as he swung the gold watch back and forth.
2. Flo's dog *concentrated* on the bone in her hand and didn't look away even when a cat walked past.
3. Tom likes all sports but has decided to *concentrate* on baseball.
4. Beth *concentrates* on her dancing every afternoon instead of playing outside.

and Verbalize...

_____

_____

_____

concept: a general idea or thought; a mental picture

Visualize...

1. The lion-tamer's new *concept* of training young tigers seems a little dangerous, especially the part about letting them sleep in his bed.
2. The *concept* of equal protection under the law is an important part of American democracy.
3. Describe your plan again slowly, so I can get a better *concept* of it in my mind.
4. Ron always has to have a *concept* of what his picture is going to look like before he begins brushing the paint on the paper.

and Verbalize...

_____

_____

_____

concert: a musical show

Visualize...

1. More than 50,000 people attended the rock *concert* in the football stadium.
2. The conductor lifted his baton and the *concert* began—first the violins and cellos, then the clarinets and French horns.
3. Everyone in the auditorium stood up and began to clap when the *concert* was over.
4. Have you seen your favorite singer at a live *concert* or only on a music video?

and Verbalize...

_____

_____

_____

condition: the way that a person or thing is

Visualize...

1. The stray cat was in terrible *condition*, especially its fur, which was matted into dirty tangles.
2. The runners didn't get tired because they were in good *condition*.
3. My old car is still in good *condition*, so I'm not going to buy a new one for a while.
4. What *condition* was Frank's house in after the tornado?

and Verbalize...

_____

_____

_____

conductor: a person who directs a musical group; a person on a train or bus who collects tickets and helps passengers

Visualize...

1. At the last minute the *conductor* lost his baton, so he had to use a ruler to lead the orchestra.
2. The band *conductor's* face was red and his hair was flying as he stood on his toes and waved his arms wildly.
3. The train *conductor* wore a black uniform and a hat with a silver band that said "*Conductor*."
4. One of the passengers called the *conductor* to the back of the bus when Martha took her pet rabbit out of her coat pocket.

and Verbalize...

_____

_____

_____

connection: the place where two things are put together; the act of putting things together; a link between people

Visualize...

1. The *connection* sparked and shorted out because the blue wire was tied to the red wire instead of to the yellow wire.
2. "I'm going to call you on another line because the *connection* is bad and I can hardly hear you," Wanda told her mother.
3. The *connection* of our washing machine to the hot water outlet took about three minutes.
4. "What is your *connection* to Fred?" Jeff asked Frank. "Is he your brother or cousin?"

and Verbalize...

_____

_____

_____

conquer: to overcome by force; to gain control of

Visualize...

1. The ancient Romans *conquered* almost all of the western world.
2. A mouse can't *conquer* a lion but it can conquer an ant.
3. At last, hungry and tired, the brave mountain climber *conquered* Mt. Wilson and put up an American flag.
4. "I'm going to try to *conquer* my smoking habit," Uncle Joe said, throwing his cigarettes into the trash can.

and Verbalize...

_____

_____

_____

conquest: the act of taking over by force; the act of gaining control over

Visualize...

1. Millions of Indians died in the Spanish *conquest* of Mexico.
2. Mark slammed his history book shut. "I'm tired of reading about the *conquest* of one country by another one," he said.
3. The discoveries of Dr. Salk led to the *conquest* of polio.
4. Sir Edmund Hilary's *conquest* of Mt. Everest was a great achievement.

and Verbalize...

_____

_____

_____

conservation: the protection of natural resources

Visualize...

1. Because the climate has been so dry, it's especially important to practice water *conservation*.
2. Ron doesn't practice *conservation*. He throws empty bottles and cans in the garbage instead of recycling them.
3. The lives of many wild animals depend on our *conservation* of forests and other wilderness areas.
4. "Whoever poured the oil into the creek didn't care much about the *conservation* of the environment," Ruby said, looking down at the dirty water.

and Verbalize...

_____

_____

_____

considerable: a lot

Visualize...

1. *Considerable* damage was done to our furniture when the roof leaked and the rain poured in.
2. A hundred acres is a *considerable* amount of land for one person to farm by himself.
3. After Agnes broke her arm, she had a *considerable* pain and had to take a pill to get to sleep.
4. "I paid a *considerable* price for that new pogo stick," Frank said, "so I want you to take good care of it."

and Verbalize...

_____

_____

_____

construct: to build

Visualize...

1. The boys used old boards to *construct* a clubhouse in the backyard.
2. How many months did it take the carpenters to *construct* José's new house?
3. Pam *constructed* a model airplane and her little sister tore it apart.
4. Did you *construct* the doghouse by yourself or did your father help you put it together?

and Verbalize...

_____

_____

_____

contempt: scorn, lack of respect

Visualize...

1. Tom has *contempt* for Greg—Tom never says anything kind to him.
2. The cruel basketball coach had *contempt* for any of the boys who couldn't make a basket.
3. The thief showed *contempt* for the police by stealing the squad car from in front of the police station.
4. "You treat me with *contempt* when you lie to me and think I won't know the difference," Dan's father said.

and Verbalize...

_____

_____

_____

C

contestant: a person in a contest

Visualize...

1. The winning *contestant* on the quiz show won a shiny red car and a trip to Alaska.
2. Della and Jerome were the last two *contestants* left in the spelling bee.
3. There were three prizes and three *contestants*, so everyone won something.
4. Every year *contestants* from all the states compete to be Miss America.

and Verbalize...

_____

_____

_____

continent: one of the seven large areas of land on the Earth

Visualize...

1. The United States is on the North American *continent*.
2. Australia is the smallest of the seven *continents*.
3. When I took the boat from Brazil to Nigeria, I went from the *continent* of South America to the *continent* of Africa.
4. Scientists believe that once all the *continents* were connected and formed a single land mass.

and Verbalize...

_____

_____

_____

contrast: a big difference between persons or things

Visualize...

1. There's a sharp *contrast* between Rex and Ted when it comes to horsemanship: Rex can ride at a gallop and Ted falls off when his horse is standing still!
2. June's sad expression was in vivid *contrast* to her usual cheerful smile.
3. The *contrast* between the noisy city and the calm, quiet country made Mr. Finch yearn for his farm.
4. The *contrast* between Pam's height and Ed's shortness made the two of them unlikely skating partners.

and Verbalize...

_____

_____

_____

cooperate: to work together

Visualize...

1. Everyone in the kitchen *cooperates* at dinner time: Pam's father sets the table, her mother puts the food on the plates, and Pam and her sister carry things into the dining room.
2. Dan tried to help the baby put on her shoes, but she wouldn't *cooperate*: she kicked her legs and curled up her toes.
3. Stan *cooperated* with the police by giving them the license number of the getaway car.
4. The baseball team never learned to *cooperate*, so it wasn't surprising that they lost all of their games.

and Verbalize...

_____

_____

_____

courageous: very brave

Visualize...

1. The *courageous* fireman ran into the blazing house to save the sleeping child.
2. Lucy did a *courageous* thing when she walked into her new school alone.
3. A soldier has to be very *courageous* to be awarded the Congressional Medal of Honor.
4. "The *courageous* acts of five brave women saved our town from the flood," the mayor said.

and Verbalize...

_____

_____

_____

create: to make

Visualize...

1. We *created* a cool place to sit in the summer by planting shade trees in our backyard.
2. These islands were *created* by the eruptions of underwater volcanoes.
3. Blowing sand *creates* a dangerous situation because drivers can't see each other or the road.
4. The opposite of *creating* something is destroying something.

and Verbalize...

_____

_____

_____

C

creative: artistic or inventive

Visualize...

1. Della's *creative* use of blues, purples, and greens made the living room look like an undersea cave.
2. "I'm not very *creative*," Agnes complained. "All I can make from a lump of clay is a lump of clay."
3. The *creative* scientist invented a car that could run on water.
4. The *creative* students used wood and cloth to make a model of the space shuttle.

and Verbalize...

_____

_____

_____

crest: the highest part; the tuft of feathers on a bird's head

Visualize...

1. Bill finally reached the *crest* of the hill and looked down at the valley below.
2. In the distance the *crests* of the blue mountains were topped with snow.
3. The white *crest* of the wave broke over the swimmer as he dived through the green water.
4. Some birds have bright *crests* of feathers on their heads.

and Verbalize...

_____

_____

_____

crevice: a narrow crack or split

Visualize...

1. A rattlesnake slithered out from a *crevice* in the red rock.
2. The earthquake made a series of long *crevices* in the ice field.
3. An elephant's thick gray skin is covered with big wrinkles that look like *crevices*.
4. "I found the missing dime," said Hortense. "It fell into a *crevice* in the floor."

and Verbalize...

_____

_____

_____

crew: a team of people who work together

Visualize...

1. The captain of the ship ordered the *crew* to swab the deck.
2. How many people are on the flight *crew* of that airplane?
3. The cleanup *crew* swept the floor of the auditorium after the big dance.
4. "Come to dinner," Mrs. Smith told Mark after he and his friends had finished painting her fence, "and bring the whole *crew.*"

and Verbalize...

_____

_____

_____

crust: the hard outside part or coating of something

Visualize...

1. Dan always cuts the *crusts* off his sandwiches because he only likes the soft inside part of the bread.
2. The tray of water wasn't frozen solid but had only a thin *crust* of ice across the top.
3. Wanda used cookie crumbs to make the *crust* of the coffee cake.
4. My mother's apple pie has the best *crust.*

and Verbalize...

_____

_____

_____

cunning: clever, sly

Visualize...

1. The *cunning* fox hid behind the tree and waited for the rabbit to come out of its hole.
2. The robber was very *cunning*: he walked into the bank dressed like a policeman.
3. Raccoons are *cunning* animals that can open jars with their paws.
4. Our dog is very *cunning* about avoiding a bath. Last time he rolled over and played dead.

and Verbalize...

_____

_____

_____

C

current: air or water moving in one direction; a flow of electricity (n)

Visualize...

1. The swimmer was nearly swept away by the river's swift *current*.
2. A strong high-altitude wind *current* blew many clouds into the sky above the valley.
3. José flipped the light switch, the electric *current* went through the wire, and the light bulb flashed on.
4. The electric saw wouldn't work because its cord was broken and the *current* from the wall socket couldn't reach the saw's motor.

and Verbalize...

_____

_____

_____

current: belonging to the present time (adj)

Visualize...

1. Susan likes her *current* teacher better than the one she had last year.
2. Is that the *current* T.V. Guide, or the one from last week?
3. You have to keep in touch with *current* events if you want to know what's going on in the world.
4. Hollywood actors who are among the *current* big stars include Tom Cruise and Roger Rabbit.

and Verbalize...

_____

_____

_____

custom: something usually done by a group of people

Visualize...

1. One of the Indian tribe's *customs* was for the men to paint their faces and sing a song about a bear before they went hunting in the forest.
2. It's the *custom* in Ted's family to give each other presents on Valentine's Day.
3. In the United States it's a *custom* to go on a family picnic or have a barbecue on July 4th.
4. I was new in the country and didn't know the *customs* of the people, so I often looked like a fool!

and Verbalize...

_____

_____

_____

Chapter 4

The D's

daily: happening every day

Visualize...

1. Martha takes a *daily* vitamin with her orange juice at breakfast.
2. We don't take the *daily* paper—only the Sunday edition.
3. "I bathe *daily*, shop weekly, and go on vacation yearly," Mrs. Smith said.
4. Tom used to go to the doctor once a year, but since he got sick he has to make a *daily* visit to the hospital.

and Verbalize...

_____

_____

_____

dart: a small arrow (n)

Visualize...

1. Wanda threw the *dart* at the target—and hit the bull's-eye!
2. "It's easy to tell our *darts* apart," Fred said to Frank. "Yours have green feathers on the end and mine have blue feathers."
3. The *darts* of the spear gun were tied to fishing lines so the fish couldn't swim away after they were hit.
4. The Indian in the Amazon rain forest used a blowgun to shoot poison *darts*.

and Verbalize...

_____

_____

_____

D

dart: to move quickly and suddenly (v)

Visualize...

1. The school of fish *darted* into the deep water when Rod waded into the lake and tried to catch them.
2. The robber *darted* around the corner before the policeman could catch him.
3. I hit the brakes just in time when the child *darted* in front of my car.
4. The halfback stopped, faked to his right, then *darted* for the sideline to catch the ball.

and Verbalize...

_____

_____

_____

data: facts, figures, and other items of information

Visualize...

1. Have you entered the necessary *data* into the computer?
2. Seismographs—machines that record movements of the Earth—provided important *data* on the recent San Francisco earthquake.
3. The scientist compiled all the *data* and then began to analyze what they meant.
4. Have the *data* on this year's forest fires been collected and organized?

and Verbalize...

_____

_____

_____

dazzle: to make almost blind by too much light; to impress with something very showy or brilliant

Visualize...

1. The bright light from the camera's flashbulb *dazzled* Lucy, and for a minute she couldn't see anything.
2. The sun's reflection in the water was *dazzling*, so Tim looked away and put on his sunglasses.
3. The chest of gold coins, rubies, and pearls *dazzled* the greedy pirates. They just stared without speaking.
4. All the men at the party were *dazzled* by the beautiful woman in the long silver evening gown.

and Verbalize...

_____

_____

_____

debris: trash; broken pieces of something

Visualize...

1. There was a lot of *debris* along the edge of the highway, mostly cans and candy wrappers thrown from cars.
2. The sea gulls swooped down and began to pick through the *debris* at the dump.
3. *Debris* from the plane crash lay scattered across the pasture: a wing, part of the tail, some broken glass.
4. Rex found a broken rudder when *debris* from the wrecked ship floated up on the beach.

and Verbalize...

_____

_____

_____

dedicate: to set apart for a special purpose or use; to present something in honor of someone or some special cause

Visualize...

1. Gus decided to *dedicate* more time to learning how to play the piano.
2. Mr. Finch *dedicated* his weekend to cleaning up his messy yard.
3. The statue of the soldier was *dedicated* to all the men and women who fought for their country.
4. The author *dedicated* her latest book to her children.

and Verbalize...

_____

_____

_____

dedicated: devoted, very interested and involved

Visualize...

1. José is a *dedicated* baseball player—he practices three hours every day.
2. If Della were a *dedicated* musician, she would practice the piano more.
3. Mr. Mendoza is a *dedicated* father who spends three hours every night helping his two boys with their homework.
4. Mary is a *dedicated* basketball fan and comes to every game and all the practices.

and Verbalize...

_____

_____

_____

D

defend: to guard or protect

Visualize...

1. The bank guard carries a gun to *defend* the bank from robbers.
2. A soldier's job is to *defend* his country when war is declared.
3. A good way to *defend* your house against burglars is to lock all the windows and doors.
4. The loyal mother hen *defended* her chicks by running at the cat who wanted to eat them.

and Verbalize...

_____

_____

_____

delay: to put off till a later time; to slow down

Visualize...

1. The umpire decided to *delay* the start of the baseball game until the rain stopped.
2. Can we *delay* the meeting for an hour so I can look at the data?
3. The heavy snow *delayed* traffic on the highway, so Mr. Finch was an hour late for his dentist's appointment.
4. The heavy snows *delayed* the climbers, forcing them to spend two nights on the mountain instead of one.

and Verbalize...

_____

_____

_____

delight: to make very happy; to become very happy

Visualize...

1. The clown's surprise arrival at the party *delighted* the children.
2. The hostess *delighted* her guests with a wonderful turkey, a ham, and a chocolate cake for dessert.
3. Bob's parents are *delighted* with his new girlfriend because she's smart and kind.
4. Flo was *delighted* with her shiny new red bicycle.

and Verbalize...

_____

_____

_____

delta: a triangle of land at the mouth of a river

Visualize...

1. The river's current carried the rich mud downstream and deposited it in the *delta*.
2. The rich farmland of the *delta* is sometimes flooded by the river when the rains are heavy.
3. We steered our boat between islands in the *delta*, then entered the river's mouth and started upstream.
4. Tim and Tom like to fish for the big striped bass that live in the waters of the *delta*.

and Verbalize...

_____

_____

_____

demonstrate: to explain, prove, or show clearly; to take part in a public meeting or parade to show your strong feelings

Visualize...

1. Joe watched while Phil *demonstrated* to Joe the correct way to of swinging a golf club.
2. The scientist used a diagram to *demonstrate* how his new invention could make electricity.
3. Mark's father held a sign and walked up and down the street with the other workers who were *demonstrating* for better pay at the factory.
4. Five of us were *demonstrating* for equal rights for all ethnic groups when we were arrested in front of the courthouse .

and Verbalize...

_____

_____

_____

depart: to go away or leave

Visualize...

1. Thousands of fans began *departing* the stadium after the game was over.
2. Electronic boards at the airport show when different planes arrive and *depart*.
3. The train was supposed to *depart* at 3:30 p.m., so we arrived at the station by 3:00.
4. The senator shook everyone's hand before he got into his helicopter and *departed* for Washington.

and Verbalize...

_____

_____

_____

D

dependable: able to be trusted

Visualize...

1. Our baby sitter is very *dependable*. She never breaks an appointment, she's always on time, and she always remembers to make the kids take their baths.
2. Gus' car is *dependable*—it always starts and never breaks down.
3. Our weatherman is not *dependable*—when he says it's going to be sunny it snows!
4. "Our milkman is as *dependable* as the sun," Rex said. "He's here every morning."

and Verbalize...

_____

_____

_____

deposit: to put money or valuable things in a bank or other safe place; to put

Visualize...

1. Mrs. Mendoza gets paid every Friday afternoon and always goes directly to the bank to *deposit* her paycheck.
2. Why don't you *deposit* that valuable jewelry in a bank safe-deposit box, instead of leaving it on your dresser?
3. Hortense *deposited* her lunch box on the drain board in the kitchen before she went outside to play.
4. "Would you *deposit* that letter in the mailbox for me?" Stan's mother asked.

and Verbalize...

_____

_____

_____

depth: the distance from top to bottom or from front to back

Visualize...

1. The *depth* of the mine shaft was over a mile and the miners took elevators to get up and down.
2. It was safe to dive headfirst into the pool because its *depth* was over 12 feet.
3. The submarine could go deep into the sea, but it couldn't go safely beyond a certain *depth*.
4. "At what *depth* did you locate the sunken treasure?" I asked the scuba diver.

and Verbalize...

_____

_____

_____

descend: to move from a higher place to a lower one

Visualize...

1. "Come down to breakfast!" Jerome's mother called up to him, so he crawled out of bed and *descended* the stairs slowly.
2. The airplane *descended* in wide, slow circles before it landed.
3. The helicopter *descended* toward the aircraft carrier.
4. The diving bell *descended* through the dark ocean waters, a long string of bubbles rising above it.

and Verbalize...

_____

_____

_____

deserve: to have a right to

Visualize...

1. Della *deserved* some of the cookies because she helped her mother bake them.
2. Pam *deserves* to be rich, because she always works hard and saves all of her money.
3. Jeff never studied or did any of his homework, so he *deserved* the bad grades on his report card.
4. After practicing hard all week, I *deserve* a starting position on the team.

and Verbalize...

_____

_____

_____

desire: a strong wish or longing

Visualize...

1. Agnes had a strong *desire* for Italian food, so she ordered a large cheese-and-pepperoni pizza.
2. Ed's sister and her boyfriend got engaged because they had a *desire* to get married.
3. The pirates attacked one ship after another because of their *desire* for treasure.
4. "I have no *desire* to fight anymore," the bloody, defeated boxer told the crowd.

and Verbalize...

_____

_____

_____

D

desolate: lonely and bleak; ruined

Visualize...

1. The ghost town was *desolate*—all the buildings were empty and the only sound was the wind.
2. The *desolate* town of One Palm is surrounded only by desert and miles and miles of cactus.
3. After the war the country was left *desolate*—open stretches of bombed land, burnt trees, cities in ruins.
4. Crumbling walls and fallen ceilings were all that remained of the *desolate* castle.

and Verbalize...

_____

_____

_____

desperate: reckless because of having no hope; very bad or hopeless

Visualize...

1. I sold my watch because I was *desperate*—all of our money was gone and we had to buy food.
2. The *desperate* refugees left the sinking ship and swam toward land.
3. The farmer's financial situation was *desperate* after the rain ruined his cotton crop.
4. The victims of the car crash were in *desperate* shape and Dr. Gray feared that some of them might not live.

and Verbalize...

_____

_____

_____

destination: the place where someone or something is going

Visualize...

1. Adam was on the wrong train because his *destination* was Boston and the train was going to New York.
2. Mr. Finch was halfway to his *destination* when his car broke down.
3. "There's no address on this letter," the postman said. "How am I supposed to know its *destination*?"
4. The falling leaves have no *destination* but only go where the wind blows them.

and Verbalize...

_____

_____

_____

determination: great willpower to do something

Visualize...

1. The explorer had lost his way but not his *determination.* He walked for days through the jungle until he finally saw a village ahead.
2. Lars had great *determination* and finished the long race even though his feet were bleeding.
3. It took a lot of *determination* and studying for Ron to raise his grades from "D's" to "A's."
4. The mountaineer showed great *determination* when he climbed Mt. Everest by himself.

and Verbalize...

_____

_____

_____

develop: to bring or come gradually into being

Visualize...

1. It took several days for the naked baby birds to *develop* feathers.
2. At first Beth could hardly throw a ball, but now she has *developed* into the best pitcher on the baseball team.
3. Professor Lopez spent many years *developing* his machine for turning iron into gold.
4. Photographers *develop* their photographs in a "darkroom"—a room with no light except a red light bulb which won't hurt the film.

and Verbalize...

_____

_____

_____

device: something made for a special use

Visualize...

1. You could become rich if you invented a *device* that pulled weeds by itself.
2. The vacuum cleaner is a labor-saving *device,* like the dishwasher and the electric can opener.
3. The *device* for cracking nuts is called a "nutcracker."
4. The old man exclaimed, "What *device* will they think of next? Now they have a *device* to send letters through a phone line!"

and Verbalize...

_____

_____

_____

63

D

devise: to think up

Visualize...

1. We *devised* a way to bring the sunken pirate ship to the surface.
2. The prisoners *devised* a plan of escape: they would use their spoons to dig a tunnel.
3. Dr. X was trying to *devise* a process that would allow people to go forward and backward in time.
4. "I've *devised* a way to fly," Flo said. "I'll wear these wings and this cap with the propeller."

and Verbalize...

_____

_____

_____

devote: to give effort, attention, or time to some purpose

Visualize...

1. Lucy *devoted* two hours a day to her piano lessons.
2. When he wasn't at work, Mr. Mendoza *devoted* all his time to his children.
3. The children *devoted* the whole summer to building the tree house.
4. Mr. Smith could have become a millionaire, but he *devoted* his life to helping others and never thought about making money.

and Verbalize...

_____

_____

_____

devour: to eat greedily and completely; to destroy with great force

Visualize...

1. The big dinosaur killed the little dinosaur and *devoured* it, every bit of it, until only the bones were left.
2. Lucy said, "I'm so hungry I could *devour* a horse."
3. The hot flames *devoured* the house and part of the garage before the firemen could put the fire out.
4. The rushing flood waters *devoured* a chunk of the river bank, and the bridge began to collapse.

and Verbalize...

_____

_____

_____

diagonal: slanted, going up and down at an angle

Visualize...

1. The crossed lines of an "X" aren't vertical or horizontal but *diagonal*.
2. A "W" is made up of four *diagonal* lines. Two *diagonal* lines make a "V."
3. A zigzag line is made up of many *diagonal* lines.
4. I made two triangles by cutting a square in half along a *diagonal* line.

and Verbalize...

_____

_____

_____

diameter: a straight line that cuts a circle in half

Visualize...

1. If you cut an orange along its *diameter*, you cut the orange in half.
2. The Earth is about 25,000 miles around; its *diameter* is about 8,000 miles.
3. Is the *diameter* of a baseball greater or larger than the *diameter* of a basketball?
4. The *diameter* of the moon is smaller than the *diameter* of the Earth.

and Verbalize...

_____

_____

_____

diet: the foods a person or animal usually eats; a special food program

Visualize...

1. Dr. Gray told the kids that their regular *diet* should include lots of fruits and vegetables.
2. Is a monkey's *diet* made up only of bananas?
3. While he was training for the big fight, the boxer was on a high-protein *diet*.
4. "Oh no," Mr. Haug said, trying to hook his belt. "It's time for me to go on another *diet*."

and Verbalize...

_____

_____

_____

D

difficult: hard to do

Visualize...

1. Is it *difficult* or easy for you to stand on your head?
2. Gus had trouble with some of the *difficult* math problems, so he decided to work on the easier ones first.
3. It was a *difficult* drive up to Strawberry Lake—the road was steep and narrow and very muddy from the last rainstorm.
4. The boat had a *difficult* time entering the bay because a strong wind was blowing and the waves were high.

and Verbalize...

_____

_____

_____

digest: to break down food in the stomach into usable forms; to understand completely

Visualize...

1. A cow's stomach can *digest* hay but a person's stomach can't.
2. Ed chewed and swallowed ten green apples but then had trouble *digesting* them.
3. It took Mrs. Smith over an hour to read and *digest* the school report.
4. My car was wrecked a week ago, but I still haven't *digested* the fact that from now on I'll be walking instead of driving.

and Verbalize...

_____

_____

_____

director: a person who supervises and guides the work of others

Visualize...

1. The *director* of the play told the actors that the sword fight didn't look real enough.
2. The hospital is run by a board of *directors*.
3. All the nurses in the hospital work under the *Director* of Nursing, a woman named Mrs. Payn.
4. The *director* of the evening news told the anchorwoman to stop for a commercial.

and Verbalize...

_____

_____

_____

discipline: control of one's actions, behavior, and thoughts; punishment given to train or correct someone

Visualize...

1. Phil has a lot of *discipline*. He gets up every morning at 5:00 and runs six miles.
2. It takes *discipline* to stay on a diet and not snack between meals.
3. The principal made the boys rake leaves after school as *discipline* for running up and down the halls.
4. What *discipline* did your father give you when he found out you skipped school yesterday?

and Verbalize...

_____

_____

_____

discover: to find

Visualize...

1. When Ruby climbed the tree she *discovered* a nest of baby robins.
2. Ted was walking in the park when he *discovered* a gold watch on the ground.
3. Susan looked through her history book and finally *discovered* the answer to her teacher's question.
4. Did Christopher Columbus really *discover* America?

and Verbalize...

_____

_____

_____

display: a show or exhibit (n)

Visualize...

1. Tom went to to see the *display* of antique guns at the museum.
2. I looked at the big *display* of cameras in the window of the camera shop.
3. There were over 200 pairs of shoes in the window *display*.
4. "Of all the *displays* at the car show, the '32 roadster was the best," Pam told Bill.

and Verbalize...

_____

_____

_____

D

display: to show (v)

Visualize...

1. Maria *displayed* her paintings at the art show in the park.
2. In order to *display* his skill, Magic put on a basketball-shooting contest.
3. Little Willy *displayed* his anger by yelling, screaming, and crying.
4. The car company *displayed* its newest model at the auto show.

and Verbalize...

_____

_____

_____

dissolve: to mix evenly with a liquid; to bring to an end

Visualize...

1. *Dissolve* this red Kool-Aid in a pitcher of water and you'll have some tasty punch.
2. I sucked the green lifesaver and it *dissolved* in my mouth.
3. The president *dissolved* the club because there weren't enough members.
4. After hearing the lies he told about me, I decided to *dissolve* my friendship with Jeff.

and Verbalize...

_____

_____

_____

distinguish: to see the difference between certain things; to see; to prove yourself skillful or admirable

Visualize...

1. The miner in the dark cave couldn't *distinguish* between daytime and nighttime.
2. Everyone needs to *distinguish* between right and wrong.
3. The people on shore could *distinguish* a faint, blinking light across the foggy bay.
4. Jerome *distinguished* himself as an excellent student when he got all "A's" on his report card.

and Verbalize...

_____

_____

_____

distrust: to not trust

Visualize...

1. Flo *distrusted* Tom after she saw him cheating off her paper.
2. If you *distrust* Beth, why did you give her the key to your jewelry box?
3. Mr. Finch used to trust everyone, but since his farm was robbed he has begun to *distrust* even his friends.
4. "It's a terrible thing to *distrust* people," Mr. Wong said, "but you have to be careful with strangers."

and Verbalize...

_____

_____

_____

diver: a person who works or swims under water

Visualize...

1. The *divers* put on air tanks and black rubber wet suits and then jumped into the blue sea.
2. The *diver* discovered the treasure chest inside the sunken ship.
3. Navy *divers* swam under the battleship, looking for cracks and holes in its hull.
4. The skin *diver* saw hundreds of green and red and bright yellow fish.

and Verbalize...

_____

_____

_____

draft: a current of air; a sketch, plan, or rough copy of something written

Visualize...

1. I began to shiver when I felt the *draft* of frosty air coming under the door.
2. Mrs. Mendoza opened the oven door and a *draft* of hot air nearly burned her face.
3. Mr. Smith drew up a *draft* of the plans for his new office, then went to talk to the construction company.
4. Ruby wrote three *drafts* of her paper before she was finally satisfied with it.

and Verbalize...

_____

_____

_____

D

drama: a story written for actors to perform; excitement and suspense, or an exciting and suspenseful situation

Visualize...

1. Lucy stayed up too late watching an exciting *drama* on T.V.
2. One of the best movie *dramas* made for children is "The Black Stallion."
3. Some court trials are full of *drama*, but many can be very boring.
4. Flo is standing at the window watching the *drama* next door: a small gray cat is about to jump on a sleeping bulldog.

and Verbalize...

_____

_____

_____

dwell: to live somewhere; to keep thinking about

Visualize...

1. Mrs. Jones used to *dwell* in the country but now she *dwells* in the city, in an apartment building not far from the park.
2. Gray squirrels *dwell* in trees but ground squirrels *dwell* in underground burrows.
3. When she's lonely, Agnes spends a lot of time *dwelling* on the past.
4. "I know you're sad about losing the chess match," Ruby's mother told her, "but try not to *dwell* on it."

and Verbalize...

_____

_____

_____

dynamite: an explosive mixture

Visualize...

1. The *dynamite* exploded with a loud roar, throwing stones and great clouds of dust into the air.
2. The construction crew used *dynamite* when they dug the tunnel through the mountain.
3. Everyone ran for cover when the brush fire reached the stacked boxes of *dynamite*.
4. "When Mr. Finch and Mr. Mendoza get together, it's *dynamite*," said Agnes. "They argue <u>all</u> the time."

and Verbalize...

_____

_____

_____

dynamo: an electric generator; a person who is energetic and forceful

Visualize...

1. How many *dynamos* does the town power plant have?
2. The dam's falling water turns the turbines of the *dynamos* to make electricity.
3. Mrs. Lopez is a real *dynamo*. She does a hundred things a day and never gets tired.
4. Mary and I are completely different. She's a *dynamo* and I'm a dead battery.

and Verbalize...

_____

_____

_____

Chapter 5

The E's

economy: the management of the resources of a community, country, etc.; the careful use of money and other things to reduce waste

Visualize...

1. The *economy* of Cuba depends on the sale of sugar made from sugar cane.
2. When the *economy* slows down, some people lose their jobs and have to look for other work.
3. "We'll have to practice *economy* all week if we're going to go to the movies on Friday," Mark's father said as he looked at his checkbook.
4. The scientist spoke with *economy* —he used very few words.

and Verbalize...

_____

_____

education: schooling, or the knowledge gained from a teacher

Visualize...

1. You have to go to school if you want to get a complete *education.*
2. People without any *education* are unable to read or write.
3. Pete received his college *education* at the University of Texas.
4. "If you don't go to school every day, how are you going to get an *education?*" asked Jake.

and Verbalize...

_____

_____

_____

eerie: strange and scary

Visualize...

1. The wind whined like someone in pain, and the tree branches cast *eerie* shadows along the wall.
2. Rod got an *eerie* feeling when he heard the door to his room creak open.
3. "What's that *eerie* sound?" Tim asked. "It sounds like a ghost dragging a chain across the floor."
4. That was an *eerie* movie, especially the part where the villain turned into a moth and flew away.

and Verbalize...

_____

_____

_____

effect: impression or feeling; something that happens because of something else

Visualize...

1. The blue and green colors in the room created an *effect* of coolness.
2. The movie director wanted more skeletons and spider webs for an eerier *effect*.
3. One *effect* of the heavy spring rains is that all the purple wild flowers are blooming early.
4. Greg's face turning green was one *effect* of his smoking the cigar.

and Verbalize...

_____

_____

_____

efficient: working well, getting good results without wasted time or effort

Visualize...

1. The *efficient* baker made ten pies in 15 minutes and popped them all into the big oven.
2. It's more *efficient* to use a rake than to pick up leaves one by one with your hands.
3. This small car is more *efficient* than that big car because it uses less gasoline to go the same distance.
4. Which is more *efficient* for heating a house—electricity or gas?

and Verbalize...

_____

_____

_____

elaborate: complicated and fancy

Visualize...

1. The *elaborate* chandelier had 3,000 lights shaped like roses, tulips, and daffodils.
2. The *elaborate* dinner began with steak, lobster, and crab, and ended with four different desserts.
3. "I like simple cotton dresses," Della said, "instead of *elaborate* ones with ruffles and fancy ribbons."
4. The *elaborate* tent had its own bathroom and kitchen.

and Verbalize...

_____

_____

_____

elder: an older person

Visualize...

1. Mary was always nice to her grandparents because her mother told her to respect her *elders*.
2. Mrs. Smith's mother has lived in this town for 70 years—she is one of the *elders* of the community.
3. The *elders* of the Indian tribe met and decided to go south before the bad winter weather arrived.
4. The islanders believed that after the *elders* died they went to live on an island in the sky.

and Verbalize...

_____

_____

_____

elevate: to raise to a higher level

Visualize...

1. Mr. Finch used the floor jack to *elevate* his car so he could crawl under it and look at the motor.
2. When Agnes has a bad cold, she uses two or three pillows to *elevate* her head.
3. The hot stove *elevated* the temperature of the kitchen so much that Martha had to open a window.
4. When people begin to argue they always start to *elevate* their voices.

and Verbalize...

_____

_____

_____

E

embed: to set firmly in something

Visualize...

1. Ted swung his hammer, *embedding* the spike deeply in the tree's trunk.
2. The construction workers *embedded* iron bars in the wet cement to make the wall stronger.
3. The antique gold bracelet was heavily *embedded* with rubies and other gems.
4. Ancient sea shells were *embedded* in the green rocks.

and Verbalize...

_____

_____

_____

emerge: to come out; to become known

Visualize...

1. The ground hog *emerged* from his hole when the sun came out.
2. At last the sun *emerged* from behind the dark clouds.
3. Last year Josh *emerged* as the best player on the football team.
4. Illiteracy—the inability to read and write—has *emerged* as a big problem in our country.

and Verbalize...

_____

_____

_____

employee: a person who works for someone else

Visualize...

1. Ms. Mendoza is not an *employee*—she owns her own business.
2. On Friday, the boss paid all of his *employees* four 2 week's work.
3. Our factory has 40 *employees*: 6 managers and 34 workers.
4. José's brother used to work at the bank, but now he's an *employee* at the new ice cream parlor.

and Verbalize...

_____

_____

_____

empty-handed: having nothing to show for your efforts

Visualize...

1. We fished all day but we didn't catch anything, so we had to come home *empty-handed.*
2. The football team tried hard but they just couldn't score—they came away *empty-handed.*
3. Tom's father was tired of working hard all year and ending up *empty-handed,* so he decided to look for a better job.
4. The boys couldn't find any ripe blackberries and had to return to the cabin *empty-handed.*

and Verbalize...

_____

_____

_____

enable: to allow

Visualize...

1. A good education *enables* you to look for a good job.
2. The big engine in his sports car *enables* Phil to drive 100 miles per hour.
3. The pay raise at work *enabled* Mrs. James to buy new skates for her children.
4. The special wet suit *enabled* the diver to swim in water that was icy cold.

and Verbalize...

_____

_____

_____

encircle: to go around; to surround

Visualize...

1. A bracelet *encircles* June's wrist; a necklace *encircles* her neck.
2. A high fence *encircled* the private grounds of the mayor's mansion.
3. The general ordered his troops to attack after they *encircled* the enemy.
4. A mob of excited fans *encircled* the movie star—all you could see was the top of her blonde head and one arm waving.

and Verbalize...

_____

_____

_____

E

encouragement: something said or done to give hope and courage

Visualize...

1. Gus' teacher told him how well he read. Her *encouragement* helped him decide to read the 500-page book.
2. My father's cheers gave me *encouragement* as I ran the race.
3. Dr. Gray gave Tim *encouragement* after his accident by telling him that soon he would be walking again.
4. Most people do better if they receive *encouragement* instead of criticism.

and Verbalize...

_____

_____

_____

endure: to put up with; to keep going

Visualize...

1. We all sat at the dinner table and *endured* another one of Uncle Bob's long, boring war stories.
2. Mrs. Jones can't *endure* the snow any more—she's thinking of moving to Florida where it is sunny and warm.
3. The runner was exhausted but he *endured* and finally crossed the finish line.
4. The wild waves crashed against the hull and swept over the deck, but the little boat *endured* until it reached land.

and Verbalize...

_____

_____

_____

enormous: huge

Visualize...

1. A mouse is small, a horse is big, and an elephant is *enormous*. It is biggest of all!
2. The 747 is an *enormous* plane which can hold over 300 passengers.
3. An iceberg is an *enormous* chunk of ice floating in the ocean.
4. Pam had an *enormous* amount of homework—three chapters to read, two papers to write, and a long page of math problems!

and Verbalize...

_____

_____

_____

entertain: to interest and amuse

Visualize...

1. My father smiled and then laughed so I knew the movie *entertained* him.
2. The clown threw a pie into the air, slipped on a banana peel, and turned a somersault to *entertain* the children who came to the circus.
3. The comedian tried to *entertain* the audience but his jokes weren't funny and everyone went to sleep.
4. The parents played cards to *entertain* themselves while the children watched "The Wizard of Oz."

and Verbalize...

_____

_____

_____

enthusiasm: a strong feeling of excitement and interest about something

Visualize...

1. The crowd cheered with *enthusiasm* when the home team scored six points and won the game.
2. Ruby was full of *enthusiasm* about her new dancing class. She couldn't wait to go!
3. At first Jeff loved baseball, but after a while he lost his *enthusiasm* and decided to quit the team.
4. Our class expressed a lot of *enthusiasm* when the teacher said that we were all going to build a boat and sail to Tahiti.

and Verbalize...

_____

_____

_____

entry: the act of entering; a place through which you enter; something written in a book, list, diary, or other record

Visualize...

1. We had tickets, so we had no trouble gaining *entry* to the concert.
2. The main *entry* to the big department store has six double doors.
3. Beth wiped away her tears, then lifted her pen and wrote another *entry* in her diary.
4. Agnes looked at the last *entry* on her shopping list and pushed her cart toward the bakery section.

and Verbalize...

_____

_____

_____

environment: the air, the water, the soil, and all the other things around a person, animal, or plant; surroundings

Visualize...

1. Pollution is ruining the *environment*—it's poisoning the earth, air, and water.
2. Parrots and cockatoos live in a tropical *environment* where it is warm and moist.
3. The library provides a calm, quiet *environment* for studying.
4. William grew up in a criminal *environment*, but he was lucky—he got an education and made a success of his life.

and Verbalize...

_____

_____

_____

epidemic: a big outbreak of a disease

Visualize...

1. The flu *epidemic* began on the East Coast and slowly spread across the country.
2. After the measles *epidemic* hit our school, the classrooms were almost empty.
3. The doctors tried to stop the *epidemic* by giving everyone shots.
4. "If we don't isolate that virus, we're going to have an even bigger *epidemic* on our hands," Dr. Gray told Phil and Flo.

and Verbalize...

_____

_____

_____

equality: the quality or condition of being equal

Visualize...

1. The idea of human *equality* means that everyone has the same right to live in dignity.
2. There would be no racial prejudice if everyone believed in *equality*.
3. Some people don't want to accept the *equality* of men and women.
4. The judge couldn't choose a winner because of the *equality* of the three contestants.

and Verbalize...

_____

_____

_____

equator: an imaginary line around the middle of the Earth

Visualize...

1. The *equator* divides the Earth into the Northern and Southern Hemispheres.
2. Mr. Mendoza crossed the *equator* when he traveled from the United States to Argentina and Brazil.
3. If you measure the length of the *equator*, you're also measuring the circumference of the earth—about 25,000 miles.
4. Is Australia north or south of the *equator*?

and Verbalize...

_____

_____

_____

era: a period of history

Visualize...

1. My grandfather and I grew up in different *eras*. In his *era* there were horses and wagons, and in mine there were cars, planes, and rockets.
2. Is that old car with the fins from the 1960's or from some earlier *era*?
3. One *era* ended and another *era* began when the Berlin Wall fell.
4. "Well, it's the end of an *era*," Stan said when the great baseball player came to bat for the last time in his career.

and Verbalize...

_____

_____

_____

erosion: a wearing away, washing away, or eating away by wind, rain, or sand

Visualize...

1. Wind *erosion* carried away the rich topsoil, and now crops won't grow in our valley.
2. The *erosion* of the pasture began when the river overflowed and washed some of the earth away.
3. After the forest fire, we planted grass and new trees to protect the naked hillside from *erosion*.
4. "Centuries of blowing sand caused the *erosion* of those curved red rocks," Professor Lopez told his geology class.

and Verbalize...

_____

_____

_____

E

erupt: to explode; to throw out hot, melted rock

Visualize...

1. A fire *erupted* in the factory when a spark fell into a can of gasoline.
2. The crowd *erupted* in a loud cheer when our team made a touchdown.
3. When the volcano *erupted*, fire shot into the sky and red-hot lava flowed into the town below.
4. The sky turned dark when the volcano *erupted* and clouds of ash blocked the sun.

and Verbalize...

_____

_____

_____

essential: necessary, basic

Visualize...

1. A wagon's most *essential* parts are its wheels—without them the wagon couldn't move!
2. It's *essential* that you graduate from high school if you want to get a good job.
3. Cream is an *essential* ingredient in ice cream. You can't make ice cream without it!
4. Is building model airplanes an *essential* task or something you do for fun?

and Verbalize...

_____

_____

_____

establish: to set up or begin

Visualize...

1. It's important to *establish* a clear goal before you can begin a project.
2. "Did Dad begin his company?" Jerome asked. "No, the company was *established* by your grandfather in 1920," his mother answered.
3. "We need to *establish* a base camp before we begin to explore," Indiana Jones said to his friends when they reached the edge of the jungle.
4. The first settlers *established* a town on the banks of the wide and peaceful river.

and Verbalize...

_____

_____

_____

evaporate: to change from a liquid to a gas; to fade away, to disappear

Visualize...

1. The sun was hot, and the water in the children's plastic pool began to *evaporate* into the air.
2. The mist over the lake *evaporated* as the sun came out, and soon the sky was blue again.
3. Ruby bought one dress after another until all her money had *evaporated*.
4. Greg's big lead began to *evaporate*, and soon Ted passed him and went on to win the race.

and Verbalize...

_____

_____

_____

event: happening

Visualize...

1. There must be some kind of *event* in the football stadium tonight because all of the field lights are on.
2. Flo thought that graduating from college was the most important *event* of her life.
3. A series of unfortunate *events*—a storm breaking the mast, the crew getting sick, the food going bad—forced the captain to turn his ship around and head for home.
4. The fall of the Soviet Union is one of the two or three most important historical *events* of this century.

and Verbalize...

_____

_____

_____

evidence: proof

Visualize...

1. When the police found the woman's fingerprints on the gun, they had *evidence* that she was the one who had fired it.
2. The lawyer presented the *evidence* to the jury and hoped they would agree that his client was innocent.
3. "What *evidence* do you have that I tracked in the mud?" Susan asked. "Hmm," she said, when her father pointed to her dirty sneakers.
4. Broad green leaves and thick stems are *evidence* of a healthy tomato plant.

and Verbalize...

_____

_____

_____

evident: easy to tell

Visualize...

1. It was *evident* that Rex was hungry because we could hear his stomach growling.
2. It was *evident* that Flo had been crying because there were still tears on her cheeks.
3. It was *evident* that Jake's broken bicycle could not be fixed—the frame was bent in half.
4. The sun was going down as we left town, and it became *evident* that we wouldn't get to the lake before dark.

and Verbalize...

_____

_____

_____

evil: very bad

Visualize...

1. The *evil* witch turned the prince into a frog and locked him in a cage.
2. Is letting the air out of someone's tire a good or *evil* thing to do?
3. The *evil* child hid her grandmother's glasses under a brick in the backyard.
4. Adolf Hitler was one of the most *evil* men in the history of the world.

and Verbalize...

_____

_____

_____

exhaust: to make tired; to use up

Visualize...

1. Ted had to keep stopping to rest because the long, uphill hike to Hidden Lake *exhausted* him.
2. The long wheat harvest *exhausted* Mr. Finch—he looked thin and pale and his face showed new wrinkles.
3. The ship could only drift with the currents once it had *exhausted* its fuel supplies.
4. Rex had *exhausted* his allowance for the week and had to borrow five dollars from Tom.

and Verbalize...

_____

_____

_____

exhausting: very tiring

Visualize...

1. Mr. Wong was so tired after his *exhausting* trip that he went straight to bed without brushing his teeth.
2. Ted won't listen, so it's *exhausting* to try to talk to him.
3. Professor Lopez's long and *exhausting* lecture made many people in the audience begin to yawn and feel restless.
4. "This week has been *exhausting*," Mrs. Mendoza said. "Let's go out to dinner—I'm just too tired to cook."

and Verbalize...

_____

_____

_____

exhibit: to show or display

Visualize...

1. The farmer won a blue ribbon when he *exhibited* his huge watermelon at the county fair.
2. The gifted artist *exhibited* her newest paintings at the city museum.
3. All the children in the class *exhibit* a talent for blowing big bubbles with their bubble gum.
4. Pam and Beth both *exhibit* an ability to get along well with others.

and Verbalize...

_____

_____

_____

exhibition: a public display of objects or skills

Visualize...

1. Are you going to the art museum to see the *exhibition* of modern sculpture?
2. Phil bought a ticket to the new car *exhibition* at the city auditorium.
3. Ms. Jones gave an *exhibition* of first aid procedures to our class.
4. The gold crown was the most impressive piece in the Egyptian archeology *exhibition*.

and Verbalize...

_____

_____

_____

existence: being alive, real, present, or intact

Visualize...

1. Our house and farm and even the big tree were there before I was born and came into *existence*.
2. Would you believe in the *existence* of ghosts if you saw one on a dark and stormy night?
3. "The *existence* of gold dust in this stream makes me believe the hills are full of gold ore," Mr. Drake said.
4. Is the old wagon still in *existence* or did it finally fall apart?

and Verbalize...

_____

_____

_____

expand: to become larger; to make larger

Visualize...

1. The balloon *expanded* and *expanded* and *expanded* until it couldn't *expand* anymore—and then it exploded!
2. The snake's body *expanded* into a funny shape when the snake swallowed the rat.
3. We *expanded* our house by adding on a bedroom and a family room.
4. Mrs. Kim decided to *expand* her book on wildflowers by writing another chapter.

and Verbalize...

_____

_____

_____

expect: to look forward to something you think will probably happen; to count on something because it is proper or necessary

Visualize...

1. Tom kept looking out the window because he was *expecting* his father to arrive at any moment.
2. Lucy *expected* to get a Christmas gift from her grandmother, but she didn't know what it would be.
3. "I *expect* you to do a better job of cleaning up your room," Mark's mother told him, holding up the old sandwich she'd found under his bed.
4. Our parents *expected* us to treat our elders with respect, and so we always did.

and Verbalize...

_____

_____

_____

expedition: a journey with a special purpose; the people, supplies, and means of transportation involved in such a journey

Visualize...

1. Tom and Tim went on an *expedition* to find the lost city of Atlantis.
2. The scientists discovered a new kind of penguin on their research *expedition* to the South Pole.
3. The military *expedition* crossed the desert by night to take the enemy by surprise.
4. A hundred pioneers and a long line of horses, pack mules, and wagons made up the *expedition* that was searching for a new route to California.

and Verbalize...

_____

_____

_____

explorer: a person who travels to a place to discover new things

Visualize...

1. Was Christopher Columbus the first *explorer* to discover America?
2. In Jules Verne's book <u>Journey to the Center of the Earth</u>, a band of *explorers* go on an expedition to the center of the earth.
3. The *explorers* Lewis and Clark traveled by foot, by canoe, and on horseback in what is now the western United States.
4. Who was the first *explorer* to reach the South Pole?

and Verbalize...

_____

_____

_____

extend: to make or become longer; to stretch or reach; to offer

Visualize...

1. Will that fishing pole *extend* or is that as long as it gets?
2. Why don't you *extend* your vacation and stay over another day?
3. *Extend* your arms at your sides and run in place.
4. I want to *extend* my thanks to you for all the help you've given me.

and Verbalize...

_____

_____

_____

extension: something added on; an extending in time

Visualize...

1. The new *extension* to our house will have a bedroom and a bath.
2. I'm familiar with the old library but I haven't been inside the new *extension*.
3. The banker granted Dan an *extension* on his loan so he could have more time to pay it back.
4. The *extension* of the school year from May into June made the parents happy and the students sad.

and Verbalize...

_____

_____

_____

extinct: no longer found on the Earth; no longer active

Visualize...

1. Dinosaurs are *extinct*. None of them are living now on the Earth.
2. The dodo bird—a gentle, clumsy bird that couldn't fly—became *extinct* in the 1600's.
3. California condors are large birds that have almost become *extinct*. Now the chicks are being hatched in zoos.
4. People like to climb the *extinct* volcano and look down at the blue lake inside the crater.

and Verbalize...

_____

_____

_____

Chapter 6

The F's

fabulous: amazing; wonderful

Visualize...

1. The *fabulous* wealth of the king allowed him to buy a ruby the size of a baseball and anything else he wanted.
2. Babe Ruth's most *fabulous* year was 1927, when he hit 60 home runs.
3. "We took a ship down the coast of Mexico, then flew to Brazil," Ms. Marten told her friends. "It was a *fabulous* vacation!"
4. "How do you feel?" the reporters asked the new Miss Universe. She shook her long black curls and said, "*Fabulous!*"

and Verbalize...

_____

_____

_____

facility: a building, room, or equipment that serves a special purpose

Visualize...

1. The computer *facility* is open 24 hours a day.
2. The hospital had *facilities* for 200 emergency cases.
3. Phil asked the landlord if the apartment building had laundry *facilities*.
4. "I don't have the *facilities* to take care of more bears," the exhausted zoo keeper said.

and Verbalize...

_____

_____

_____

F

factor: something that makes something else happen

Visualize...

1. The slippery road was one of the *factors* that caused the auto accident.
2. "What *factors* allowed you to win the race?" Mr. Jones asked. "Speed, endurance, and the will to win," Greg answered.
3. For most people, money is a big *factor* when they decide which new car to buy.
4. "My parents' encouragement was a big *factor* in my success," said the movie star as she accepted her award.

and Verbalize...

_____

_____

_____

fade: to become less bright

Visualize...

1. Ed had his car repainted when it began to *fade* from dark blue to light blue.
2. Martha washed her red dress so many times it *faded* to pink.
3. My blue shirt *faded* when I left it out on the clothesline for two weeks.
4. Rex knew the book was old because the pages had *faded* to a brownish yellow.

and Verbalize...

_____

_____

_____

famous: known by many people

Visualize...

1. Movie stars are *famous* people because their faces are known to millions of people.
2. My brother became *famous* when his record became a big hit and his music video was on television.
3. Mr. Wong wasn't rich or *famous* but he didn't care because his family and friends loved him.
4. "Remember, if you become *famous* you won't have the privacy you have now," Bill's mother said.

and Verbalize...

_____

_____

_____

fascination: a strong attraction to, or interest in, something

Visualize...

1. Mr. Brown has a *fascination* with the game of chess. He thinks about it all the time and plays every chance he gets.
2. Agnes goes to the planetarium three times a day because she has a *fascination* with astronomy.
3. Old coins hold a *fascination* for José and he collects them whenever he can.
4. The cat watched with complete *fascination* as the sparrow fluttered around in the bird bath. "Hmm, could be lunch!" the cat thought to himself.

and Verbalize...

_____

_____

_____

fatigue: the condition of being tired

Visualize...

1. The young men felt *fatigue* when they moved Mrs. White's piano down the stairs, up the street, and into her new apartment.
2. After running a mile I didn't feel *fatigue*—I felt strong and fresh and ran on for another few blocks.
3. "You're suffering from *fatigue*," Dr. Gray said. "You need to rest and not work so hard."
4. Last night Beth complained of *fatigue* and this morning she said she was too tried to get out of bed.

and Verbalize...

_____

_____

_____

fearsome: scary

Visualize...

1. The *fearsome* creature in the horror movie had three mouths, five eyes, and a chain saw.
2. The storm's huge waves were *fearsome*, and the frightened sailors feared they might drown.
3. The *fearsome* display of lightning terrified the horses in the corral.
4. "There's nothing *fearsome* about Fang," Agnes said. "He's a sweet, gentle dog who wouldn't even bite a flea."

and Verbalize...

_____

_____

_____

feast: a big meal made for a special event

Visualize...

1. Our Thanksgiving *feast* included a turkey, sweet potatoes, salad, rolls with butter, and pumpkin pie for dessert.
2. We held a *feast* and invited the whole block to eat with us when my brother came home from the Army.
3. A "luau" is a big outdoor *feast* in Hawaii.
4. "I thought you said a 'snack,' not a '*feast*,'" Phil said to Flo when he saw all the food on the kitchen table.

and Verbalize...

_____

_____

_____

fertile: able to produce plants or young easily and plentifully

Visualize...

1. "This land is very, very *fertile*," Mr. Finch told his visitors. "Drop a seed into the ground on Monday, and by Friday you've got an apple tree!"
2. The Central Valley of California is very *fertile*—it produces more food than any other valley in the world.
3. What makes the difference between barren desert and *fertile* farmland? Water.
4. The Appaloosa mare was healthy and very *fertile*—she had 8 colts in 12 years.

and Verbalize...

_____

_____

_____

fervent: having or showing deep feeling or being intensely devoted

Visualize...

1. The *fervent* football fans waved flags and cried when their team lost the game.
2. The soldiers began to cheer and clap their hands when the general gave his *fervent* speech.
3. Jerome's father is a *fervent* chess player—he'll talk to you for hours about his favorite moves or who his favorite chess players are.
4. "I have a *fervent* belief in the goodness of our country," the president told the T.V. audience.

and Verbalize...

_____

_____

_____

festival: a celebration

Visualize...

1. The music *festival* began with a parade down Elm Street by 30 marching bands.
2. After the Watermelon *Festival* the park was littered with soggy paper plates, green-striped watermelon rinds, and shiny black seeds.
3. Ruby found a little clay pot shaped like a rabbit at the art *festival.*
4. When the Greens' give a party, it's a real *festival:* Mr. Green hangs white paper lanterns from the trees and Mrs. Green serves food under a big red tent.

and Verbalize...

_____

_____

_____

figure: a symbol that stands for a number or word; a shape or form; an important person (n)

Visualize...

1. The numerical *figure* for "four" is "4." The *figure* for "per cent" is "%."
2. Which of these three *figures* do you like best: the circle, the square, or the triangle?
3. Something that had the *figure* of a very tiny man descended the steps of the flying saucer.
4. No matter who he is, the President of the United States is always an important *figure* in the world.

and Verbalize...

_____

_____

_____

figure: to compute; to think (v)

Visualize...

1. Ed used the adding machine to *figure* how much money he owed Bill.
2. The teller at the bank *figured* how much interest Pam's account had earned.
3. Rex stayed up late trying to *figure* what to do with Spot's eight new puppies.
4. The movie's plot was hard to follow and Jake had a hard time trying to *figure* it out.

and Verbalize...

_____

_____

_____

flee: to run away

Visualize...

1. Lars saw the little white cat *flee* for the bushes when the big dog ran barking into the yard.
2. The bank robbers *fled* the scene when they heard the sirens of the police cars.
3. During the flood, people were *fleeing* to stay ahead of the rising waters.
4. "Did you *flee* or stand and fight?" the captain asked his soldiers.

and Verbalize...

_____

_____

_____

flexible: able to bend and not break, not rigid, easily bent

Visualize...

1. The new garden hose was *flexible* and Tom had no trouble winding it up into a tight circle.
2. The hard plastic was brittle and not *flexible*—it broke when Rod tried to bend it.
3. I never thought glass was *flexible*, but in a strong wind I saw our window bend out and then go flat again without breaking.
4. Because Jeff's right hand was in a cast and his fingers weren't very *flexible*, he had to button his shirt with his left hand.

and Verbalize...

_____

_____

_____

flicker: to grow bright and then dim and then bright in a shaky way

Visualize...

1. During the storm the lights *flickered* every time the wind blew the power lines.
2. The candles began to *flicker* in the draft from the open window.
3. The T.V. screen *flickered* silver and blue in the dark living room.
4. The fire *flickered* and went out before Rex could get another log from the woodpile.

and Verbalize...

_____

_____

_____

founder: the person who starts or establishes something

Visualize...

1. Thomas Jefferson was one of the *founders* of America. He wrote the Declaration of Independence.
2. The *founder* of The Roaring 20's Club was Mr. Trask, who first organized it in 1925.
3. The *founder* of the great city did not live long enough to see it completed.
4. The *founders* of the scholarship fund set aside a million dollars to help deserving students go on to college.

and Verbalize...

_____

_____

_____

fragile: delicate, not strong, frail

Visualize...

1. The *fragile* china cup shattered when Dan dropped it on the rug.
2. Agnes packed the glasses and dishes carefully, then wrote "*Fragile*" on the outside of the box.
3. The *fragile* old woman sat in the sunshine, a blanket wrapped around her thin shoulders.
4. "I used to be a *fragile* child," Babe said, "but working outdoors made me stronger."

and Verbalize...

_____

_____

_____

froth: a mass of bubbles

Visualize...

1. Flo shook the bottle of cola, opened it, and a stream of brownish *froth* shot out.
2. The tired racehorse had a white *froth* on his mouth after he finished running the race.
3. There was a *froth* of tiny white bubbles at the bottom of the waterfall.
4. The mad dog's mouth was covered with a white *froth* or foam.

and Verbalize...

_____

_____

_____

F

function: purpose; a formal gathering (n)

Visualize...

1. The *function* of a hammer is to hit a nail and drive it into the wood.
2. "What's the *function* of this device?" asked Mr. Harris, holding up a small wooden box with a handle on the side.
3. Greg and Ruby each received an award at the school *function* last night.
4. My mother was hosting a *function* at the Women's Club, so we helped her with the tablecloths and the punch bowl.

and Verbalize...

_____

_____

_____

function: to work or to serve (v)

Visualize...

1. You can't *function* very well at school if you don't get enough sleep the night before.
2. The soldier's gun wouldn't *function*, so he threw it to the ground and ran for cover.
3. The stadium *functioned* as both a sports arena and an outdoor concert hall.
4. "My straw hat also *functions* as a butterfly net," Tom said as he waved his hat in the air.

and Verbalize...

_____

_____

_____

fundamental: basic

Visualize...

1. Learning to throw a baseball is a *fundamental* part of learning to be a baseball player.
2. Reading is a *fundamental* learning skill. You have to know how to read if you want to learn about anything else.
3. "One plus one equals two" is a *fundamental* truth of arithmetic.
4. "Exercising is a *fundamental* part of building a strong, trim body," Mr. Smith said.

and Verbalize...

_____

_____

_____

furnace: a large enclosed metal box where heat is produced

Visualize...

1. We use the *furnace* in the winter to warm up our house, and the air conditioner in the summer to cool it down.
2. Agnes turns up the *furnace* after dark when the house begins to get chilly.
3. Many old *furnaces* used to burn coal, but new ones use natural gas.
4. Pam's basketball melted when she left it too close to the *furnace.*

and Verbalize...

_____

_____

_____

furnish: to provide; to supply with furniture or equipment

Visualize...

1. Our hens *furnish* us with a daily supply of brown eggs.
2. "You *furnish* the food, I'll do the cooking," Martha told Hazel.
3. Rex *furnished* his living room with a brown tweed sofa and matching chairs.
4. The school workshop is *furnished* with many power tools, including saws, drills, and electric sanders.

and Verbalize...

_____

_____

_____

futile: unsuccessful, useless

Visualize...

1. The man tried to reach the raft with a long stick but his effort was *futile* and the raft floated away without him.
2. The baseball was already past June, but she made a *futile* dive for it anyway.
3. Mrs. Smith tried to get Fred to like math, but she knew it was *futile*—all he cared about was music.
4. Our attempt to buy tickets for the concert was *futile*—they were all sold out.

and Verbalize...

_____

_____

_____

Chapter 7

The G's

gain: to get or add something as a result of your efforts; to increase in weight

Visualize...

1. Mary *gained* 20 minutes more for breakfast by driving to work instead of walking.
2. "What do you *gain* by being mean?" Mark asked his grouchy boss.
3. Everyone cheered as Frank *gained* the lead in the 100-yard dash.
4. "I *gained* 100 pounds from all those holiday meals," whined Wanda.

and Verbalize...

_____

_____

_____

galaxy: a very large group of stars

Visualize...

1. Our sun is just one of millions of stars in the Milky Way *galaxy*.
2. There are many, many *galaxies* in the known universe.
3. The movie "Star Wars" takes place in a *galaxy* far, far away.
4. "Maybe there are people living somewhere in another *galaxy*," Professor Lopez told the astronomy class.

and Verbalize...

_____

_____

_____

G

gap: a hole or empty space

Visualize...

1. The cows always get out of the barn through the *gap* in the wall.
2. The *gap* in Beth's mouth is where she lost her front tooth.
3. There's a *gap* in this book where the pages were torn out.
4. "Bill has a *gap* in his memory," Dr. Gray said. "He can't remember the accident, only waking up in the hospital afterward."

and Verbalize...

_____

_____

_____

gasp: a quick, short breath (n)

Visualize...

1. Della dived deep into the lake, then swam to the surface and took a *gasp* of air.
2. My mother's *gasps* filled the room as my sister modeled the new, skimpy swimming suit.
3. Tim let out a *gasp* when he got into the cold shower.
4. The audience in the movie theater let out one loud *gasp* as the monster turned and started toward the nice old man.

and Verbalize...

_____

_____

_____

gasp: to take a quick, short breath (v)

Visualize...

1. Greg *gasped* for air as his friends pulled him from the freezing water of the pond.
2. Agnes *gasped* when she saw all the candles on her birthday cake.
3. "I'm trying to run 10 miles today," *gasped* the tired jogger. "Do you think I'll make it?"
4. My father *gasped* when he saw the huge dent in the side of his car.

and Verbalize...

_____

_____

_____

gauge: an instrument for measuring; a standard of measurement (n)

Visualize...

1. The gas *gauge* on the car showed "E" for "empty."
2. The airplane pilot checked all his lights and *gauges*, especially the *gauge* showing oil pressure.
3. Degrees are a *gauge* of temperature, of hotness and coldness.
4. The man's huge muscles were a *gauge* of his great strength.

and Verbalize...

_____

_____

_____

gauge: to measure accurately; to estimate or judge (v)

Visualize...

1. The scientist used a special device to *gauge* the amount of pollution in the air.
2. "The altimeter *gauges* altitude," the pilot told his student.
3. Rex *gauged* the distance between himself and the bear as about 15 or 20 feet.
4. "It's hard to *gauge* how long it will take to finish the castle," the stonemason told the king.

and Verbalize...

_____

_____

_____

gear: a wheel with teeth on the edge; equipment for a particular purpose

Visualize...

1. The watchmaker opened the watch and checked all the little *gears* that were going around and around inside the watch.
2. The truck wouldn't run because the teeth were broken off the main *gear*.
3. When he was ready to go to Bear Lake, Tom packed the car with his clothes, food, and fishing *gear*.
4. *Gear* for skiing—boots, skis, poles—can be very expensive.

and Verbalize...

_____

_____

_____

gem: a stone that is worth a lot of money

Visualize...

1. Diamonds, rubies, and emeralds are all costly *gems*.
2. The pirate's treasure chest held no precious *gems* but only bits of colored glass.
3. The queen's crown was set with sparkling *gems*.
4. "The woman in the blue evening gown is wearing a necklace set with blue *gems*," Lucy whispered to June. "Yes," June answered, "those are sapphires."

and Verbalize...

_____

_____

_____

generation: all the people born about the same time

Visualize...

1. My father's *generation* was born during the 1940's. My *generation* was born during the 1970's.
2. "There are three *generations* in this photo," said my mother, pointing to a picture of my grandfather, my father, and my brother.
3. Our *generation* is facing many environmental problems, especially the poisoning of our air and water.
4. "We have to take care of the earth so the next *generation* will have a clean and decent place to live," Mrs. Smith told her class.

and Verbalize...

_____

_____

_____

geology: the study of the earth's crust; features of the earth's crust

Visualize...

1. Pam collects all kinds of rocks because she's interested in *geology*.
2. Mark didn't know his *geology*—he couldn't tell the difference between real gold and fool's gold.
3. "Do you know the *geology* of this area?" I asked Ted. "The ground you're standing on was once the bottom of a great ocean!"
4. "When we talk about the *geology* of Mexico," Professor Lopez said, "we need to talk about valuable minerals—gold and silver and gems."

and Verbalize...

_____

_____

_____

gigantic: very large, huge

Visualize...

1. The towering mountain was *gigantic*. It was over 20,000 feet tall.
2. The moon is not green cheese but a *gigantic* ball of rock.
3. King Kong was a *gigantic* make-believe ape. He was so large he could hold a person in the palm of his hand.
4. Some dinosaurs were small, some were large, and many were *gigantic*.

and Verbalize...

_____

_____

_____

gill: the part of a fish or tadpole that lets it breathe underwater

Visualize...

1. The little *gills* of the goldfish moved back and forth as it breathed air from the water.
2. People have lungs, and fish have *gills*.
3. Whales don't have *gills* because they aren't fish but mammals.
4. The fish on the bottom of the boat were flopping around, opening and closing their *gills*.

and Verbalize...

_____

_____

_____

gland: a part of the body that makes needed fluids from materials in the blood

Visualize...

1. Saliva *glands* make your mouth water when you smell something good to eat.
2. The pituitary *gland* helps people grow.
3. When Judy got sick the *glands* on her neck and under her arms hurt.
4. "Your heart is an organ, not a *gland*," Dr. Gray said.

and Verbalize...

_____

_____

_____

G

glimmer: to give off a dim, unsteady light

Visualize...

1. A few stars *glimmered* but Venus shone brightly in the early evening sky.
2. The green light at the end of the dock *glimmered* across the dark lake.
3. A single candle *glimmered* at the window of the castle tower.
4. The sun *glimmered* at the distant opening of the cavern.

and Verbalize...

_____

_____

_____

glimpse: a short, quick look

Visualize...

1. Rex caught one *glimpse* of the jewels before the pirate slammed the lid of the treasure chest.
2. Just a *glimpse* of the movie was enough for Bill. He didn't want to see any more.
3. The pretty girl didn't give Jeff and Ron even a *glimpse* as she walked past them on the sidewalk.
4. "Did you get a *glimpse* of his face before he hit you and everything went dark?" the policeman asked the injured man.

and Verbalize...

_____

_____

_____

glossy: shiny

Visualize...

1. Della brushed her horse's coat until it was smooth and *glossy* black.
2. Look how Beth's *glossy* black hair shines in the sunlight!
3. June polished her leather shoes until they were so *glossy* she could see her face reflected in them.
4. "Should I use *glossy* or flat paint on the wheelbarrow?" Greg asked.

and Verbalize...

_____

_____

_____

gorge: a deep, narrow canyon (n)

Visualize...

1. The boys pushed the boulder over the edge of the cliff and watched it fall into the *gorge.*
2. The river looked like a shining silver ribbon at the bottom of the steep *gorge.*
3. The guard rail kept the blue car from running off the road and falling into the *gorge.*
4. The helicopter lifted the injured hiker from the dangerous *gorge.*

and Verbalize...

_____

_____

_____

gorge: to stuff yourself with food (v)

Visualize...

1. Carl made himself sick by *gorging* on pizza and ice cream at the party.
2. Amanda *gorges* on popcorn and cookies when she feels sad and lonely.
3. The cat *gorged* on tuna fish, hamburger, and a plate of chicken when someone left the refrigerator door open.
4. The starving deer *gorged* themselves on the hay the park rangers laid out.

and Verbalize...

_____

_____

_____

graceful: beautiful or pleasing in design, movement, or style

Visualize...

1. Swans are very *graceful* when they glide across smooth water.
2. Mary couldn't decide who was more *graceful*, the ice skater or the ballet dancer.
3. The actress moved her hands in a *graceful* way when she talked.
4. The ostrich looked clumsy when it stood next to the *graceful* flamingo.

and Verbalize...

_____

_____

_____

gradual: happening slowly

Visualize...

1. For most actors, success isn't sudden but *gradual*—it takes them years to become well-known.
2. Did the Ice Age begin as a *gradual* change in climate, or did everything turn cold overnight?
3. "There will be *gradual* cooling this week," said the weatherman. "It will be 70 degrees on Monday, 68 degrees by Wednesday, and 66 degrees by Friday."
4. The illness is a *gradual* one—first you get a cough, then a slight fever, a headache, and finally red spots on your feet.

and Verbalize...

_____

_____

_____

grandparent: a grandfather or grandmother

Visualize...

1. My mother's parents and my father's parents are all my *grandparents*.
2. Only one of Rod's *grandparents* is still living—his father's mother.
3. Flo's *grandparents* on her mother's side live in Chicago, in a big house near the lake.
4. Ruby's *grandparents* give her toys when she goes to visit them.

and Verbalize...

_____

_____

_____

graze: to eat grass for food

Visualize...

1. The black-and-white horse got sick from *grazing* in the weeds.
2. Farmer Finch milks his cows in the morning before he puts them out to *graze* in the pasture.
3. Pam's neighbor has sheep *grazing* in his yard so he won't have to mow the lawn.
4. "Now draw a picture of blue horses *grazing* in a yellow meadow," Ms. Long told her art students.

and Verbalize...

_____

_____

_____

G

grit: small pieces of sand or stone

Visualize...

1. The farmer wore a cotton mask so he wouldn't breathe in dust and *grit* as he plowed the bare field.
2. The miner's face was covered with dark *grit* when he rode the coal car to the opening of the mine.
3. The oil in the motor needed to be changed because it was dirty and full of *grit*.
4. Martha closed all the windows but *grit* from the dust storm still got into the house.

and Verbalize...

_____

_____

_____

growth: process of becoming larger as time passes

Visualize...

1. Rod's *growth* was fast—he was getting an inch taller every month.
2. Springville's *growth* was enormous—now the town covered the whole valley and the slopes of the hills.
3. Professor Lopez used a ruler to check the *growth* of the white mice in the cage.
4. Stan's tire business is having a steady *growth*—each month Stan sells more tires than the month before.

and Verbalize...

_____

_____

_____

guarantee: a promise to repair or replace something within a certain period of time; anything that makes a result certain (n)

Visualize...

1. Phil's new lawnmower comes with a 90-day *guarantee* on all parts and labor.
2. The *guarantee* on Greg's car had run out, so when it broke down Greg had to pay for the repairs himself.
3. "There's no *guarantee* that this green medicine will help," warned Dr. Gray.
4. A college education improves your chances of getting a good job, but it's no *guarantee*.

and Verbalize...

_____

_____

_____

G

guarantee: to make sure; to promise (v)

Visualize...

1. Farmer Finch built his garden wall out of stone to *guarantee* that it would last.
2. Good food, exercise, and sleep don't *guarantee* you'll <u>never</u> get sick.
3. "I *guarantee* your wife will love it," the barber said, patting Mr. Smith's short haircut.
4. The painter *guaranteed* the new paint would last for 10 years.

and Verbalize...

_____

_____

_____

gust: a quick, strong rush of wind

Visualize...

1. A *gust* of wind blew Della's purple hat off.
2. A rainy *gust* blew wet maple leaves against the window.
3. The breeze wasn't steady but kept coming and going in *gusts* that bent the palm trees.
4. A sudden *gust* crossed the lake and knocked Rex's toy sailboat on its side.

and Verbalize...

_____

_____

_____

gymnastics: physical exercises that require skill, balance, and strength

Visualize...

1. In gym class we practice *gymnastics* on a thick rubber mat. We do somersaults, rolls, and handstands.
2. One of the first things you learn in *gymnastics* is how to fall and roll correctly.
3. June practiced her *gymnastics* by dropping from the high rings and turning a somersault before she reached the ground.
4. *Gymnastics* is one of many events in the Olympics.

and Verbalize...

_____

_____

_____

Chapter 8

The H's

habitat: the place where an animal or plant naturally lives and grows

Visualize...

1. The eucalyptus forests of Australia are the only natural *habitat* for koala bears.
2. The *habitat* of the largest tortoises in the world is the Galapagos Islands.
3. Ferns need a moist, warm *habitat*, like a tropical rain forest.
4. Our family jokes that my hungry teenage brother's *habitat* is the refrigerator.

and Verbalize...

_____

_____

_____

hammock: a kind of bed made of canvas or netting that is suspended by rope at both ends

Visualize...

1. Ron's *hammock* is a heavy rope net tied between two trees in the backyard.
2. On a lazy summer day it's pleasant to lie in a *hammock* and look up at the sky.
3. Lucy's cat likes to take a nap in the backyard *hammock*.
4. You have to be careful when you turn over in a *hammock* or you might roll out.

and Verbalize...

_____

_____

_____

hardy: tough, able to put up with harsh conditions

Visualize...

1. The iceplant is a *hardy* plant that grows in sand and needs very little water.
2. The old goat was *hardy*. He roamed around the farm, eating cans and corncobs and spiny weeds.
3. Eskimos are *hardy*. They live in houses made of ice, and hunt and fish for their food in frozen waters.
4. Uncle Jake was a *hardy* man who lived alone in a cabin with no running water or electricity.

and Verbalize...

_____

_____

_____

hare: an animal like a rabbit but a little larger

Visualize...

1. A cottontail is a rabbit, but a jack rabbit is a *hare*.
2. The *hare's* ears and back legs are longer than the rabbit's.
3. In the story "The Tortoise and the *Hare*," the turtle beats the *hare* in a race.
4. "Some *hares* carry diseases and are not safe to eat," the hunter warned Tim.

and Verbalize...

_____

_____

_____

harvest: the gathering in of a crop when it is ripe (n)

Visualize...

1. It's time for the plum *harvest* when the plums are big and purple and sweet.
2. The pumpkin *harvest* is in October, right before Halloween.
3. Usually planting time is in the spring and the *harvest* is in the fall.
4. Farmer Finch hurried to finish the cotton *harvest* because a rainstorm was coming that would damage his crop.

and Verbalize...

_____

_____

_____

harvest: to gather crops (v)

Visualize...

1. Farmer Finch *harvested* his cotton by driving a cotton picker up and down the white rows of cotton.
2. Lucy and Della wore gloves to protect their hands from the sharp spines when they *harvested* the blackberries.
3. Greg didn't like to *harvest* wheat because the dust and straw made him sneeze and itch.
4. "Are you *harvesting* those apples or eating them?" Mr. Smith asked Jeff and Mark when he saw their empty buckets.

and Verbalize...

_____

_____

_____

haunting: strange and hard to forget

Visualize...

1. Della couldn't stop thinking about the sad and *haunting* movie she had seen.
2. The song Pam heard on the radio was *haunting*—beautiful and odd. She kept humming it at work.
3. The woman's white face in the train window made a *haunting* picture—I couldn't get it out of my mind.
4. The story of Edward Scissorhands—the man who had scissor blades instead of fingers—is a *haunting* one.

and Verbalize...

_____

_____

_____

haven: a place of safety or shelter

Visualize...

1. The old church was a *haven* for homeless people who had nowhere to go.
2. The peaceful cabins along the lake are a *haven* for people tired of city life.
3. Lucy made her barn into a *haven* for animals hurt by hunters.
4. Mr. Mendoza's quiet home is a *haven* for him after a day in his loud, busy office.

and Verbalize...

_____

_____

_____

H

heave: to lift, pull, push, or throw something heavy

Visualize...

1. The men sweated and strained and finally *heaved* the old refrigerator out of the kitchen and onto the back porch.
2. Mark grunted as he picked up the sack of potatoes and *heaved* it into the corner of the shed.
3. Fred and Frank said, "One, two, THREE!" and *heaved* the old sofa onto the back of the red truck.
4. Flo *heaved* the pack onto her back and adjusted the straps.

and Verbalize...

_____

_____

_____

hedge: a row of bushes or low trees planted close together

Visualize...

1. We planted a *hedge* of flowering shrubs to keep people and animals from crossing our lawn.
2. The prince had to cut his way through a *hedge* of briars to reach the castle and the sleeping princess.
3. The horse jumped the low *hedge* and galloped off across the open field.
4. "Can we borrow your clippers to trim our *hedge*?" Tim asked Mrs. Smith.

and Verbalize...

_____

_____

_____

height: the distance from top to bottom

Visualize...

1. Ruby grew three inches in *height* last year, from 4 feet 11 inches to 5 feet 2 inches.
2. The *height* of the elm tree in Ted's backyard is about 25 feet.
3. Your driver's license shows your weight, *height*, and the color of your eyes and hair.
4. "Two hundred pounds is too much weight for someone of your *height*," Dr. Clark said to Santa Claus.

and Verbalize...

_____

_____

_____

hemorrhage: to bleed a great deal

Visualize...

1. Nurse Jones wrapped a bandage tightly around the wound to keep it from *hemorrhaging.*
2. It's very serious when a patient begins to *hemorrhage* during an operation.
3. The injured man began to *hemorrhage* when the large artery broke.
4. "It's just a little cut," Stan told his crying brother. "You're not *hemorrhaging.*"

and Verbalize...

_____

_____

_____

heroic: courageous, daring, or desperately energetic or resourceful

Visualize...

1. Jeff was *heroic* when he went into the burning building to save the child.
2. The single parent raising three children alone is as *heroic* as a mountain climber.
3. The bus driver made a *heroic* effort to keep the bus from sliding off the icy road.
4. The teacher was *heroic* as she tried to work with a class of 45 five-year-olds.

and Verbalize...

_____

_____

_____

hibernate: to spend the winter sleeping

Visualize...

1. Some animals *hibernate* during the winter. They go into a deep sleep until spring comes.
2. The scientist crawled into the freezing cave where the bear was *hibernating.*
3. "I need a rest," Mrs. Marten said. "I'd like to quit my job and spend the next few months *hibernating.*"
4. The bear wasn't awake but *hibernating,* so Flo pulled out one of his whiskers for a souvenir.

and Verbalize...

_____

_____

_____

hire: payment for the use of a thing or the work of a person (n)

Visualize...

1. "I'm not for *hire*," the detective told Phil. "I'm on vacation this week."
2. Are these motor boats for *hire* or are they private boats?
3. After Dr. Gray began working, she arranged for the *hire* of a cook.
4. "You can get a boat for *hire* or you can swim to the island," the rude man at the dock told Rex.

and Verbalize...

_____

_____

_____

hire: to pay for the use of a thing or the work or services of a person (v)

Visualize...

1. Hortense *hired* a car and a driver because she didn't know how to drive.
2. The storekeeper *hired* me to deliver groceries at a salary of five dollars an hour.
3. Bob's mother was going to *hire* a gardener, but Bob said he would take care of the yard for free.
4. Farmer Finch *hired* a crew of students to help him harvest his tomatoes.

and Verbalize...

_____

_____

_____

historic: very important and not likely to be forgotten

Visualize...

1. An *historic* day for this country was the day the Civil War began.
2. The murder of President Kennedy was a sad *historic* event.
3. July 4 is an *historic* date because it marks the signing of the Declaration of Independence.
4. "This is an *historic* occasion," Martha laughed when Gus put on a suit for the first time.

and Verbalize...

_____

_____

_____

hoard: to get and save carefully for future use

Visualize...

1. In the fall squirrels *hoard* nuts for the winter.
2. Scrooge was a greedy and selfish man who got rich by *hoarding* his money and never giving any of it away.
3. Flo's grandmother *hoards* used tin foil and string in a closet that's full to the brim.
4. The store shelves were empty because people began to *hoard* food when the hurricane approached.

and Verbalize...

_____

_____

_____

holster: a leather case for holding a handgun

Visualize...

1. Little Jimmy wore a cowboy vest, a big hat, and two *holsters* for his toy guns.
2. Movie cowboys always wear their *holsters* on their hips.
3. The detective's shoulder *holster* made a bulge under his jacket.
4. "Don't shoot!" shouted the hero. "My *holsters* are empty and I can't find my guns!"

and Verbalize...

_____

_____

_____

homesick: sad because of being away from one's home or family

Visualize...

1. Della wrote letters from camp every day because she was so *homesick* for her family.
2. Jerome was *homesick* for palm trees and the blue Pacific after he moved from California to Colorado.
3. Mary was *homesick* for the green mountains near her village in Mexico.
4. "I never get *homesick* when we go on vacation," Stan said. "I love to travel."

and Verbalize...

_____

_____

_____

H

homestead: a house, sheds and barns, and the land around them

Visualize...

1. Our family's *homestead* is in North Dakota, but only my grandfather still lives there.
2. Beth's *homestead* had enough pasture for 200 cows and at least 50 horses.
3. Bob's *homestead* is way back in the hills, between the lake and the old silver mine.
4. "Welcome to the old *homestead!*" Mr. Finch said, throwing open the front door of his 100-year-old ranch house.

and Verbalize...

---

home town: the town in which a person was born or grew up

Visualize...

1. I'm often homesick for my *home town* and all my relatives who still live there.
2. Mrs. Jones has lived in Chicago for years, but her *home town* is San Francisco.
3. The astronaut's *home town* gave him a big parade when he returned from walking on the moon.
4. "I'd never return to this little place if it weren't my *home town*," the rich man said. "But I was born here."

and Verbalize...

---

hood: a head covering often fastened to the collar of a coat; the part of a car that fits over the engine and that can be raised and lowered

Visualize...

1. Beth's blue raincoat has a big *hood* that helps keep her head dry.
2. The *hood* of the king's dark cape covered his gold crown.
3. Phil lifted the *hood* of his car to check the oil.
4. "Oh no," Mr. Wong said to Flo as they drove up the hill. "There's black smoke coming from under the *hood!*"

and Verbalize...

---

hoop: a strip of wood or metal formed into a ring or circle

Visualize...

1. The boy made a "basket" when he threw the basketball through the metal *hoop*.
2. Six metal *hoops* held the big wooden barrel together.
3. The juggler threw ten silver *hoops* into the air.
4. The lion tamer got the tiger to jump through the burning *hoop*.

and Verbalize...

---

horizon: the line where the earth and the sky seem to meet

Visualize...

1. The people on the dock watched the white ship sail away until it disappeared below the *horizon*.
2. I couldn't see the *horizon*—it was impossible to see where the dark sea ended and the dark sky began.
3. There were clouds on the *horizon* and Della knew a rainstorm was coming.
4. The sun rises on the eastern *horizon* and sets on the western *horizon*.

and Verbalize...

---

horizontal: flat or level, parallel to the horizon

Visualize...

1. The top of the table is *horizontal* and its legs are vertical.
2. The long leg of an "L" is a vertical line, and the short leg is a *horizontal* line.
3. Tim drew two *horizontal* lines. "Those are railroad tracks," he told his mother.
4. The blinds on our living room windows are *horizontal*, but the ones in the bedroom are vertical.

and Verbalize...

H

horseshoe: a U-shaped metal plate that is nailed to a horse's hoof

Visualize...

1. The blacksmith made four iron *horseshoes* for the black stallion's hooves. The *horseshoes* fit perfectly.
2. The cowboy had to get off and walk when his horse lost one of its *horseshoes*.
3. There's a story in our town about a rich man whose horses all wore silver *horseshoes*.
4. Some people believe *horseshoes* are good luck, and nail them above the doors of their houses.

and Verbalize...

_____

_____

_____

host: a person who entertains guests; a large number

Visualize...

1. Rex is a good *host* because he makes his guests feel at home.
2. Dan's *host* at the castle was the king himself.
3. All the corn stalks were beaten flat when the *host* of soldiers crossed the field.
4. A *host* of people filled the town square and all the streets around it.

and Verbalize...

_____

_____

_____

humor: the funny or amusing side of things (n)

Visualize...

1. Mrs. Jones never laughs because she has no sense of *humor*.
2. Everyone laughed, but there was no *humor* in Tim's making fun of the new boy at school.
3. "I can't see the *humor* in someone slipping on a banana peel," Della said, getting up from the floor.
4. Tom thought the Three Stooges were very, very funny, but Tim couldn't see the *humor* in Moe hitting Larry and Curly.

and Verbalize...

_____

_____

_____

humor: to give in to the wishes of a person (v)

Visualize...

1. Lucy's father wanted her to learn poetry, so she *humored* him by reading a poem at dinner every night.
2. Phil got tired of always *humoring* Flo and never telling her what he really thought.
3. Pam wanted to have a picnic in the living room. "I know it's strange," she said, handing us some plates, "but *humor* me."
4. "*Humor* me," Bill said. "Wear the silver dress to the party even if you don't want to."

and Verbalize...

_____

_____

_____

husky: big and strong

Visualize...

1. Mrs. Marten's daughter is a *husky* child with big arms and legs.
2. The boy worked on the farm all summer and came home tanned and *husky*.
3. Stan was sick as a baby, but by the time he was three he was a *husky* little boy.
4. Ruby is thin and not very strong but her sister is *husky*.

and Verbalize...

_____

_____

_____

hut: a small, roughly-made shelter

Visualize...

1. The wise man was happy living in his simple *hut* made of mud and straw.
2. The hikers stayed overnight in a stone *hut* along the trail.
3. The shack was more of a *hut* than a house, but it was warm and its roof kept the rain from coming in.
4. In the fairy tale, the old witch lived alone in a *hut* at the edge of the woods.

and Verbalize...

_____

_____

_____

Chapter 9

The I's

icicle: a pointed, hanging stick of ice formed from dripping water

Visualize...

1. All winter a row of *icicles* hung from the edge of the cabin's roof.
2. The car was covered with snow and had *icicles* hanging from its bumpers.
3. The explorer had *icicles* hanging from his beard as he planted his flag at the South Pole.
4. "This *icicle* is like a popsicle!" Pam laughed as she held the long cone of ice in her hand.

and Verbalize...

_____

_____

igloo: an Eskimo's small, rounded house made of blocks of hard snow

Visualize...

1. An *igloo* looks like a domed beehive made of ice.
2. The Eskimos fitted the blocks of snow together like bricks when they built the *igloo*.
3. The tired Eskimo was glad to see the round outline of his *igloo* in the distance.
4. Some Eskimos in Alaska still live in *igloos*, but many now live in wood houses.

and Verbalize...

_____

_____

_____

I

ignore: to pay no attention to

Visualize...

1. Della *ignored* the ringing of the telephone. She pretended she didn't hear it and kept playing the piano.
2. My dog brings me his leash when he wants to go for a walk, but when I'm tired I try to *ignore* him.
3. Mrs. Lopez is a good mother because she doesn't *ignore* her children when they need to talk to her.
4. "Don't *ignore* me!" Mrs. Gray said to her husband when he opened up his newspaper at dinner.

and Verbalize...

_____

_____

_____

illiterate: unable to read or write

Visualize...

1. Jeff's uncle can't sign his name or read any street signs because he is *illiterate*.
2. When Gus learned to read he was no longer *illiterate*.
3. Many *illiterate* adults have a hard time finding good jobs.
4. Stan was a famous football player, but he couldn't read the newspaper stories about himself because he was *illiterate*.

and Verbalize...

_____

_____

_____

illusion: something that seems to be real but is not

Visualize...

1. It was just an *illusion* when the magician made the white rabbit disappear—the rabbit was really hidden in his pants.
2. The car's darkly-tinted windows gave the *illusion* that it was always night outside.
3. The castle towers appeared higher than the clouds but it was only an *illusion*.
4. "I've lost my *illusions* about Hollywood," the young actress said. "It's not as wonderful as I thought."

and Verbalize...

_____

_____

_____

illustrate: to make clear or explain; to draw a picture or diagram to explain or decorate something written

Visualize...

1. Professor James flapped his arms at his sides, trying to *illustrate* his point about the way birds fly.
2. Johnny dived into the swimming pool to *illustrate* that he wasn't afraid of deep water.
3. Mr. Wong used pen and ink to *illustrate* the story about the dragon who lived on a rain cloud.
4. Farmer Finch *illustrated* his new book on gardening with colorful drawings of blooming flowers.

and Verbalize...

_____

_____

_____

image: a picture or other likeness of a person or thing

Visualize...

1. The *image* of the man's face on the T.V. screen was blurry and hard to see.
2. When you listen to someone talking on the radio, you have to create an *image* in your mind of what that person looks like.
3. The white swan curved its long neck to see the mirror *image* of itself in the blue water.
4. Lucy's *image* of the perfect dessert is a slice of chocolate cake with a scoop of vanilla ice cream on top.

and Verbalize...

_____

_____

_____

imaginary: existing only in the mind

Visualize...

1. Unicorns don't really exist. A unicorn is an *imaginary* animal that looks like a beautiful white horse with a long, straight horn on its forehead.
2. Della has an *imaginary* friend named Tip that only she can hear and see.
3. Most people think the lost city of Atlantis is *imaginary*, but Ted and Pam think it's real, and that it's hidden somewhere under the sea.
4. "Mark's great wealth is only *imaginary*," Fred explained. "He has a hundred, not a million dollars."

and Verbalize...

_____

_____

_____

imagination: the act or power of forming pictures in the mind, especially of things that aren't present

Visualize...

1. In Fred's *imagination* the cardboard box was really a castle where a king and queen lived.
2. Beth was sure a ghost was in her bedroom, before she realized it was just her *imagination*—the ghost was only the white curtain blowing at the window.
3. "You have a vivid *imagination*," Agnes told Timmy after she read his story about the undersea city.
4. "Your picture of an elephant doesn't look like an elephant," Tom said. "Use your *imagination*," Ted answered.

and Verbalize...

_____

_____

_____

impress: to have a strong effect on someone's thoughts or feelings

Visualize...

1. Gus always *impresses* people when he juggles ten sharp knives in the air.
2. The Grand Canyon's majestic size *impressed* Flo.
3. Della's singing voice *impressed* José so much that he couldn't stop clapping and cheering.
4. "Do I *impress* you with my size?" the elephant asked the mouse.

and Verbalize...

_____

_____

_____

improvement: a change for the better

Visualize...

1. Lucy made a big *improvement* in her reading after she began visualizing what she read.
2. Dr. Gray checked Rex every day after his accident to make sure he was showing some *improvement*.
3. The farmers hoped for an *improvement* in the weather after five days of rain had flooded all the fields.
4. "This is a big *improvement!*" Hortense said when she finished painting her bedroom purple. "The old color was awful!"

and Verbalize...

_____

_____

_____

inch: to move very slowly

Visualize...

1. It took 20 minutes for the brown turtle to *inch* its way across the road.
2. The caterpillar *inched* along the stem, taking one bite and then another out of the big green leaf.
3. The mountain climbers *inched* carefully along the narrow ledge.
4. "It was foggy and I had to *inch* my way along the curving road," the bus driver explained when he arrived late.

and Verbalize...

_____

_____

_____

incline: a surface that slopes or slants

Visualize...

1. Mr. Smith had to shift the car into first gear to drive up the steep *incline*.
2. The giant boulder rolled down the *incline* and crushed the empty red truck.
3. Tim pulled the green wagon up the *incline* and then let it roll back down.
4. "The tomato patch doesn't look level," Farmer Finch said. "I think it has a slight *incline*."

and Verbalize...

_____

_____

_____

increase: to grow in size; to add to

Visualize...

1. Della's family *increased* from four people to six people when the twins were born.
2. Greg's weight began to *increase* because he ate chocolate cake for dessert every night.
3. Farmer Finch *increased* Mark's pay from three dollars to four dollars an hour.
4. June *increased* her savings by putting 30 more dollars into the bank.

and Verbalize...

_____

_____

_____

I

incredible: unbelievable or astonishing

Visualize...

1. Greg made an *incredible* amount of money when he discovered gold in his own backyard.
2. Tom thought it was *incredible* when he heard that Mrs. Smith's eight-year-old son was so smart he was going to start high school.
3. The opera singer's *incredible* voice broke Dan's glasses and the mirror on the wall.
4. "Rex's story about traveling to Mars is pretty *incredible*," said Professor Lopez.

and Verbalize...

_____

_____

_____

indefinite: not clear or exact, vague

Visualize...

1. Mrs. Smith's vacation plans were *indefinite*—she didn't know when she'd go to the coast.
2. Bob and Mary planned to get married in June, but the actual wedding date was *indefinite*.
3. The air was smoggy and the green hill was only an *indefinite* brown smudge in the distance.
4. The wildlife photographer planned to live in Africa for an *indefinite* number of years. He didn't know when he might return to America.

and Verbalize...

_____

_____

_____

indicate: to be a sign of; to show or point out

Visualize...

1. Those black clouds above the hills *indicate* a rainstorm by morning.
2. Beth's sad face and red eyes *indicated* that she had been crying.
3. Nurse Jones *indicated* with a wave of her hand that Dr. Gray was ready to see us.
4. "Please *indicate* your answers by checking the right boxes," Professor Lopez said as he handed out the tests.

and Verbalize...

_____

_____

_____

individual: separate or single; belonging to only one person or thing

   Visualize...

   1. In a big class, it's hard for the teacher to give each student *individual* attention.
   2. Tim thinks of his 100 earthworms as *individual* pets and has a name for each one of them.
   3. Everyone's fingerprints are *individual*—no two people have the same prints.
   4. The pattern of each snowflake is as *individual* as a person's fingerprint.

   and Verbalize...

   _____

   _____

   _____

industry: any large-scale business, especially manufacturing; steady effort, hard work

   Visualize...

   1. How many cars and trucks does the auto *industry* make a year?
   2. The steel *industry* produces the big beams needed to build skyscrapers.
   3. Rod's *industry* in studying his Spanish was repaid by a good grade on the final test.
   4. Mr. Jones increased Ruby's pay because of her reliability and *industry*.

   and Verbalize...

   _____

   _____

   _____

influence: the power to produce an effect on others without using force or a command

   Visualize...

   1. Professor Brown thinks the *influence* of T.V. on children is not very good.
   2. Greg was upset because he had very little *influence* on his boss' decisions.
   3. Dr. Gray had a lot of *influence* over her friends because they respected her.
   4. Pat's *influence* on Della can be seen in the bright skirts and blouses Della wears.

   and Verbalize...

   _____

   _____

   _____

I

information: facts

Visualize...

1. If you want *information* about places to camp, call the Park Service.
2. The police detective gathered *information* about the bank robbery.
3. The powerful new telescope should collect a lot of *information* about the strange red star.
4. Rod didn't know Flo's telephone number so he called *Information* to find out.

and Verbalize...

_____

_____

_____

ingenious: clever, imaginative, and original

Visualize...

1. June's cat is *ingenious*—he has learned to open the door of the cupboard where his cat food is kept.
2. Only an *ingenious* machine like the computer can do ten different things in ten seconds.
3. The music box is *ingenious*: two little dancers move back and forth and bow to each other as the music plays.
4. "Tom is *ingenious*," Lucy said. "He hooked his television to his telephone and now he can see me when I talk to him."

and Verbalize...

_____

_____

_____

inhabit: to live in or on

Visualize...

1. Over seven million people *inhabit* New York City.
2. Hundreds of little green frogs *inhabit* the pond behind Mary's house.
3. Monkeys, brightly-colored birds, and all kinds of insects *inhabit* the tropical jungle.
4. No one *inhabits* a ghost town.

and Verbalize...

_____

_____

_____

inject: to put a liquid inside or into something by using a needle

Visualize...

1. Nurse Jones was going to *inject* me with some flu medicine, but then she asked me if I'd rather take the blue-and-white capsule.
2. "Ouch!" Jeff cried when the doctor *injected* him with a long, sharp needle.
3. Professor Lopez *injected* some red dye into the green water in the test tube.
4. When a rattlesnake bites someone, it *injects* poison through the holes at the ends of its fangs.

and Verbalize...

_____

_____

_____

injury: harm or damage done to a person or thing

Visualize...

1. The car accident left Ron with cuts and bruises but no serious *injury*.
2. The bicyclist hit by the speeding car was taken to the hospital because of his *injuries*.
3. The train jumped the tracks but luckily there were no *injuries* among the 200 passengers.
4. The *injury* to the horse's leg wasn't bad—soon the white stallion would run again in a race.

and Verbalize...

_____

_____

_____

inscription: words carved or written on something

Visualize...

1. The *inscription* on the inside of Mrs. Finch's wedding ring gives the date she was married.
2. The team won the final game and received a big trophy with the *inscription* "STATE CHAMPIONS."
3. "BEST OF LUCK" was the *inscription* on the gold watch Mr. Smith's company gave to him.
4. The archeologists found an ancient tablet with a long *inscription* on it, but no one could read the strange writing.

and Verbalize...

_____

_____

_____

I

inspiration: a sudden flow of good ideas; a person or thing that causes the flow of good ideas

Visualize...

1. The poet was full of *inspiration* and so he wrote and wrote.
2. The composer had no inspiration *inspiration*, so he worked on his car instead of writing a new symphony.
3. "You are my *inspiration!*" Dan said to Flo when he finished his 30-page love poem.
4. "Believe it or not, a dragonfly's wing was my *inspiration* for the new plane," the inventor said.

and Verbalize...

_____

_____

_____

instruct: to teach; to order

Visualize...

1. Lucy *instructed* Jerome in the use of the big green computer.
2. Mrs. Smith began *instructing* her husband in the right way to fry an egg.
3. Dr. Gray *instructed* Wanda to take a green pill in the morning and a blue pill at lunch.
4. The policeman *instructed* Lars to go down into the cellar because the wild tornado was coming closer.

and Verbalize...

_____

_____

_____

instrument: a tool or mechanical device; something that is played to make musical sounds

Visualize...

1. The dentist used one shiny *instrument* after another as she worked on Greg's bad tooth.
2. All of the pilot's *instruments* began to beep and flash when the plane flew through the black thundercloud.
3. Professor Lopez used a special *instrument* to test the green air inside the pyramid.
4. "Do you play a musical *instrument?*" Mr. Wong asked. "I play three *instruments*," June said. "The trumpet, the trombone, and the piano."

and Verbalize...

_____

_____

_____

insulate: to keep from becoming too hot or too cold; to protect

Visualize...

1. The polar bear's thick layer of fat *insulates* him from the freezing snow and icy sea.
2. Walls two feet thick *insulated* the inside of the castle from the burning desert sun.
3. The knights made a circle around the king to *insulate* him from danger.
4. The high mountains *insulated* the castle from attack.

and Verbalize...

_____

_____

_____

intelligence: the ability to think, learn, and understand

Visualize...

1. Flo's *intelligence* helped her learn the new computer system in three days.
2. The monkey proved its *intelligence* when it made itself a peanut-butter-and-jelly sandwich and then poured a glass of milk.
3. It took a lot of *intelligence* to build a rocket that could fly to the moon.
4. Does it take more *intelligence* to build dangerous weapons or to know not to use them.

and Verbalize...

_____

_____

_____

intelligent: smart

Visualize...

1. The very *intelligent* boy played the piano while he did math problems in his head.
2. The *intelligent* horse stamped its hoof three times when Farmer Finch asked, "What's one plus two?"
3. Einstein was a very *intelligent* scientist but he often wore socks that didn't match.
4. Goofy is sweet but he's not as *intelligent* as Mickey Mouse.

and Verbalize...

_____

_____

_____

intense: very great or strong, extreme

Visualize...

1. The heat of the lava from an erupting volcano is *intense*.
2. Few plants or animals can live in the *intense* cold of the Antarctic. The frigid air freezes even your breath.
3. The pressure on a doctor in the operating room can be *intense* because the patient's life depends on the doctor's skill.
4. Richard Burton was an *intense* actor with a deep voice and flashing eyes.

and Verbalize...

_____

_____

_____

interior: the inside

Visualize...

1. Mr. Mendoza painted the *interior* of his house in January, but decided to wait until spring to paint the outside.
2. The outside of the old house looked terrible, but the *interior* was bright and pretty, almost brand-new.
3. The *interior* of the sea shell was shiny, smooth, and pink.
4. In "Beauty and the Beast," the Beast is ugly on the exterior but nice on the *interior*.

and Verbalize...

_____

_____

_____

international: between or among different nations

Visualize...

1. The famous actor had an *international* following—he had fans all over the world.
2. Los Angeles and New York City both have *international* airports, with flights leaving every few minutes for countries around the world.
3. "Do you sell your dried fruit only in the United States, or do you have an *international* market?" Mr. Wong asked Farmer Finch.
4. "Our company is *international*," Mr. Smith explained to his visitors. "We have offices in Berlin, London, and Tokyo."

and Verbalize...

_____

_____

_____

inventor: a person who thinks up new devices and machines

Visualize...

1. Rex's uncle is an *inventor*—he's trying to build a car that can run on sunlight instead of gasoline.
2. Alexander Graham Bell was the *inventor* of the telephone.
3. The Wright brothers were *inventors* who wanted to fly. They invented one of the first airplanes.
4. No one knows which man or woman was the *inventor* of the wheel.

and Verbalize...

_____

_____

_____

investigate: to look into carefully in order to find the facts

Visualize...

1. The boys took lanterns and flashlights when they went to *investigate* the haunted house.
2. Policemen ask people questions and look for evidence when they are *investigating* a crime.
3. The astronauts took samples of rock as they *investigated* the surface of the moon.
4. The fireman sifted through the ashes as he *investigated* the cause of the fire.

and Verbalize...

_____

_____

_____

isolate: to separate or set apart from a group

Visualize...

1. The king wanted to be alone so he *isolated* himself in a castle on an island in the middle of the sea.
2. The teacher *isolated* Ron in the empty hallway when Ron wouldn't behave in class.
3. Greg's mother *isolated* him from the other children until he got over the measles.
4. "We must *isolate* the virus and study it," Dr. Gray said. "That's the first step toward finding a cure for the disease."

and Verbalize...

_____

_____

_____

I

issue: a published magazine that is part of a series; a point or problem to be debated (n)

Visualize...

1. Martha read an article on space flight in the latest *issue* of <u>Time</u> magazine.
2. A new *issue* of <u>Sports Illustrated</u> comes out every month.
3. The senator is well-informed: he has a good grasp of the major *issues* in education, employment, and crime prevention.
4. "Our relations with Central America will be an important *issue* in the presidential race this year," Mrs. Lopez said.

and Verbalize...

_____

_____

_____

issue: to come out; to give out (v)

Visualize...

1. Curls of blue smoke *issued* from the log cabin's chimney.
2. The wonderful smell of freshly-baked bread *issued* from the kitchen.
3. The busy policeman *issued* 25 speeding tickets in one day.
4. "When I *issue* an order I want it obeyed!" the angry general shouted to his men.

and Verbalize...

_____

_____

_____

Chapter 10

The J's & K's

jester: a person who told jokes to amuse the king or queen

Visualize...

1. The *jester* wore a cap with bells, and acted like a clown, turning somersaults and making up songs and rhymes.
2. *Jesters* were the only people in the castle who could make fun of the king.
3. Sometimes the playing card called a "joker" has a *jester's* face on it.
4. *Jesters* were also called "fools," but they were often the wisest people in the kingdom.

and Verbalize...

_____

_____

_____

jewelry: decorations for the body: rings, bracelets, and necklaces

Visualize...

1. Bill gave Beth some *jewelry*—a gold ring and a diamond necklace from the pirate's treasure chest.
2. Rubies, emeralds, and sapphires are costly gems used in expensive *jewelry*.
3. Martha's favorite piece of *jewelry* is a simple string of pearls.
4. "This piece of *jewelry* has been in our family for years," Agnes said when she gave June the silver bracelet.

and Verbalize...

_____

_____

_____

J-K

jockey: a person who rides horses in races

Visualize...

1. A *jockey* must be small and very light so his weight won't slow down his horse.
2. Fred went to the racetrack to watch his favorite *jockey* ride in the race.
3. *Jockeys* wear high boots, caps, and brightly-colored shirts called "silks."
4. The winning *jockey* held up a big gold trophy that was filled with red roses.

and Verbalize...

_____

_____

_____

kangaroo: an animal of Australia with small front legs and large, powerful back legs for jumping

Visualize...

1. A *kangaroo* stands and hops on its back legs and uses its heavy tail for balance.
2. *Kangaroos* have thick soft fur and long ears like a rabbit's.
3. The baby *kangaroo* peeked out from its mother's pouch.
4. The fence at the zoo was high so the *kangaroos* wouldn't jump over it and escape.

and Verbalize...

_____

_____

_____

kneel: to go down on one or both knees

Visualize...

1. Ron had to *kneel* and then crawl on all fours to get under the fence.
2. The hunter *knelt* behind the brown bush as the deer came to drink at the stream.
3. The soldiers *knelt* behind the barricade so the bullets wouldn't hit them.
4. "*Kneel* when you speak to me!" shouted the angry king.

and Verbalize...

_____

_____

_____

knowledge: information gained by study or experience

Visualize...

1. The doctor has a lot of *knowledge* about diseases and how to cure them.
2. Georgia grew up on a ranch, so she has *knowledge* about training horses.
3. The astronomer had lots of *knowledge* about the stars, but not much *knowledge* about cooking a hamburger.
4. "I'm innocent!" said the accused man. "I have no *knowledge* of this crime."

and Verbalize...

_____

_____

_____

knuckle: a place on a finger where two bones are joined

Visualize...

1. The queen slid the diamond ring over her *knuckle* to get it off.
2. Max skinned his *knuckles* trying to climb over the high brick wall.
3. Mary's grandfather has swollen *knuckles* because of his arthritis.
4. You "crack" your *knuckles* by flexing your finger joints and making them "pop."

and Verbalize...

_____

_____

_____

Chapter 11

The L's

label: a piece of paper or cloth that can be stuck or sewn to an object to tell something about it (n)

Visualize...

1. June knew the bottle of blue liquid was poison because of the skull and crossbones on the *label*.
2. At the clothing store Albert looked for a shirt whose *label* said "Extra Large."
3. Tom's little sister took all the *labels* off the cans, so Tom never knew what can he was opening for lunch.
4. Beth read the *label* on the bug poison before she went outside to squirt the giant ant.

and Verbalize...

_____

_____

_____

label: to mark an object to tell something about it (v)

Visualize...

1. Dan's mother *labeled* all of his clothes with his initials before he left for summer camp.
2. Ted *labeled* the jar "Apple" after Ruby put the apple jelly inside.
3. Rod and Jeff didn't *label* any of the boxes, so now they'll have to open every one to find out what's inside.
4. "*Label* that folder 'March' and put all this month's bills inside it," Flo told Phil.

and Verbalize...

_____

_____

_____

labor: work; effort of childbirth

Visualize...

1. Mr. Smith hired carpenters but he also put a lot of his own *labor* into building his new house.
2. It cost Mark $25 for parts and $200 for *labor* to have his car fixed!
3. "Making this cake takes too much *labor*," grumbled Greg.
4. Mrs. Smith went into *labor* at 4 a.m. and her baby was born at noon.

and Verbalize...

_____

_____

_____

lagoon: a small, shallow body of water usually connected to a larger body of water

Visualize...

1. The *lagoon* around a tropical island is separated from the open sea by a coral reef.
2. White foam on the reef shows where the *lagoon* ends and the deep water begins.
3. The water in tropical *lagoons* is green and clear, but the deep water outside the reef is dark blue.
4. When the tide is very low, you can walk across the *lagoon* to the reef.

and Verbalize...

_____

_____

_____

landmark: something which marks an historical place or event; something easily seen which marks location

Visualize...

1. The old farmhouse is a county *landmark*. It was built by the first settler in this valley.
2. The stone *landmark* with the bronze plaque stands where the famous duel was fought.
3. The *landmark* showing where the gold was buried was a big rock with a long crack running through it.
4. "That tree is your *landmark*," Bart said. "When you see it, you turn right to get to the ranch."

and Verbalize...

_____

_____

_____

lantern: a lamp with a cover to protect the light from wind and rain

Visualize...

1. The *lantern* we use when we go camping is very bright and makes a hissing sound.
2. June's mother likes to hang white paper *lanterns* from the trees whenever she has a dinner party outside.
3. Kerosene *lanterns* have a cloth wick you can raise or lower to make the light brighter or dimmer.
4. The farmer lit a *lantern* and went out to the barn to check on the baby calf.

and Verbalize...

_____

_____

_____

laughter: sounds people make when they are happy or amused

Visualize...

1. The children howled with *laughter* when the clown slipped on the banana peel.
2. June knew the movie must be funny when she heard loud *laughter* coming from the theater.
3. There was *laughter* from the audience when the comedian told a joke about his mother-in-law.
4. "It was embarrassing," Rex said. "I told a joke and there wasn't any *laughter*, not even a giggle."

and Verbalize...

_____

_____

_____

launch: to start; to put into the water or send up into the air

Visualize...

1. The company planned to *launch* its new line of lunch boxes just before school opened in September.
2. The new T.V. series about the talking horse was *launched* in the fall.
3. Prince Charles broke a bottle of champagne across the hull of the new cruise ship just before it was *launched.*
4. The rocket was *launched* and the astronauts were on their way to the moon.

and Verbalize...

_____

_____

_____

L

lava: the burning melted rock that flows from a volcano

Visualize...

1. Red glowing *lava* flowed slowly downhill from the crater of the volcano.
2. It's dangerous to be in the direct path of *lava* when a volcano erupts.
3. "This rock that looks like black glass is cooled *lava*," Professor Lopez explained to Beth and Pam.
4. A river of *lava* buried the ancient city of Pompeii.

and Verbalize...

---

lean: without fat (adj)

Visualize...

1. The greyhound isn't a stocky but a *lean* dog that can run faster than a rabbit.
2. *Lean* meat is better for you than meat that has a lot of fat in it.
3. "I'm not skinny, I'm just *lean*," Bill said when his mother tried to get him to eat a third helping.
4. The stray dog had a *lean* and hungry look.

and Verbalize...

---

lean: to stand at a slant instead of straight; to rest against something for support (v)

Visualize...

1. Hortense *leaned* over the fence to pick some orange poppies from the neighbor's flower bed.
2. The famous Tower of Pisa in Italy *leans* quite a bit to one side.
3. Rod *leaned* the ladder against the side of the house so he could climb up and patch the leaky roof.
4. "Della doesn't have any family or friends," Lucy explained. "She doesn't have anybody to *lean* on when things get tough."

and Verbalize...

---

leash: a strap or chain fastened to a dog or other animal to keep it from straying

Visualize...

1. The miner used a rope for a *leash* when he took his pet wolf for a walk.
2. The big red dog pulled the *leash* from his master's hand and ran after the rabbit.
3. Only dogs on *leashes* were allowed in the town park.
4. "Put a *leash* on your monkey," the policeman told Susan. "You can't let it run free like that."

and Verbalize...

_____

_____

_____

legend: a story that may or may not be true that is passed down through the years

Visualize...

1. People care about the *legend* of King Arthur and his knights because it is about love and honor.
2. An American *legend* is the story of George Washington cutting down the cherry tree.
3. My grandfather believed the *legend* of the Lost Dutchman Mine and spent many years looking for gold in the Superstition Mountains of Arizona.
4. "There's a *legend* about this knife," Rex said. "My grandfather told my father that it was made from a chunk of a shooting star."

and Verbalize...

_____

_____

_____

legendary: not real; very famous

Visualize...

1. El Dorado is a *legendary* city whose streets are paved with gold.
2. "Are Paul Bunyan and his blue ox Babe real or *legendary* figures?" Bob asked Flo.
3. Babe Ruth was a *legendary* baseball player who hit 60 home runs in one season.
4. Tom Smith's appetite is *legendary*—everyone in town knows that Tom can eat two steaks, four eggs, and ten pancakes for breakfast.

and Verbalize...

_____

_____

_____

L

leisure: time to rest or to do things you like

Visualize...

1. Does Rex have any *leisure*, or is he busy building houses all the time?
2. Stan doesn't believe in *leisure*—he never rests or plays but only works.
3. Machines were supposed to give people more *leisure* but most of us work more now than ever.
4. Beth's mother has very little *leisure*—she works seven days a week at Don's Cafe.

and Verbalize...

_____

_____

_____

leopard: a large wild cat covered with black spots that lives in Africa and Asia

Visualize...

1. The yellow fur of the *leopard* is covered with hundreds of small black spots.
2. *Leopards*, cheetahs, tigers, and lions are all members of the cat family.
3. When people say, "A *leopard* can't change his spots," they mean that a person can't change the way he or she is.
4. The *leopard* waited on his branch as the careless monkey began to climb the tree.

and Verbalize...

_____

_____

_____

level: height; position or rank (n)

Visualize...

1. When the Blue River flooded it rose to a *level* of 60 feet.
2. The water *level* in the trough had dropped and now the gray horse had to stretch his neck to get a drink.
3. Mr. Smith worked his way up through the different *levels* of the ice cream company until he became the chairman of the board.
4. Jeff's *level* of ability in reading and writing is much higher since he took the special summer school class.

and Verbalize...

_____

_____

_____

level: an instrument for showing whether a surface is horizontal (n)

Visualize...

1. Carpenters use a *level* to make sure what they are building is exactly horizontal.
2. A *level* has a little window with a bubble in it. The bubble moves back and forth and shows when things are crooked or straight.
3. Hortense carried a hammer, a saw, a box of nails, and a *level*.
4. Mr. Smith used a *level* to make sure his new pool table was perfectly horizontal.

and Verbalize...

_____

_____

_____

level: having the same height everywhere; of equal height (adj)

Visualize...

1. Rex rolled the ball but it stopped and rolled back to him because the floor wasn't *level*.
2. The old table wasn't *level*—it leaned to one side, because two of its legs were too short.
3. The bottom of the elephant's long ear was *level* with the zoo keeper's eyes.
4. "Are the fence posts *level* with one another, or are some of them higher than the rest?" Greg's father asked him as they built the new fence.

and Verbalize...

_____

_____

_____

level: to scrape to the same height; to aim; to be truthful (v)

Visualize...

1. The builder *leveled* the ground with a bulldozer before he poured the foundation for the house.
2. Farmers *level* their fields so water will flow evenly and reach all the thirsty plants.
3. Flo *leveled* her rifle at the target and then pulled the trigger.
4. "Are you going to *level* with me or not?" Dan's father asked. "I want the true story about the monkey in the kitchen."

and Verbalize...

_____

_____

_____

L

lifetime: the period of time that a person or thing is alive

Visualize...

1. Professor Lopez explained that the blue fly had a *lifetime* of only a few days.
2. Martha's grandfather lived his entire *lifetime* on a cattle ranch in western Montana.
3. In your *lifetime* men and women from Earth may land on Mars.
4. "I don't like to waste time," Beth explained. "I've got a thousand things to do and only one *lifetime* to do them in."

and Verbalize...

_____

_____

_____

limit: the point or line where something ends; maximum quantity allowed

Visualize...

1. Mary and Gus drove to the city *limits* and then beyond them, out into the green countryside.
2. The scientist believed there must be more galaxies beyond the known *limits* of the universe.
3. "No, three is my *limit*," Tim said, when Lucy asked him if he wanted another hamburger.
4. "The speed *limit* on the highway is 55 miles per hour, but in town it's 25," the policeman explained as he wrote Lars a ticket.

and Verbalize...

_____

_____

_____

lizard: an animal with a long body and tail, four legs, and scaly skin

Visualize...

1. A *lizard* is a reptile, a cold-blooded animal like an alligator or a snake.
2. The small brown *lizard* shot out its long tongue to catch the buzzing fly.
3. "The chameleon changes colors to hide itself," Professor Lopez explained, pointing to the green *lizard* on the green leaf.
4. The marine iguana is a rare *lizard* that swims in the ocean and eats seaweed.

and Verbalize...

_____

_____

_____

L

location: the place where something is

Visualize...

1. Lars and Stan looked and looked but couldn't find the *location of* the buried treasure.
2. June's red dog keeps digging up bones and moving them to new *locations*.
3. José's vacation house is in a beautiful *location*—there's a forest at his front door and the ocean at his back door.
4. The director shot his movie on *location* in Brazil instead of using the fake jungle in the studio in Hollywood.

and Verbalize...

_____

_____

_____

loneliness: being alone and wanting to be with others

Visualize...

1. The dog in the pet store whined because it suffered from *loneliness*—all of the other dogs had been sold.
2. *Loneliness* isn't a problem for Hortense now that she has a kitten to keep her company.
3. Mr. James felt great *loneliness* when he lived in the lighthouse at the edge of the distant sea.
4. "My biggest problem was *loneliness*," Lars said, when he returned from sailing around the world in a one-man boat. "There was no one to talk to."

and Verbalize...

_____

_____

_____

loom: a frame or machine for weaving cloth (n)

Visualize...

1. Aunt Agnes likes to weave cloth place mats and napkins on her wooden *loom*.
2. Lucy wove the yarn back and forth through the strings of the *loom*.
3. Navajo women and men use large *looms* to weave rugs with beautiful designs.
4. Factory *looms* are huge and loud, and are run by electric motors.

and Verbalize...

_____

_____

_____

L

loom: to appear dimly or vaguely as a large, threatening shape (v)

Visualize...

1. Rex and Mark jumped out of the way when the big truck *loomed* suddenly through the thick fog in front of them.
2. The hunter grabbed his rifle as the grizzly bear *loomed* above the opening of the tent.
3. At sunset the western mountains *loomed* above the valley, casting long shadows across the fields and town.
4. "Don't look now, but there's a black-caped vampire *looming* over your shoulder," Pam whispered to Della in the darkened castle.

and Verbalize...

_____

_____

_____

lumber: wood that has been cut into boards (n)

Visualize...

1. The loggers cut down the pines and hauled them to the mill to be sawed into *lumber.*
2. Oak is a hardwood and one of the most expensive kinds of *lumber.*
3. "Be careful of this rough *lumber*," Bill said. "It'll give you splinters because it hasn't been planed."
4. "You're going to need a lot more *lumber* to finish that stable," Mr. Finch told Flo and Gus. "You've got to build another wall."

and Verbalize...

_____

_____

_____

lumber: to move along heavily (v)

Visualize...

1. The bear *lumbered* across the meadow, his big body slow and heavy.
2. The orange cat got away easily when the Great Dane tried to *lumber* after it.
3. The moving van had a string of 20 cars behind it as it *lumbered* up the mountain.
4. The huge football players *lumbered* into the locker room after losing the game.

and Verbalize...

_____

_____

_____

lunge: to move forward suddenly

Visualize...

1. The dog watched the cat walk across the room, then suddenly *lunged* at it with a loud bark and bared teeth.
2. The fighters danced around the boxing ring, *lunging* at each other but not landing any punches.
3. Pam raced across the field, stumbled, then *lunged* for the baseball and caught it just as it was about to hit the ground.
4. Ted *lunged* for the runaway baby carriage as the speeding car turned the corner.

and Verbalize...

_____

_____

_____

lurch: a sudden rolling or swaying movement

Visualize...

1. Jerome's baby sister took her first step with a *lurch*, then fell down.
2. The old blue car slipped out of gear and with a *lurch* began rolling down the hill toward the intersection.
3. The pirate with the wooden leg has a *lurch* in his walk.
4. "The phone rang, and I woke up with a *lurch*," Susan explained. "That's how I bumped my head."

and Verbalize...

_____

_____

_____

Chapter 12

The M's

machinery: machines; the moving, working parts of a machine

Visualize...

1. Della's brother likes to work with *machinery* and plans to be a car mechanic.
2. The old farm *machinery*—the cotton picker, the hay rake, and the spray rig—sat rusting in the barnyard.
3. The *machinery* of the jammed typewriter was full of dirt and dust and grime.
4. "We use a lot of oil to keep this *machinery* running smoothly," the mechanic said, pointing to the gears and levers and spinning wheels.

and Verbalize...

_____

_____

_____

magnet: a piece of iron that draws other iron objects toward it

Visualize...

1. Bob's horseshoe-shaped *magnet* picked up bits of iron from the dirt.
2. The big crane in the junkyard used a giant *magnet* to pick up the wrecked car.
3. Flo used a *magnet* to find the needle that was lost in the hay stack.
4. The lamp was like a *magnet* to the moths—they were all attracted to its bright light.

and Verbalize...

_____

_____

_____

M

maintain: to keep in good condition or repair; to declare to be true; to uphold or defend

Visualize...

1. Dr. Gray pays Jerome to do her gardening—Jerome *maintains* her lawn and flowers and trees.
2. Mr. Wong *maintains* his car by having the oil changed every 2,000 miles.
3. The man on trial for bank robbery *maintained* his innocence throughout the trial, but he was found guilty anyway.
4. The army *maintained* its position along the river until nightfall.

and Verbalize...

_____

_____

_____

majestic: grand or noble-looking

Visualize...

1. The Grand Canyon is *majestic*.
2. From his hotel room Dan had a *majestic* view of the snowy mountains and the blue lake reflecting the mountains.
3. The Arabian stallion is a *majestic* animal—no horse is more beautiful, or has a prouder bearing.
4. The ship was *majestic*, with large white sails and shining decks and a blue flag with three gold crowns across it.

and Verbalize...

_____

_____

_____

major: largest, most important

Visualize...

1. The *major* part of Ruby's first day at work was spent meeting people and learning what her duties would be.
2. "Is brushing your teeth of *major* or minor importance in maintaining healthy teeth and gums?" Dr. Gray asked the students.
3. The *major* role in a play or movie is called the "lead."
4. "Mr. Clark is the *major* stockholder in our corporation," the president of the ice cream company told Rex. "He owns 55% of the shares."

and Verbalize...

_____

_____

_____

mammal: warm-blooded animal that has hair or fur—female mammals have glands that produce milk

Visualize...

1. Whales may look like fish, but they are really *mammals*.
2. The blue whale is the largest *mammal* and the largest animal to ever live on earth.
3. Human beings, dogs, cats, cows, and horses are *mammals*. Snakes, lizards, alligators, and turtles are reptiles.
4. Giraffes are the *mammals* with the longest necks.

and Verbalize...

_____

_____

_____

mammoth: an extinct large elephant with hairy skin and long curved tusks (n)

Visualize...

1. Cave men killed *mammoths*, ate them, and used their skins for clothes.
2. Ancient men painted pictures of *mammoths* on the walls of their caves.
3. The last *mammoth* died thousands of years ago.
4. Intact *mammoths* have been found frozen in big blocks of ice.

and Verbalize...

_____

_____

_____

mammoth: huge (adj)

Visualize...

1. Digging the Panama Canal was a *mammoth* job that took years.
2. The *mammoth* cargo plane could hold ten tanks, six helicopters, four jeeps, and 50 soldiers.
3. "The grizzly bear looks *mammoth* when it stands on its hind legs and waves its paws over your head," Rod said. "I was terrified."
4. The mountain was *mammoth*—its peak was higher than the clouds.

and Verbalize...

_____

_____

_____

M

maneuver: to move or manipulate skillfully

Visualize...

1. The pilot *maneuvered* the helicopter just above the water so the man in the life raft could grab the rope ladder.
2. Drivers on New York streets go very fast, *maneuvering* quickly in and out of traffic.
3. In two minutes Mr. Finch *maneuvered* the clumsy caterpillar up the ramp and onto the trailer.
4. The cowboy rode quickly from one side to the other as he *maneuvered* the cows through the gate and into the corral.

and Verbalize...

_____

_____

_____

manipulate: to handle or operate; to manage by clever use of personal influence

Visualize...

1. The artist *manipulated* his pencil skillfully, quickly sketching Ruby's pretty face.
2. Greg was good at *manipulating* a boat—he steered us safely through the dangerous reef and into the open sea.
3. By pretending to be unhappy, Della *manipulated* her father into buying her the new dress.
4. The boss knew how to *manipulate* his employees by promising them more money or threatening to pay them less.

and Verbalize...

_____

_____

_____

manufacture: to make things, especially by machine and in large numbers

Visualize...

1. The shoe factory by the river *manufactures* 4000 pairs of shoes a day.
2. Cars are *manufactured* on an assembly line, where each person does one specialized job over and over.
3. Rex's uncle owns a small business that *manufactures* gears for cuckoo clocks.
4. The "U.S.A." stamped on the back of the wristwatch tells us where it was *manufactured*.

and Verbalize...

_____

_____

_____

marvel: to feel wonder and astonishment

Visualize...

1. Pam always *marvels* at the wonderful dinners Aunt Martha makes in 20 minutes.
2. The young father *marveled* at the way his little boy could sleep anywhere, anytime.
3. Flo *marveled* at the hundreds of gold coins and sparkling jewels in the pirate's treasure chest.
4. "I *marvel* at your calmness," Stan said to the captain as the ship began to sink slowly beneath them.

and Verbalize...

_____

_____

_____

massive: huge

Visualize...

1. The *massive* stone that rolled down the mountain was the size of a bus.
2. The *massive* crowd filled the huge stadium and overflowed into the city streets.
3. The fallen tree was *massive* and blocked four lanes of traffic.
4. King Kong lifted his *massive* head and screamed when the airplane attacked him.

and Verbalize...

_____

_____

_____

mast: a long pole that holds a ship's sails

Visualize...

1. Three wide, white canvas sails flew from the main *mast* of the ship.
2. A black flag with a skull and crossbones flew from the *mast* of the pirate's ship.
3. The sailor climbed the *mast* to the crow's-nest to look for land.
4. The sailing ship slowly sank, until only the tip of the *mast* was above the water.

and Verbalize...

_____

_____

_____

master: expert; a person who has power or authority over others

Visualize...

1. The Dutch painter Van Gogh was a *master* at using colors, especially bright yellows and oranges and reds.
2. Lars is an experienced mason and a *master* at building brick chimneys.
3. "Are you the *master* of the house?" the saleswoman asked Dan when he opened the front door. "No," Dan said, "my father is."
4. "A dog obeys its *master*, but a cat is its own *master*," Della's little brother explained to her.

and Verbalize...

_____

_____

_____

material: what a thing is made from or used for; a fabric, cloth

Visualize...

1. Concrete and steel are two kinds of building *materials* used to construct skyscrapers.
2. Della bought the *materials* f or fixing the fence at the hardware store.
3. Ruby chose a light cotton *material* for the summer dress she was making.
4. Wool is a good *material* for clothes if you live in a cold climate.

and Verbalize...

_____

_____

_____

mature: having reached full growth or development; ripe

Visualize...

1. When those young trees are *mature*, they will be over 35 feet tall.
2. Eric is 40 years old but he is about as *mature* as a teenager.
3. When the tomatoes are *mature* they will be dark red, sweet, and very juicy.
4. A Santa Rosa plum isn't *mature* until it turns a dark purple.

and Verbalize...

_____

_____

_____

melody: a series of musical notes that make up a tune; the main tune in a piece of music

Visualize...

1. The song "Danny Boy" has a sad *melody* that makes many people cry when they hear it.
2. Most love songs have slow, tender *melodies.*
3. Flo and Tim write songs together—Flo writes the *melodies* and Tim writes the words or "lyrics."
4. In this piece of music, the piano carries the *melody* and the violins and harp give the harmony.

and Verbalize...

_____

_____

_____

merchandise: goods sold in stores

Visualize...

1. The store clerks were stacking new *merchandise* on the shelves after the big sale.
2. "This is very nice *merchandise*," Lucy said as she lifted the set of dinner knives from the display case.
3. The department store keeps most of its *merchandise* in a warehouse.
4. When Mr. Cooper went out of the tire business he had to sell all his *merchandise.*

and Verbalize...

_____

_____

_____

mermaid: an imaginary woman with the tail of a fish who lives in the ocean

Visualize...

1. The *mermaid* would be a beautiful woman if she had legs instead of a tail.
2. The sailor in the story loved a *mermaid*, and he was sad when she swam out to sea and left him.
3. *Mermaids* are supposed to be able to live only in the water.
4. A "merman" is a male *mermaid.*

and Verbalize...

_____

_____

_____

M

mesh: an open space in a net, sieve, or screen

Visualize...

1. A mosquito net has a very small *mesh* so mosquitoes can't fly through it.
2. "Chicken wire" has a six-sided *mesh* about the size of a quarter and is used in chicken coops.
3. The *mesh* of our screen door has little rips in it from where our cat has climbed with his claws.
4. "*Mesh*" stockings are stockings dancers wear. They look like black netting.

and Verbalize...

_____

_____

_____

meter: the basic unit of length in the metric system of measurement (a meter is just over 39 inches; an instrument which measures the amount of something

Visualize...

1. A mosquito net has a very small *mesh* so mosquitoes can't fly through it.
2. "Chicken wire" has a six-sided *mesh* about the size of a quarter and is used in chicken coops.
3. The *mesh* of our screen door has little rips in it from where our cat has climbed with his claws.
4. "*Mesh*" stockings are stockings dancers wear. They look like black netting.

and Verbalize...

_____

_____

_____

method: the way of doing something

Visualize...

1. A good *method* for doing laundry is to sort clothes into "colors" and "whites."
2. Pam's neighbor has a strange *method* of mowing his lawn: he borrows his brother's sheep on Saturday and lets them graze all day.
3. "What's the best *method* for getting grease spots out of the rug?" Della asked Bob. "I just dropped the turkey."
4. The "scientific *method*" is an orderly way of asking questions and collecting information about things.

and Verbalize...

_____

_____

_____

metric: a system of measurement based on the meter and the gram

Visualize...

1. People in Europe use the *metric* system for measuring distance and weight.
2. You can use the *metric* "kilometer" or the American "mile" to measure distance.
3. "Kilos" are the *metric* measurement, "pounds" the American one.
4. Professor Lopez has a set of *metric* tools for his VW car—his wrenches are "sized" in millimeters instead of fractions of an inch.

and Verbalize...

_____

_____

_____

microphone: an instrument that turns sound into electrical signals and makes the sound louder

Visualize...

1. "Testing, testing," the musician said into the *microphone*, and his voice filled the auditorium.
2. The audience couldn't hear Hortense's speech, so someone brought her a *microphone* to amplify her voice.
3. Most *microphones* are attached to a wire and sit in a metal stand, but others are wireless and portable.
4. The singer whispered "I love this audience" into the *microphone* and everyone smiled and applauded.

and Verbalize...

_____

_____

_____

midnight: twelve o'clock at night—the end of one day and the start of the next

Visualize...

1. At *midnight* the worried queen woke up to hear the clock strike 12 times.
2. Noon is 12 p.m. and *midnight* is 12 a.m.
3. Cinderella's carriage turned into a pumpkin at *midnight*.
4. Each new year begins one second after *midnight* on December 31, 1991—New Year's Eve.

and Verbalize...

_____

_____

_____

migration: a movement from one place to settle in another

Visualize...

1. The *migration* of birds flying south for the winter often begins as early as September.
2. Monarch butterflies have a *migration* that takes them from the California coast to a valley in central Mexico.
3. The *migration* of the grey whales is from Alaska to the Gulf of California.
4. Early American settlers followed a *migration* which took them west to open country.

and Verbalize...

---

mineral: a material or substance that is dug out of the earth

Visualize...

1. Gold and silver are precious *minerals* that are mined from the earth.
2. Oil is a liquid *mineral* that is pumped out of the earth through a well.
3. Coal is a soft, black-colored *mineral* that is burned for fuel.
4. "Is Spot an animal, vegetable, or *mineral*?" Flo's little brother asked. "Spot is a rock," Flo said. "He is a *mineral*."

and Verbalize...

---

miniature: a very small copy or model

Visualize...

1. Some people collect glass bottles with *miniatures* of ships inside them.
2. The little figurine on Beth's desk is a *miniature* of the Statue of Liberty.
3. Mr. Wong spent a year building a *miniature* of the Eiffel Tower in his garage.
4. Model airplanes are *miniatures* of real airplanes.

and Verbalize...

---

mirror: a flat, silver-backed glass in which you can see yourself

Visualize...

1. Ruby always stops to look at herself whenever she sees a *mirror*.
2. The Invisible Man could never see his reflection in a *mirror*.
3. Mark held up a *mirror* to see if his fake mustache was still glued on.
4. The blue lake was like a *mirror*—in its still waters the clouds and mountains were reflected.

and Verbalize...

_____

_____

_____

mitten: a covering for the hand

Visualize...

1. A *mitten* has one space for your fingers and one space for your thumb.
2. *Mittens* are warmer than gloves because your fingers keep one another warm.
3. You can't use a pair of scissors when you're wearing *mittens*.
4. Tim wore a green stocking cap, a blue scarf, and red *mittens* when he went outside to build a snowman.

and Verbalize...

_____

_____

_____

mob: a crowd, especially one that is lawless and disorderly

Visualize...

1. An angry *mob* gathered outside the jail after the trial was over.
2. "Go home," the sheriff told the *mob*, "I'm not going to let anything happen to my prisoner."
3. "I don't like rock concerts," Jeff said, "because the *mobs* make me nervous."
4. A *mob* of children raced out of the movie theater and filled the sidewalk so no one could pass by.

and Verbalize...

_____

_____

_____

moist: slightly wet, damp

Visualize...

1. After the gentle rain the flower bed was *moist* but not muddy.
2. Agnes wiped the smeared lipstick from her mouth with a *moist* Kleenex.
3. Frank checked the towels in the dryer, but they were still *moist.*
4. I thought the roof was leaking because the ceiling felt *moist.*

and Verbalize...

_____

_____

_____

moisture: a slight wetness, dampness

Visualize...

1. The potted plant was dry as a bone—there wasn't a drop of *moisture* in its soil.
2. June caught her breath and wiped the *moisture* from her face after running up the stairs.
3. "This little sprinkle of rain is good," Mrs. Mendoza said. "We really need the *moisture.*"
4. The water bottle was almost empty—there was just a little *moisture* at the bottom.

and Verbalize...

_____

_____

_____

mold: a furry fungus that grows on food and damp surfaces; a hollow form that allows a liquid to dry or harden into a certain shape (n)

Visualize...

1. Mary held up the carton of green cottage cheese. "Oh no," she said, "*mold*!!"
2. The empty house was cold and moist and there was *mold* growing on the curtains.
3. Flo makes Jello in a copper *mold* shaped like a starfish.
4. The candle maker poured the hot wax into a *mold* to make a big square candle.

and Verbalize...

_____

_____

_____

mold: to make into a special shape (v)

Visualize...

1. The sculptor *molded* the big lump of clay until it looked like the face of Thomas Jefferson.
2. Johnny used his fork to *mold* his potatoes into a tall mountain.
3. The concert musician tried to *mold* his daughter spent in the wilderness.

and Verbalize...

_____

_____

_____

molten: melted by heat

Visualize...

1. *Molten* steel is poured into molds to cool and harden.
2. Lava is *molten* rock which flows like liquid fire from a volcano.
3. Glassblowers blow into special tubes to form *molten* glass into different shapes.
4. The *molten* wax of a candle is as hot as the candle's flame.

and Verbalize...

_____

_____

_____

monitor: a person with special duties; a device which records or checks (n)

Visualize...

1. The blackboard *monitor* cleaned the blackboards every day after school.
2. The test *monitor* handed out tests and pencils to the students. "Keep your eyes on your own papers," he said.
3. The mechanic used an exhaust *monitor* to make sure the car wasn't spewing too much pollution into the air.
4. In a T.V. studio the *monitor* is a T.V. screen which shows the picture being broadcast.

and Verbalize...

_____

_____

_____

M

monitor: to check or keep watch over (v)

Visualize...

1. The scientist *monitored* his instruments daily to make sure they were working correctly.
2. The young mother *monitored* her child's progress at school by talking to the teacher every week.
3. The nurse closely *monitored* the T.V. screen that showed the sick man's heartbeats.
4. The librarian *monitored* the children in the library, whispering to them to read and not talk.

and Verbalize...

---

moonlit: lighted by the moon

Visualize...

1. The *moonlit* lake looked like a pool of molten silver.
2. The woman stood in the open doorway, her *moonlit* hair a white glow around her face.
3. On a *moonlit* night you can often see your shadow on the ground.
4. We walked down the *moonlit* road between dark trees and pale flowers.

and Verbalize...

---

mortal: unable to live forever, subject to death; able to cause death; very serious, extreme

Visualize...

1. Will Superman live forever, or is he *mortal?*
2. Knowing you are *mortal* makes you realize how precious time is.
3. The soldier suffered a *mortal* wound in the battle and died that night.
4. Stan has a *mortal* fear of snakes—even a harmless gopher snake makes him tremble.

and Verbalize...

---

mosquito: a thin buzzing insect that leaves itchy bites

Visualize...

1. When a *mosquito* bites you, it sucks some of your blood and leaves an itchy bump.
2. *Mosquitoes* make a whining sound when they buzz around your head.
3. One *mosquito* in Della's bedroom was enough to keep her awake all night.
4. On a humid summer night you can spend all your time slapping at *mosquitoes*.

and Verbalize...

_____

_____

_____

motion: movement; a request for a vote (n)

Visualize...

1. The rocking *motion* of the boat made Fred sleepy, but it made Frank sick.
2. With a *motion* of his arm the policeman signaled that I could cross the street.
3. "I make a *motion* we vote on this bill <u>tonight</u>," the tired senator said.
4. "I second Pam's *motion* to adjourn the meeting early," Rex said. "I've got to get home to watch Bart Simpson on T.V."

and Verbalize...

_____

_____

_____

motion: to signal or direct by making a gesture (v)

Visualize...

1. The waitress *motioned* us to follow her to a table by the window.
2. Mr. Wong *motioned* Agnes out of the room. "I have to talk to you right now," he whispered when she met him in the hallway.
3. When Mark heard his mother's voice he turned around and saw her *motioning* to him from across the room.
4. Lucy thought her father was *motioning* to her, but he was just brushing away a fly.

and Verbalize...

_____

_____

_____

mountaintop: the top of a mountain

Visualize...

1. Pines grow up the sides of this mountain, but the *mountaintop* is just bare rock.
2. Climbers often put up a flag when they reach the *mountaintop*.
3. Some people in Peru live in small villages on *mountaintops*.
4. The pilot saw only a carpet of white cloud and here and there snow-covered *mountaintops* sticking up.

and Verbalize...

_____

_____

_____

mulch: leaves or straw spread on flowerbeds to help plants grow

Visualize...

1. Lars mixes grass clippings and leaves to make *mulch* for his garden.
2. Mary bought a bag of *mulch* at the nursery for her rosebushes.
3. A *mulch* made out of leaves and vegetable scraps is called "compost."
4. To a weak, hungry plant, rich *mulch* is like a wonderful dinner.

and Verbalize...

_____

_____

_____

mummy: a body that is preserved after death by a special process the Egyptians used, which included the wrapping of the body with cloth

Visualize...

1. The ancient Egyptians buried their dead as *mummies*—bodies wrapped in long strips of cloth.
2. The *mummies* of the Pharaohs—Egyptian kings—were placed in burial chambers deep inside the pyramids.
3. Archeologists have also found *mummies* of dogs and cats.
4. Some ancient *mummies* studied by scientists still have hair and skin.

and Verbalize...

_____

_____

_____

muscle: the tissue in the bodies of people and animals that can be tightened or loosened to make the body move; strength

Visualize...

1. The long *muscle* in the back of your leg is called a "hamstring."
2. Dan likes to flex his arm so people can feel his *muscles*.
3. Ed didn't have enough *muscle* to budge the refrigerator.
4. "Frank's team played hard, but they didn't have the *muscle* and we finally wore them down," Ted explained.

and Verbalize...

_____

_____

_____

musical: a play or motion picture with songs, choruses, and dances (n)

Visualize...

1. "My Fair Lady" is a *musical* about a poor girl who begins a new and happier life when she learns to speak better English.
2. The *musical* "South Pacific" is set on a tropical island with swaying palm trees and green lagoons.
3. In the *musical* "Cats," the actors dress like cats, with whiskers, long tails, and paws instead of hands.
4. "West Side Story" is a *musical* based on Shakespeare's "Romeo and Juliet."

and Verbalize...

_____

_____

_____

musical: able to make music; sounding beautiful or pleasing like music (adj)

Visualize...

1. Everyone in the band played a different *musical* instrument.
2. Stan's sister is very *musical*, but Stan can't carry a tune.
3. "Let's listen to the *musical* call of the meadowlark," Professor Lopez said as he started the tape recorder.
4. Mr. Finch loved his wife not only for her kindness and beauty but also for her hauntingly *musical* voice.

and Verbalize...

_____

_____

_____

Chapter 13

The N's

nation: a country; a group of people sharing the same history, culture, and language

Visualize...

1. Canada is the *nation* just north of the United States.
2. Spain, France, Italy, Germany, and Switzerland are some of the *nations* in Europe.
3. The movie "Dances with Wolves" is about the Native Americans who made up the Sioux *nation*.
4. "Alien *Nation*" is a movie about a group of people who come to Earth from another planet.

and Verbalize...

_____

_____

_____

navigate: to sail, steer, or direct a ship or plane

Visualize...

1. The captain *navigated* his ship through the locks of the Panama Canal.
2. The ship's navigator checked his maps before he advised his captain how to *navigate* through the dangerous reef.
3. Rex had to *navigate* the rough seas blindly when the dense fog descended.
4. A pilot *navigates* his plane with the help of his co-pilot and his navigator.

and Verbalize...

_____

_____

_____

N

needle: a small, slender piece of steel used for sewing; the piece of thin steel the medicine flows through when a doctor gives you a shot; the thin, pointed leaf of a pine tree; the tiny part of a record player that rides on the record and picks up the sound

Visualize...

1. "I'll thread the *needle* if you'll sew on the button," Pam said to Ted.
2. "Shots don't hurt that much, bit I still get frightened whin I see that shining *needle*," Professor Lopez confessed to Flo.
3. The *needles* on a pine tree don't fall off when winter comes.
4. The record sounds scratchy because the *needle* on the stereo is worn out.

and Verbalize...

_____

_____

_____

nerve: a bundle of fibers that carries signals between the brain and spine and other parts of the body

Visualize...

1. Greg's back hurts because a slipped disc in his spine is pinching a *nerve*.
2. The dentist gave Della a shot to deaden the *nerve* before he started to drill her tooth.
3. The *nerves* in June's hand sent a quick message to her brain—"Hurry, your hand is burning! Lift it off the stove!"
4. "I drank five cups of coffee and now my *nerves* are jumpy," Professor Lopez explained when he dropped all his books.

and Verbalize...

_____

_____

_____

network: an interconnected system of lines or wires; an interconnected system or group, especially of T.V. or radio stations

Visualize...

1. The spider's web was a complicated *network* of slender silk cables.
2. I could hardly see the stars through the *network* of telephone lines and T.V. antennas.
3. The three main T.V. *networks* in the United States are ABC, NBC, and CBS.
4. Bank of America has a *network* of banks across the country.

and Verbalize...

_____

_____

_____

170

nightfall: dusk, the time when night comes

Visualize...

1. On summer nights the children were supposed to be home before *nightfall.*
2. All along the street the porch lights of the houses came on at *nightfall.*
3. The cowboys rode fast to reach their camp before *nightfall.*
4. "Twilight" is the brief period between daytime and *nightfall.*

and Verbalize...

_____

_____

_____

nomad: a person who belongs to a group of people who have no permanent home, but move from place to place

Visualize...

1. Gypsies are the famous *nomads* of eastern Europe.
2. Some Arab tribes are *nomads* who travel back and forth across the desert.
3. Many Native Americans were *nomads* who moved their teepees across the plains as they followed the buffalo.
4. "The tribe of African *nomads* moved from place to place in search of pasture for their cattle," Professor Lopez explained to Stan.

and Verbalize...

_____

_____

_____

nook: a cozy little corner; a small, out-of-the-way place or compartment

Visualize...

1. Ted always eats at the little table in the breakfast *nook* instead of in the dining room.
2. The waiter showed Della and Dan to a warm *nook* by the fireplace.
3. Joyce keeps her personal papers in a special *nook* in her desk.
4. "If you are looking 'in every *nook* and cranny,' you are looking in every small place you can think of," Mrs. Smith told her students.

and Verbalize...

_____

_____

_____

N

normal: standard or usual

Visualize...

1. Mark said he had a fever but his temperature was *normal* when Dr. Gray read the thermometer.
2. It isn't unusual but *normal* for sharks to have three rows of teeth.
3. It's *normal* for a child to begin walking about the age of one.
4. The *normal* pattern for most people is to work during the day and sleep at night.

and Verbalize...

_____

_____

_____

numerous: many

Visualize...

1. The king had *numerous* shirts and pairs of pants but only one gold crown.
2. Dan telephoned Della *numerous* times, not just once or twice.
3. "I can't marry you," Beth said, returning Bill's ring. "Your faults are too *numerous* to mention."
4. June stopped taking cable T.V. because the *numerous* channels were giving her too many choices.

and Verbalize...

_____

_____

_____

Chapter 14

The O's

oar: a long paddle used to row a boat

Visualize...

1. The motor was out of gas so Gus had to use the *oars* to row the boat to shore.
2. Rowboats have *oars*, kayaks, canoes, and small rafts have paddles.
3. Little loops called "*oar* locks" keep the *oars* in place while you row.
4. The ancient Romans used slaves to man the many *oars* of their ships or "galleys."

and Verbalize...

_____

_____

_____

observe: to see, notice, watch; to follow a law or rule

Visualize...

1. Lars hoped Mrs. Smith hadn't *observed* him sleeping at his desk.
2. Ruby *observed* the lab experiment and took notes for the test on Thursday.
3. "*Observe!*" said the magician, pulling a rabbit out of his hat.
4. The policeman pulled Della over and gave her a ticket for not *observing* the speed limit.

and Verbalize...

_____

_____

_____

obstacle: something that stands in the way or stops progress

Visualize...

1. The horse jumped over a hurdle, a barrel, and other *obstacles* in the ring.
2. The storm blew down one tree and then another, until the entire highway was covered with *obstacles* and no car could pass.
3. Flo's broken leg was a major *obstacle* to her going to the skating party.
4. "Normal danger is no *obstacle* to me!" shouted Superman as he leaped to stop the train.

and Verbalize...

_____

_____

_____

octopus: a sea animal with a soft body and eight long arms called tentacles.

Visualize...

1. The purple *octopus* wrapped its eight arms around the pink seashell.
2. The *octopus* let out a cloud of black ink so it could hide from the shark.
3. Although it can swim, the *octopus* usually moves by crawling along the sea floor.
4. The *octopus* used the round suckers on the underside of its tentacles to cling to the rock.

and Verbalize...

_____

_____

_____

opinion: a belief based upon what a person thinks or believes rather than what is proved or known to be true

Visualize...

1. "In my *opinion*," June said, "blue is the best color for a kitchen."
2. "I want facts, not *opinions*," the police captain told the officers who were investigating the robbery.
3. An editorial is a newspaper column that gives one writer's *opinion*.
4. Mrs. Jones had strong *opinions* about everything, even things she didn't know anything about.

and Verbalize...

_____

_____

_____

opponent: a person who is against another in a fight, contest, or discussion

Visualize...

1. The boxer watched his *opponent* enter the ring as the crowd applauded and shouted.
2. Who was John F. Kennedy's *opponent* in the 1960 presidential election?
3. The chess player watched carefully as his *opponent* began to move her queen.
4. The tennis players were *opponents* on the court, but good friends in their personal lives.

and Verbalize...

_____

_____

_____

orbit: the path that a planet or other heavenly body follows as it moves in a circle around another heavenly body

Visualize...

1. The Earth travels in an *orbit* around the sun.
2. The moon moves in its own *orbit* around the Earth.
3. Our rockets have put satellites into *orbit* around the Earth.
4. The Earth's *orbit* lies between the *orbits* of Venus and Mars.

and Verbalize...

_____

_____

_____

orchard: a piece of land on which many fruit trees are grown

Visualize...

1. Rex and June took their ladders and buckets into the *orchard* to pick apples.
2. Every tree in the *orchard* was covered with huge, dark-purple plums.
3. "It's going to take a long time to pick the pears," Mr. Finch said. "That *orchard* has more than 500 trees."
4. *Orchards* of citrus trees—lemon, orange, and grapefruit—are called "groves."

and Verbalize...

_____

_____

_____

orchestra: a large group of musicians playing music together on various instruments

Visualize...

1. Every member of the *orchestra* watched the conductor lift his baton.
2. The *orchestra* is divided into different sections—the strings, the horns, the woodwinds, and the percussions.
3. "Big bands" were *orchestras* which played popular dance music in the 1930's and 40's.
4. The L.A. Philharmonic is an *orchestra* which plays long works of music called "symphonies."

and Verbalize...

_____

_____

_____

ordeal: an experience that is painful or difficult

Visualize...

1. Jerome's long *ordeal* in the wilderness began when the bear chased him and he became separated from the rest of the campers.
2. The pilot's plane crash in the mountains was the beginning of a terrible *ordeal.*
3. Beth survived her *ordeal* on the desert island by drinking rain water and catching fish with a string and a safety pin.
4. My mother's operation and long stay in the hospital were an *ordeal* for our whole family.

and Verbalize...

_____

_____

_____

organization: a group of people working together for a specific purpose, as in an agency, club, or business; an arrangement of parts to make a whole

Visualize...

1. The Red Cross is an international *organization* that helps people in distress.
2. People from different *organizations* came to the meeting on the Amazon rain forest.
3. "The *organization* of this report is confusing," Professor Lopez said, shaking his head. "These facts are given in the wrong order."
4. The perfect *organization* of his workshop allows Mr. Finch to find any tool in less than 10 seconds.

and Verbalize...

_____

_____

_____

organize: to arrange or put together in an orderly way

Visualize...

1. June *organized* the games at the party and Lars gave out prizes to the winners
2. "If Beth doesn't *organize* her desk she's not going to be able to find anything," Mrs. Smith told Della.
3. Dan *organized* the jumbled pile of silverware into knives, forks, and spoons.
4. Lucy *organized* the old books into categories: history, science, literature, and art.

and Verbalize...

_____

_____

_____

origin: beginning or starting point; parentage

Visualize...

1. "The *origin* of the epidemic was a barrel of contaminated water," Dr. Gray told Dr. Brown.
2. The *origin* of Rex's trip was San Diego and his destination was New York.
3. Flo was the *origin* of the rumor about Beth stealing Ruby's boyfriend.
4. Rod's *origins* are Mexican and German, but for three generations his family has been American.

and Verbalize...

_____

_____

_____

ostrich: a very large bird with a long neck, long legs, and tiny wings

Visualize...

1. The *ostrich* can't fly, but it can run very fast on its long legs.
2. An *ostrich* lays a huge egg that can make an omelet for six people.
3. It's not true that an *ostrich* puts its head in the sand when it's afraid and wants to hide or flee from danger.
4. "The *ostrich* is the largest bird on Earth," Professor Lopez said. "What is the smallest bird?"

and Verbalize...

_____

_____

_____

outgrow: to grow too large for; to grow beyond or away from

Visualize...

1. Gus didn't *outgrow* this shirt—it shrank when he put it into the dryer.
2. When Tom *outgrew* his shirts and pants he gave them to his younger brother to wear.
3. Dan hopes his little sister will *outgrow* her habit of sucking her thumb.
4. Hortense is *outgrowing* comic books and beginning to read real books instead.

and Verbalize...

_____

_____

_____

outrun: to run faster or farther than

Visualize...

1. Ted was excited when he *outran* Fred and crossed the finish line first.
2. Flo *outran* the other girls and then stopped to wait for them to catch up.
3. The orange cat *outran* the blue cat and arrived first at the bowl of fresh cat food.
4. The man *outran* the two robbers, took a taxi to the airport, and escaped safely from New York.

and Verbalize...

_____

_____

_____

outstanding: better than others

Visualize...

1. "You are the *outstanding* speller in the school," Mr. Wong told Ruby when he gave her the first-prize trophy.
2. Della was the *outstanding* dancer at the big dance—everyone wanted to learn the latest steps from her.
3. Jerome's drawing was *outstanding*—the rearing horse looked as if it might jump off the paper and run away.
4. Mary is an *outstanding* acrobat because she is agile, quick, and strong.

and Verbalize...

_____

_____

_____

overcome: to beat or conquer; to be conquered or overwhelmed

Visualize...

1. Mark's little brother *overcame* his fear of water and learned to swim.
2. Frank *overcame* his serious injuries to become an excellent football player.
3. The Aztecs were *overcome* by Cortez and his Spanish army.
4. The fireman was *overcome* by smoke and had to be carried from the burning house.

and Verbalize...

_____

_____

_____

overflow: to fill up and run over

Visualize...

1. The bathtub *overflowed* because the phone rang and Beth forgot the water was running.
2. During floods, rivers *overflow* their banks and sweep across higher land.
3. "Turn off the burner!" cried Tom as the pot of boiling soup *overflowed*.
4. The young mother's heart *overflowed* with love for her new baby.

and Verbalize...

_____

_____

_____

overtake: to catch up with or pass

Visualize...

1. Only Superman can run fast enough to *overtake* a speeding train.
2. Flo *overtook* Greg and then Tim as she hurried up the hill toward the castle.
3. The Ferrrari easily *overtook* and passed the VW van.
4. The policeman turned on his siren and his flashing red lights as he tried to *overtake* the speeding getaway car.

and Verbalize...

_____

_____

_____

Chapter 15

The P's

painstaking: very careful or requiring great care

Visualize...

1. Jeff is a *painstaking* carpenter who measures every board twice before he cuts it with the saw.
2. Frank did a *painstaking* job of putting the cuckoo clock back together again.
3. "Would it be an easy or a *painstaking* task to put Humpty Dumpty back together again?" Mrs. Smith asked.
4. "Archeology is a *painstaking* profession," Professor Lopez said. "It might take years to uncover a single Aztec temple."

and Verbalize...

_____

_____

_____

paralyze: to lose or to take away the ability to move or feel in a part of the body; t o lose or take away the ability to act

1. Tim's aunt couldn't walk after she was *paralyzed* in the terrible car accident.
2. Some spiders *paralyze* their prey with poison before they eat them.
3. All the different brands of breakfast cereal *paralyzed* Greg—he couldn't decide which one to buy.
4. Fear *paralyzed* Mr. Smith—he didn't run or cry out but only stood and stared as the creatures from the spaceship approached him.

and Verbalize...

_____

_____

_____

partner: a person who joins another in a business, project, marriage, or dance

Visualize...

1. The Williams-Smith Company was run by its two *partners*, Joe Williams and Tom Smith.
2. Flo asked Rex to be her *partner* on the geology project.
3. "A marriage can work only if both *partners* want it to succeed," the marriage counselor told Mr. and Mrs. Jones.
4. When the music began, Mark started across the dance floor to find a *partner*.

and Verbalize...

_____

_____

_____

patent: a government paper which gives a person or company the right to be the only one to make, use, or sell a new invention for a certain number of years

Visualize...

1. Mr. Green invented a pair of electric socks, then quickly took out a *patent* to protect his invention.
2. Fred's aunt applied for a *patent* when she invented banana-flavored chewing gum.
3. A *patent* for music or written words is called a "copyright."
4. "Does your wonderful stew have a *patent*," Pam teased Beth, "or can anyone make it?"

and Verbalize...

_____

_____

_____

pedal: a control you push with your foot to make a machine work

Visualize...

1. Cars that have "stick shifts" have three *pedals*: the brake, the accelerator, and the clutch.
2. Riders who race bicycles have special straps to keep their feet on the *pedals*.
3. The little paddle boat began to move when Della and Jeff worked the *pedals*.
4. Stan made the big sewing machine start and stop by pressing the *pedal* with his foot.

and Verbalize...

_____

_____

_____

performer: a person who entertains the public

Visualize...

1. Ruby's brother is a *performer* who plays the saxophone in a jazz band.
2. A comedian is a *performer* who has the hard job of making complete strangers laugh.
3. All actors are *performers*, whether they are on the screen or on the stage.
4. "The show must go on" is the motto of all *performers*.

and Verbalize...

_____

_____

_____

permit: to allow

Visualize...

1. Dan always walks because his mother won't *permit* him to use the family car.
2. The librarian put a finger to her lips and pointed to the sign that read: "Talking Is Not *Permitted!*"
3. No dogs were *permitted* on the beach so Della had to lock her collie in the car.
4. "If you're very, very careful I'll *permit* you to fly the plane now," the pilot said as he let Jeff take the controls.

and Verbalize...

_____

_____

_____

persist: to refuse to stop or give up; to last or stay

Visualize...

1. The secretary told Mr. Blue that Mr. Jones wasn't in, but Mr. Blue *persisted*—he called back ten times.
2. The white cat *persisted* in her efforts to open the door to the screaming parrot's swinging cage.
3. Susan's cough *persisted* even though her sore throat was better.
4. The dark clouds *persisted* all day, and by nightfall it was raining.

and Verbalize...

_____

_____

_____

P

personality: all of a person's individual characteristics and habits; charm, likableness

Visualize...

1. People stay away from Greg's cousin because she has a cranky *personality*.
2. The twins are very different: one has an outgoing *personality* but the other one is very shy.
3. Gus picked the puppy in the litter who had the most *personality*.
4. Flo has a lot of *personality*—she's always laughing and joking and telling funny stories about herself.

and Verbalize...

_____

_____

_____

physical: having to do with the body or matter

Visualize...

1. The woman's beauty was more than *physical*—she was kind and loving and had an admirable character.
2. "Mental exercise is as important as *physical* exercise," Dr. Gray reminded Lucy's grandmother.
3. The detective examined the *physical* evidence of the crime: the gun, the empty bullet case, the bloodstain.
4. "He's a ghost—his *physical* body is dead, but his 'astral' body is alive," Martha explained to her sister as they watched the scary movie.

and Verbalize...

_____

_____

_____

pirate: a person who robs ships at sea

Visualize...

1. Captain Hook is the *pirate* in "Peter Pan."
2. Jack Hawkins found the *pirate* map that showed where the treasure was buried.
3. The *pirates* raised a black flag with a white skull and crossbones as their ship began to fire on the fort.
4. If a *pirate* captain didn't like you, he'd make you "walk the plank"—walk out on a board and jump into the sea.

and Verbalize...

_____

_____

_____

pitch: the lowness or highness of a sound in music; degree of slope (n)

Visualize...

1. "Can we start in a lower *pitch*?" Mrs. Jones asked. "I just can't sing that high."
2. Mark has perfect *pitch*—he can name any note you play on the piano.
3. Lars slipped and slid down the roof because its *pitch* was so steep.
4. The church steeple had such a sharp *pitch* that the snow would not cling to it.

and Verbalize...

_____

_____

_____

pitch: to throw; to fall forward; to violently lift and fall (v)

Visualize...

1. Gus *pitched* the baseball so fast that none of the batters could hit it.
2. Stan *pitched* a bale of hay into the horse's stall.
3. Ted slipped and *pitched* headfirst onto the frozen ice.
4. The sailboat *pitched* about in the terrible storm—first its bow and then its stern nearly sank beneath the waves.

and Verbalize...

_____

_____

_____

pivot: to turn quickly with few or no steps; to move around on a fixed point, as a wheel on an axle

Visualize...

1. The basketball player caught the ball, *pivoted*, and shot a quick basket.
2. A ballet dancer can turn in a very small circle, *pivoting* on her toes and holding her arms above her head.
3. Tom stopped, *pivoted* on his heel, and ran back to the house to get his books as the school bus approached.
4. The center pole in the merry-go-round *pivoted* slowly as the painted horses went around and around.

and Verbalize...

_____

_____

_____

plateau: a high, flat piece of land; a period or place of no change or growth

Visualize...

1. The village was built on a mountain *plateau*, with steep gorges all around and higher mountains in the distance.
2. In Switzerland you can drive up into the Alps and then suddenly find yourself on a *plateau* with meadows and a lake.
3. Mr. Finch lost ten pounds on his new diet, but reached a *plateau* at 200 and was unable to lose any more.
4. The business did very well for the first two years, then hit a *plateau* and couldn't increase its profits.

and Verbalize...

_____

_____

_____

pleasure: a feeling of enjoyment or happiness or something that gives enjoyment or happiness

Visualize...

1. Beth takes great *pleasure* in eating a slice of fresh apple pie with a scoop of vanilla ice cream.
2. Mr. Mendoza's greatest *pleasure* comes from cooking a big dinner and watching his family eat.
3. "It's a *pleasure* to meet you," Mr. Grant said, bowing and kissing Lady Wilson's hand.
4. "Is this business or *pleasure?*" Mr. Smith asked when his partner called him up on New Year's Eve.

and Verbalize...

_____

_____

_____

plenty: more than enough

Visualize...

1. Dan always made three bowls of mashed potatoes for dinner so there would be *plenty*.
2. "More coffee?" Jerome asked. "No," Agnes answered. "I've had *plenty*."
3. There were *plenty* of bedrooms in Mr. Grant's house—12 for only five people.
4. There is no longer *plenty* of unspoiled air, land, and water.

and Verbalize...

_____

_____

_____

poison: a drug or other substance that harms or kills by chemical action

Visualize...

1. Arsenic is a *poison* used for killing rats.
2. "Go ahead and try the cake I made," said Rex. "It isn't *poison.*"
3. In the detective movie, the murderer put *poison* in the coffee and then served it to his victim.
4. Like the rattlesnake's, the black widow spider's bite is full *poison.*

and Verbalize...

_____

_____

_____

pomp: splendid or showy display

Visualize...

1. Prince Charles and Princess Diana's wedding was full of *pomp* and ceremony.
2. Aunt Agnes doesn't believe in a lot of *pomp*—she just wants people to comb their hair before they come to one of her parties.
3. "*Pomp* and Circumstance" is the stuffy song that is played at high school graduations.
4. Mary serves her dolls tea with all the *pomp* of a rich lady.

and Verbalize...

_____

_____

_____

ponder: to think about carefully or deeply

Visualize...

1. Rex sat in the backyard and looked up at the stars as he *pondered* about life on other planets.
2. Mark *pondered* the math problem but he couldn't figure out how to solve it.
3. Mr. Smith *pondered* whether to go on the trip to New York, then decided not to and canceled his plane reservation.
4. "Don't stand there *pondering* the meaning of life," Stan's father said. "Get those leaves raked."

and Verbalize...

_____

_____

_____

P

popular: liked or accepted by many people

Visualize...

1. Mickey Mouse is *popular* with people all over the world.
2. Ruby is the most *popular* girl in her class because she is generous and friendly.
3. Popcorn is a *popular* international snack food.
4. A *popular* thing to do on Saturday night is to go to a movie.

and Verbalize...

_____

_____

_____

portable: capable of being easily carried

Visualize...

1. Mrs. Smith takes her *portable* typewriter with her when she goes to her mountain cabin.
2. Della's *portable* TV runs on batteries and can fit inside her purse.
3. A "laptop" computer is just what it sounds like: a *portable* computer you can use on your lap.
4. Both the snail and the turtle have *portable* "houses."

and Verbalize...

_____

_____

_____

positive: certain; confident, optimistic; not negative (electricity)

Visualize...

1. "I'm *positive* you'll like this movie," Jeff told Lars. "It's about a journey to the center of the earth."
2. Beth was *positive* she would pass the geography test because she knew the name and location of every country in the world.
3. "Dan is a very *positive* young man," Dr. Gray said. "He's never gloomy or depressed."
4. The tow truck driver started the car by hooking up jumper cables to the negative and *positive* terminals of the battery.

and Verbalize...

_____

_____

_____

possible: capable of being done or happening

Visualize...

1. Typing 100 pages in one day is hard to do, but it's *possible*.
2. It's not *possible* to walk across the Atlantic Ocean.
3. "Would it be *possible* to have this sweater back by Thursday?" June asked the man at the dry cleaning counter.
4. "It's not only *possible* but probable that your hands will freeze if you don't wear your mittens," Della told her little brother.

and Verbalize...

_____

_____

_____

poster: a large printed sign that often has a picture and can be put up on a wall

Visualize...

1. Hortense likes to put up *posters* of Michael Jackson, but Tom's posters are of Natalie Cole.
2. Wanda stared at the big *poster* of a green island surrounded by a clear blue lagoon.
3. Mr. Mendoza put up campaign *posters* all over town when he ran for city council.
4. *Posters* for the circus were tacked to every telephone pole and pasted on every bare wall.

and Verbalize...

_____

_____

_____

precise: exact, perfectly accurate

Visualize...

1. Mr. Jenkins is very *precise* about the way he likes his coffee: two spoonfuls of instant coffee, one spoonful of sugar, no milk.
2. A watchmaker works with tiny, very *precise* instruments.
3. The list gave the *precise* number of calories in 15 different vegetables.
4. "Somebody" is not a very *precise* word. "She" is more *precise*, and "Susan" is very *precise*.

and Verbalize...

_____

_____

_____

P

predicament: an unpleasant, difficult, or bad situation

Visualize...

1. Ed found himself in an embarrassing *predicament*—he'd invited four people for dinner and he had only three plates.
2. The ducks were in a terrible *predicament*—the water had frozen overnight and now they were stuck to the pond.
3. "I'm in a real *predicament*," Lucy said. "I don't have enough money to pay my rent this month."
4. "How am I going to solve this *predicament*?" sighed June. "Tom and Jack have both asked me to the dance on Saturday."

and Verbalize...

---

prediction: something a person claims will happen in the future

Visualize...

1. "My *prediction* is that our football team will win the championship this year," Mark said to Dan.
2. "The weatherman's *prediction* was right," Pam said, looking out the window. "It's starting to rain, just as he said."
3. Stock market *predictions* are hard to make, even if you're an expert.
4. The fortuneteller made her *predictions* by gazing into a crystal ball.

and Verbalize...

---

prejudice: hatred or unfair treatment of a particular group; an opinion that has been formed before all the facts are known

Visualize...

1. The civil rights movement began because of racial *prejudice* against black Americans.
2. June's uncle was the victim of age *prejudice*—no one would hire him because he was over 60.
3. In our legal system we try to avoid *prejudice* by saying an accused person is "innocent until proven guilty."
4. "Try to read this newspaper story without *prejudice*," Captain Jones told Detective Ferris. "They seem to have most of the facts right."

and Verbalize...

---

prepare: to make; to get ready

Visualize...

1. Della's mother likes to *prepare* pancakes and eggs for breakfast.
2. Mr. Smith *prepares* all the reports for his office.
3. Rex and Ted *prepared* all the gear the night before their camping trip.
4. "*Prepare* yourself to jump," the instructor told the shaking skydiver.

and Verbalize...

_____

_____

_____

preserve: to save or protect; keep the same for a long time

Visualize...

1. Our national parks *preserve* wilderness areas and the animals that live there.
2. Turning off the faucet while you brush your teeth helps *preserve* water.
3. The farmer *preserved* the apricots and peaches by cutting them in half and drying them in the sun
4. The Egyptians *preserved* their dead as mummies.

and Verbalize...

_____

_____

_____

prevailing: in general use, common; the greatest in strength or influence

Visualize...

1. In the Old West, the *prevailing* code of behavior was "Shoot first and ask questions later."
2. A *prevailing* myth is that speaking out every time you're angry is a good thing.
3. George Bush was the *prevailing* candidate for president in 1988.
4. "We will be having some warmer days," said the weatherman, "because the *prevailing* winds are now from the south."

and Verbalize...

_____

_____

_____

P

prey: an animal which another animal kills and eats (n)

Visualize...

1. The striped cat's favorite *prey* are mice, but she would consider eating the yellow canary in the cage.
2. Rabbits are the natural *prey* of coyotes.
3. Lions and tigers stalk their *prey* silently before they charge and attack them.
4. Small fish are the *prey* of big fish who are the *prey* of bigger fish.

and Verbalize...

_____

_____

_____

prey: to hunt and kill for food; to take advantage of (v)

Visualize...

1. The lion *preys* mostly on zebras, but he also likes the taste of antelope meat.
2. Sparrow hawks *prey* on mice and insects.
3. The criminal *preyed* on the elderly by selling them false health insurance policies.
4. "The Jogger" was a mugger who *preyed* on people running in the park at night.

and Verbalize...

_____

_____

_____

procedure: a way of doing something, usually by a series of steps

Visualize...

1. The policeman was following department *procedure* when he fired a warning shot before aiming at the robber.
2. The *procedure* for feeding your cat is: (1) lock the kitchen door; (2) take the bag of cat food out of its hiding place and pour a small amount in the cat's bowl; (3) hide the cat food again; (4) open the door and get out of the way.
3. The "scientific method" is an orderly *procedure* for gathering information and drawing conclusions.
4. Every office has its own special *procedures*.

and Verbalize...

_____

_____

_____

process: a number of actions done in a certain order

Visualize...

1. The first step in the *process* of learning to swim is to stand in the shallow end of the pool and blow bubbles in the water.
2. The *process* of making grapes into raisins begins with picking the grapes and laying them out in the sun to dry.
3. Drawing the plans and then pouring the foundation are the first steps in the *process* of building a house.
4. "The *process* of growing up never stops," Rex's grandfather told Rex. "I'm still learning."

and Verbalize...

_____

_____

_____

proclaim: to declare publicly and officially

Visualize...

1. The minister said to the bride and groom, "I now *proclaim* you man and wife."
2. The Emancipation Proclamation of 1863 *proclaimed* the freedom of the slaves.
3. Mr. Finch's home town *proclaimed* itself the Apricot Capital of the World.
4. When the local baseball team won the state championship, the mayor *proclaimed* a day of celebration.

and Verbalize...

_____

_____

_____

produce: to make or create something; to finance and organize the making of a movie; to show

Visualize...

1. Mr. Finch's farm *produces* marvelous tomatoes: red, sweet, juicy, and delicious.
2. The Winners' Circle is a ranch that *produces* champion racehorses.
3. Mr. Wong directed the movie and Mr. Jones *produced* it.
4. Jeff reached into his back pocket and *produced* a small green frog that said, "Grok!"

and Verbalize...

_____

_____

_____

P

professional: trained to do a special job for pay; highly skilled, expert

Visualize...

1. Joe Montana was an excellent amateur football player in college and now he's a famous *professional* player.
2. Rex's father likes to paint as a hobby, but Rex's mother is a *professional* artist.
3. Mrs. Mendoza began doing TV commercials when she was a child, and now she's a really *professional* actress.
4. Della's singing is very good—she sounds completely *professional*.

and Verbalize...

_____

_____

_____

progressive: moving forward in steps; favoring social reform; stressing individuality and creativity in education

Visualize...

1. The piano book was *progressive*, beginning with songs like "Mary Had a Little Lamb," and ending with "Moonlight Sonata."
2. My grandmother was always a *progressive* woman—she thought women should be able to hold the same jobs as men.
3. The United States is not very *progressive* in its health care—we are one of the few industrialized nations that <u>don't</u> have national health insurance.
4. The school was very *progressive*—every student wrote a play, painted a mural, or composed an opera about his favorite historical figure.

and Verbalize...

_____

_____

_____

protrude: to stick or bulge out

Visualize...

1. Flo's cat tries to hide, but he's easy to find because his tail always *protrudes* from under the bed.
2. Mr. Gray was very messy—papers and parts of old ham sandwiches were always *protruding* from his desk drawers.
3. The baby's pink stomach *protruded* over the top of his diaper.
4. "What??!!" yelled Daffy Duck, his eyes *protruding*. "Who said Bugs Bunny is funnier than I am?

and Verbalize...

_____

_____

_____

purify: to cleanse or filter

Visualize...

1. The filter on the kitchen faucet helps *purify* the water and make it safer to drink.
2. The best way to *purify* drinking water is to boil it.
3. Charcoal filters are used to *purify* the air in submarines.
4. "I want you to *purify* your language," Aunt Agnes said to her nephew. "No more swearing."

and Verbalize...

_____

_____

_____

pursuit: the act of following in order to catch up to or capture

Visualize...

1. The young spent all his time and energy in *pursuit* of fame and fortune.
2. The police car turned on its siren and lights and pulled out in *pursuit* of the speeding Chevy.
3. Nothing is quite as fast as a greyhound in *pursuit* of a jack rabbit.
4. When I read that the hero is in "hot *pursuit*" of the villain, I always imagine him riding a horse with a fiery tail and smoking hooves.

and Verbalize...

_____

_____

_____

pyramid: an object with four triangular sides that meet in a point at the top

Visualize...

1. The most famous *pyramids* in the world are the ones in Egypt.
2. Bob and Pam climbed the steps of the *Pyramid* of the Moon near Mexico City.
3. A picture of a *pyramid* with an open eye at its top is on the one-dollar bill.
4. Some people believe crystal *pyramids* have magic healing powers.

and Verbalize...

_____

_____

_____

Chapter 16

The Q's

qualify: to earn or win acceptance; to be eligible; to limit

Visualize...

1. The skater practiced at the ice rink every day for 12 years before she finally *qualified* for the Olympics.
2. You have to be an American citizen to *qualify* as a voter.
3. "You need to *qualify* what you said about your brother," my father said to me. "You don't really hate him, you're just angry with him."
4. The movie star *qualified* her answer when the reporters asked her if she wanted to get married: "I do," she said, "but only if I meet the right man."

and Verbalize...

_____

_____

_____

quality: a particular characteristic; degree of worth

Visualize...

1. June's best *qualities* are her honesty and kindness. Her worst *qualities* are her forgetfulness and laziness.
2. The most obvious *quality* of diamonds is their brilliant sparkle.
3. "The soft leather of this shoe is of the finest *quality*," the salesman told Pam.
4. The *quality* of the paint was so poor that it began peeling as soon as it was brushed on.

and Verbalize...

_____

_____

_____

quarter: one of four equal parts; an American coin worth twenty-five cents

Visualize...

1. Martha cut the pumpkin pie into *quarters* so she, Wanda, Flo, and Bill could each have a slice.
2. A football game is divided into four *quarters*, or two halves.
3. The book cost 75 cents so Tom gave the clerk three *quarters*.
4. Rex takes a lot of *quarters* for the washers and dryers when he goes to the laundromat.

and Verbalize...

_____

_____

_____

Chapter 17

The R's

rack: a wood or metal frame used for holding things

Visualize...

1. Bill got out of the shower and took a towel from the towel *rack*.
2. A coat *rack* in the hallway is a good place to hang wet raincoats.
3. My neighbor has a pretty wooden dish *rack* on the counter for drying her dishes.
4. The hunter kept his guns in a locked gun *rack*.

and Verbalize...

_____

_____

_____

raft: a kind of flat boat made by fastening logs or boards together; a rubber boat

Visualize...

1. José and Tom tied logs together with rope to make a *raft* so they could cross the river.
2. The man on the *raft* used a long pole to steer the *raft* across the pond.
3. Last summer we rode down the Colorado River on a big orange *raft*.
4. The sailors from the sinking ship climbed into life *rafts*.

and Verbalize...

_____

_____

_____

R

raging: acting in a rough or angry way

Visualize...

1. The *raging* flood rushed across the town, sweeping away houses and trees.
2. A *raging* storm's huge waves can sink a big ship.
3. The *raging* bull lowered its horns and chased Tom and Tim from the pasture.
4. The *raging* man broke all the dishes in the cupboard.

and Verbalize...

_____

_____

_____

rainstorm: a storm with a lot of rain

Visualize...

1. The last *rainstorm* we had dropped 10 inches of rain in one day.
2. Bob's roof leaks whenever there's a *rainstorm.*
3. The *rainstorm* flooded the streets and made the river rise.
4. After a *rainstorm,* all the streets look shiny and wet and the sky is bright and clear.

and Verbalize...

_____

_____

_____

ramble: to talk or write too much about too many things; to wander

Visualize...

1. We get bored and start to fall asleep when my father *rambles* on and on about cars.
2. Rex was confused when the movie began to *ramble*—first there were spaceships, then elephants, then cub scouts with a birthday cake.
3. June and Bill like to *ramble* across the countryside, stopping now and then to take pictures or rest.
4. "I'm a *rambling* man," Fred's uncle said. "I travel here and there and stay just a few months in one place."

and Verbalize...

_____

_____

_____

rapids: fast-moving waters in a river

Visualize...

1. Tom's canoe almost tipped over in the dangerous *rapids.*
2. The *rapids* of a river often begin just before a big waterfall.
3. The *rapids* were white where the rushing water splashed against rocks and boulders.
4. Bob's raft shot down the *rapids* toward the waterfall.

and Verbalize...

_____

_____

_____

raw: not cooked; with the skin rubbed off

Visualize...

1. "Are you going to cook the carrots, or are we going to eat them *raw*?" Lars asked Flo.
2. People eat cooked meat but animals eat *raw* meat.
3. The sailors hands were *raw* from sliding down the rope.
4. The bottoms of Rex's feet were rubbed *raw* from walking barefoot across the sharp stones.

and Verbalize...

_____

_____

_____

recede: to pull back or withdraw

Visualize...

1. "My hair is *receding*," my father said. "Now my forehead goes back to the top of my head!"
2. The ocean comes up to those rocks at high tide, and then *recedes* again at low tide.
3. Dan couldn't return to his house until the floodwaters had *receded.*
4. As Mr. Finch drove away, he looked back and saw his farmhouse *receding* into the distance.

and Verbalize...

_____

_____

_____

R

recognition: notice; acknowledgement, approval

Visualize...

1. Fred gained national *recognition* when 20 million people saw him on the "Tonight Show."
2. The movie star escaped *recognition* by wearing glasses and a fake moustache.
3. Mark's father received a gold wristwatch in *recognition* of his 45 years of hard work.
4. The soldier fought in the battle and received a medal in *recognition* of his bravery.

and Verbalize...

_____

_____

_____

recommend: to advise or suggest; to speak in favor of

Visualize...

1. "I *recommend* you take your umbrella today," Mr. Finch told his wife. "It's going to rain."
2. Mrs. Smith *recommended* that we study Chapters 3 and 4 for the test tomorrow.
3. Tim asked his boss to *recommend* him for the new job. "Sure, Tim," Mr. Brown said, "I'll put in a good word for you."
4. "The broiled fish is excellent," the waiter told Susan, "but I *recommend* the steak and mashed potatoes."

and Verbalize...

_____

_____

_____

recover: to get back; to get well or to return to a normal condition

Visualize...

1. Dan lost his baseball glove, then *recovered* it when he found it in the school's "Lost and Found."
2. The police *recovered* the stolen car when they caught the car thief on the highway.
3. Chicken noodle soup was the only thing Ted could eat while he *recovered* from the flu.
4. "Have you *recovered* from your cousin's visit?" Rex asked Pam. "No," Pam said, "I'm still exhausted."

and Verbalize...

_____

_____

_____

reel: to be unable to walk straight; to feel dizzy; to be shaken by a blow or shock

Visualize...

1. The drunk man *reeled* around the room when he tried to walk.
2. Jim's head was *reeling* when he got off the merry-go-round.
3. Stan *reeled* at the bad news about his sister's car accident.
4. The coach was *reeling* after José and Dan quit the baseball team the same day.

and Verbalize...

---

reflect: to throw back light or heat; to give back an image; to think back on

Visualize...

1. The dazzling tin roof *reflected* the bright sunlight.
2. The black cat jumped when it saw its face *reflected* in the mirror.
3. The still water of the lake *reflected* the huge white clouds.
4. The prisoner sat in his cell and *reflected* on all the things he'd done wrong in his life.

and Verbalize...

---

refuge: a place that is safe from danger

Visualize...

1. A wildlife *refuge* is a place where wild animals are protected from hunters.
2. Wild geese and swans swim on the ponds at the bird *refuge*.
3. Wanda's peaceful home is her *refuge* from the busy world—until the phone rings.
4. "That cave can be our *refuge* from the raging storm," Ruby told the frightened hikers.

and Verbalize...

R

refuse: to say no to

Visualize...

1. Bob's mother *refused* to let him drive her car to the movies.
2. Mary quit her job when her boss *refused* to pay her more money.
3. Rex *refused* June's request for help on her homework. "You need to do it yourself," he said.
4. Mary *refused* Bob's offer to take her to the dance because she wanted to go with José.

and Verbalize...

_____

_____

_____

regain: to get back

Visualize...

1. Flo started to fall, then *regained* her balance and skated on across the frozen lake.
2. The injured man worked hard to *regain* the ability to walk.
3. The pilot *regained* control of the spinning plane before it could crash.
4. "I practice every day," Tim said, "but I haven't been able to *regain* my ability to hit home runs."

and Verbalize...

_____

_____

_____

rehearse: to practice over and over

Visualize...

1. The actors *rehearsed* their lines for the play every day after school.
2. The clown *rehearsed* his act in front of a mirror before he performed at the circus.
3. The musicians met in the auditorium to *rehearse* before the concert.
4. Fred and Frank *rehearsed* their story before they told their father about the broken window.

and Verbalize...

_____

_____

_____

reluctant: not wanting to do something, unwilling

Visualize...

1. My dog is *reluctant* to take a bath. I have to catch him and drag him to the tub.
2. The young bird was *reluctant* to fly, so the mother bird had to push it from the nest.
3. Greg was *reluctant* to walk home at night because a dangerous lion had escaped from the zoo.
4. Phil is *reluctant* to drive very far because his car has been making a coughing sound.

and Verbalize...

_____

_____

_____

remote: far away in space or time; unlikely

Visualize...

1. Dan wants to live on a *remote* island in the middle of the South Pacific.
2. Tom's mountain cabin is very *remote*—to get there you have to use an old logging road.
3. When you play the lottery, you have only a *remote* chance of winning the prize.
4. The possibility of visitors from Mars landing in the United States is *remote*.

and Verbalize...

_____

_____

_____

renowned: very famous

Visualize...

1. The scientist was *renowned* for discovering a new kind of dinosaur.
2. The *renowned* actor's picture was always in the magazines.
3. Paris is *renowned* for its great artists and wonderful food.
4. The milk shakes at Chip's Drive-In are *renowned* for their flavor and low price.

and Verbalize...

_____

_____

_____

R

represent: to stand for; to speak for

Visualize...

1. The letters of the alphabet *represent* different sounds.
2. The letters "U.S.A." *represent* "United States of America."
3. José *represented* his home-town troop at the national Boy Scouts' meeting.
4. "I *represent* the Blue Sky Insurance Company," the young man said, "with offices in every part of the world."

and Verbalize...

_____

_____

_____

research: studies to find out facts

Visualize...

1. Jerome went to the library to do *research* for his history paper.
2. "I've done all the *research* for my paper," Bob said. "Now all I have to do is write it."
3. Medical *research* shows that most people eat too much and don't exercise enough.
4. "Years of *research* have proven that smoking is dangerous to your health," Professor Lopez reminded the class.

and Verbalize...

_____

_____

_____

reservoir: a place where water is stored

Visualize...

1. The town *reservoir* was full of water because of the heavy rains.
2. A woman in a white swimsuit was water-skiing behind a red boat on the *reservoir*.
3. The little pond behind Mr. Finch's barn is a *reservoir* for his farm.
4. "The water in the *reservoir* has been poisoned!" June cried. "Tell everyone not to drink the water!"

and Verbalize...

_____

_____

_____

resolution: decision to do something; the state or quality of being very determined

Visualize...

1. Mr. Wong's New Year's *resolution* was to quit smoking. He flushed his cigarettes down the toilet and broke all his ash trays.
2. The Senate passed a *resolution* which would give free medical care to everyone.
3. Della was filled with *resolution* about winning the big race, and ran two miles every night for practice.
4. Jeff showed *resolution* when he gave his speech—his voice was strong and clear and he looked at every member of the audience.

and Verbalize...

_____

_____

_____

resource: a supply of something useful; a source for help or information

Visualize...

1. Coal, oil, water, and land are all natural *resources*.
2. If Phil loses his job, his only *resource* will be the 200 dollars he has in the bank.
3. A jockey would be a good *resource* if you wanted to learn about horses and horse racing.
4. "The library is an excellent *resource* if you want to learn more about ancient Mexico," Professor Lopez said.

and Verbalize...

_____

_____

_____

respond: to react to something said or done

Visualize...

1. Mary's cat never *responds* when she calls him—but he comes running when he hears her pouring food into his bowl.
2. "How should I *respond* to Betty?" Ted asked. "Should I write her a letter or call her on the phone?"
3. "That lion that broke out of the zoo could be dangerous," Mark said. "VERY dangerous," June *responded* as she heard a loud roar.
4. The dog *responded* by barking and jumping over the fence when he heard a cat meowing in the neighbor's yard.

and Verbalize...

_____

_____

_____

R

restrain: to hold back

Visualize...

1. The big dog was *restrained* by a heavy leather collar and a steel chain.
2. The zoo keeper had to *restrain* the children from petting the baby elephant when it came close to the fence.
3. Red velvet ropes *restrained* people from touching the famous statue.
4. "*Restrain* yourself," my mother said when I reached for the fresh chocolate cake with cherries on top. "Save a piece for Mary and your father."

and Verbalize...

_____

_____

_____

retort: to answer sharply

Visualize...

1. "I'm going to borrow your bicycle," Rex said. "No you're not," Tom *retorted*, "unless you want a punch in the nose!"
2. "Don't speak to me like that!" Mark *retorted* when Bill made fun of him.
3. June tried to tell Tim that she was sorry, but he *retorted* angrily and walked away.
4. "I love you," Bob said, but Susan *retorted* quickly, "And every other girl you see!"

and Verbalize...

_____

_____

_____

reveal: to show or display; to make known

Visualize...

1. The mayor pulled the red cloth away, *revealing* a bronze statue of a bear holding a fish in its mouth.
2. The soldier rolled up his pants leg to *reveal* the ugly scar on his knee.
3. The answers to the crossword puzzle are *revealed* on the last page of the newspaper.
4. "I'm not going to *reveal* the name of the victim," the policeman told the crowd of yelling reporters.

and Verbalize...

_____

_____

_____

review: to study; to think back on

Visualize...

1. Fred always *reviews* the list of words the night before the spelling test.
2. Lucy *reviewed* her research notes before she began writing her paper on dinosaurs.
3. The principal said to Mark, "Let's *review* the reasons Mrs. Jones sent you to my office—beginning with the pet rat you're hiding in your pocket."
4. The old man sat on the porch and *reviewed* all the different things he had been in his life—cowboy, sailor, soldier, farmer, and businessman.

and Verbalize...

_____

_____

_____

ridicule: to make fun of

Visualize...

1. Beth cried because the other kids *ridiculed* her freckles.
2. The movie was *ridiculed* because of its bad acting, fake mountains, and the stuffed horse on wheels.
3. Ted was *ridiculed* whenever he began to sing, so after a while he only hummed.
4. "Don't *ridicule* me," warned Tom as he walked into the living room with his hand stuck in the cookie jar.

and Verbalize...

_____

_____

_____

ridiculous: too silly or false to be believed; laughable

Visualize...

1. "This is *ridiculous*," Gus said, holding up the 500-page test.
2. "No one gets sunburned by the moon," Rod said to Dan. "That's a *ridiculous* idea."
3. Stan looked so *ridiculous* in his Cher costume that everyone laughed.
4. Ted's cat has the *ridiculous* habit of sleeping with her tongue out and a paw over each eye.

and Verbalize...

_____

_____

_____

R

rigorous: hard, difficult

Visualize...

1. Bill's exercise program is *rigorous*—he has to run 10 miles a day, swim 50 laps in the pool, and do 400 sit-ups.
2. "Was your math class easy?" Lars asked. "No, it was *rigorous*," Della said, "but I studied hard and passed it."
3. "It's not a *rigorous* run," the track coach said. "My grandmother could do it on her pogo stick."
4. Wanda had a *rigorous* day pulling weeds—her back hurt, her hands were raw, and two of her fingernails were broken.

and Verbalize...

_____

_____

_____

rim: the top edge

Visualize...

1. The hot chocolate spilled when it splashed over the *rim* of the cup.
2. The children left sticky fingerprints along the *rim* of the sink.
3. "Don't get to close to the *rim* of the canyon," the forest ranger said. "If you slip, you'll fall 1,000 feet."
4. The helicopter flew over the *rim* of the volcano so Beth could take pictures of the boiling red lava in the crater.

and Verbalize...

_____

_____

_____

ripple: a very small wave

Visualize...

1. The lake was as smooth as glass—there wasn't even a *ripple* on the water.
2. The frog made round *ripples* in the water when it hopped into the pond.
3. "Those aren't waves," the angry surfer said. "Those aren't even *ripples*."
4. The wind was blowing and Ruby could see *ripples* in the red and white stripes of the flag.

and Verbalize...

_____

_____

_____

risk: the chance of danger or harm

Visualize...

1. The *risk* of being attacked by an alligator in New York City is very small.
2. Research shows that there's more *risk* in traveling by car than by airplane.
3. "No campfires this week," the ranger explained. "The *risk* of a forest fire is too great."
4. "You're taking quite a *risk*," Mr. Smith said to the boy who was juggling three knives in the air.

and Verbalize...

_____

_____

_____

robot: a machine that can do simple kinds of human work

Visualize...

1. The *robot* looked like a man but, like all other *robots*, it was only a machine.
2. *Robots* are best at doing one thing over and over.
3. The factory uses *robots* instead of men to build its new cars.
4. "The *robot's* skin is made of steel," the scientist said. "And his brain is a network of wires."

and Verbalize...

_____

_____

_____

robust: healthy and strong

Visualize...

1. The new baby was pink and *robust*, with a good appetite and a loud voice.
2. The wrestler was a *robust* young man—he had a big chest and wide shoulders and wore extra-large shirts.
3. "Walter has never been very *robust*," Mrs. Finch said. "He was sick a lot when he was very young."
4. "This oatmeal will make you *robust*," the man on T.V. said. "You'll be able to walk ten miles every afternoon without stopping to rest."

and Verbalize...

_____

_____

_____

R

rodent: a type of mammal that gnaws with large front teeth—rats and mice are common rodents

Visualize...

1. Owls eat mice, squirrels, and other small *rodents*.
2. Gophers are *rodents* that dig tunnels and holes in your lawn and eat the roots of your favorite flowers.
3. Beavers, muskrats, woodchucks, and prairie dogs are all *rodents*.
4. The world's largest *rodent* is four feet long and two feet high and lives in South America. It's called a "capybara."

and Verbalize...

_____

_____

_____

rotate: to turn in a circle; to change places or take turns

Visualize...

1. The moon *rotates* around the Earth and the Earth and moon both *rotate* around the sun.
2. The toy top spun *rotated* in a blur until it began to slow down and finally fell over.
3. During the baseball game Mark and Tim *rotated* positions—Mark took Tim's place in right field and Tim took Mark's in left field.
4. In our house we *rotate* weekday chores: I wash the dishes on Mondays, Wednesdays, and Fridays, and my brother does them on Tuesdays and Thursdays.

and Verbalize...

_____

_____

_____

routine: a set of movements done over and over in the same way; a skit or act

Visualize...

1. Sometimes the daily *routine*—getting up, going to school, coming home, eating dinner, watching T.V.—can get boring.
2. Mr. Mendoza's Saturday *routine* was always the same: golf at 8:00, lunch at 11:00, a nap at 1:00, an afternoon walk at 3:00.
3. Dr. Gray's busy *routine* keeps her moving back and forth between her office and the hospital all day long.
4. Pam and June worked up a new cheerleading *routine* to surprise the fans at Friday's football game.

and Verbalize...

_____

_____

_____

rubber: a strong, elastic, waterproof substance that comes from the milky liquid in certain tropical trees and is used to make tires, balls, etc.

Visualize...

1. The farmer put on his *rubber* boots and waded into the flooded pasture to get the stranded calf.
2. The two boys played "pirates," stabbing each other with *rubber* swords that bent and could never draw blood.
3. Rex put on his *rubber* Frankenstein mask when he went trick-or-treating.
4. The *rubber* beach ball bounced down the stairs and out the open door into the street.

and Verbalize...

_____

_____

_____

rudder: a flat piece of wood or metal fastened to the back end of a boat or airplane for steering

Visualize...

1. The pilot couldn't steer when a lightning bolt hit the *rudder* of the small plane.
2. Birds use their tails as *rudders* when they fly.
3. Ed sat in the front of the boat and José sat in the back and handled the *rudder*.
4. "The *rudder* is broken," Della said, "but we can use that extra oar to steer the boat across the lake."

and Verbalize...

_____

_____

_____

rug: a floor covering made of wool or some other thick, heavy fabric—a carpet

Visualize...

1. Mr. Jones bought a *rug* to cover the wood floor so his feet wouldn't get so cold in the winter.
2. Lucy rolled up the dirty throw *rug* and took in outside to beat it with a broom.
3. Gus is learning to weave small *rugs* on his new loom.
4. A Persian *rug* is a carefully woven carpet that can take a year or more to make.

and Verbalize...

_____

_____

_____

R

rugged: rough, uneven; sturdy, strong

Visualize...

1. The countryside was very *rugged*, with rocky hills and steep gorges.
2. John Wayne was a popular actor because of his deep voice and *rugged* good looks—he looked like a cowboy, not like an actor.
3. Phil has a *rugged* old truck he uses for hauling firewood down the bumpy dirt road.
4. The farmer's *rugged* pair of boots lasted five years before they finally wore out.

and Verbalize...

_____

_____

_____

ruler: a straight strip of wood, plastic, or metal that is marked off in inches and used for measuring; a person who leads a country

Visualize...

1. A yardstick is a *ruler* 36 inches long. Most *rulers* are a foot long.
2. It's easy to draw a straight line if you use a *ruler* to guide your pencil.
3. Queen Elizabeth I was the *ruler* of England for 45 years.
4. In a real democracy, the people are the *rulers*.

and Verbalize...

_____

_____

_____

Chapter 18

The S's

sacrifice: to give up for the sake of something or someone else; to offer something to a god

Visualize...

1. The fireman *sacrificed* his own safety to rescue the child from the burning house.
2. The brave soldier *sacrificed* his own life to save the lives of his buddies.
3. Rod was happy to *sacrifice* his Saturday nights to help June with her homework.
4. "To 'feed' the sun and keep it alive, the Aztecs in Mexico *sacrificed* humans," Professor Lopez explained.

and Verbalize...

_____

_____

_____

saddle: a padded leather seat that the rider of a horse sits on

Visualize...

1. A good rider can ride a horse bareback, but a beginning rider should use a *saddle* so he won't fall off.
2. An English *saddle* is a small, smooth *saddle*. A Western *saddle* is larger and heavier, with a knob in front called a "saddlehorn."
3. Cowboys use Western *saddles* because they can loop the end of the rope around the horn when they rope cattle.
4. The "tack room" of the barn is where the rancher keeps his *saddles*, bridles, and blankets.

and Verbalize...

_____

_____

_____

S

sapling: a small young tree

Visualize...

1. It took many years for the *sapling* to grow into a full-sized tree.
2. It takes a plum tree *sapling* about three years to produce fruit.
3. There wasn't enough light for *saplings* to grow in the shadow of the giant maple tree.
4. Oak *saplings* grow from acorns. In a way, every acorn has an oak tree inside of it.

and Verbalize...

_____

_____

_____

sash: a wide piece of cloth that is worn around the waist or over one shoulder; the wooden frame of a window

Visualize...

1. The king wore a gold crown on his head, a purple *sash* across his chest, and a sword on his belt.
2. In the beauty pageant, each girl wore a *sash* with the name of her home state written on it.
3. The window *sash* kept getting stuck whenever Lars tried to open the window.
4. When you fix a broken window, you have to cut a new piece of glass to fit into the *sash.*

and Verbalize...

_____

_____

_____

satellite: a man-made object sent into space by rocket; a heavenly body that revolves around a planet

Visualize...

1. The space shuttle often carries *satellites* into outer space and puts them into orbit around the Earth.
2. *Satellites* circling the Earth send radio and T.V. waves around the world.
3. The moon is a *satellite* of the Earth.
4. "Does Mars have any *satellites*?" Professor Lopez asked. "Yes," said Lucy, "it has two moons."

and Verbalize...

_____

_____

_____

scarce: hard to find; small in amount

Visualize...

1. The blue grapes were *scarce*. Mark looked for an hour and found only two bunches in the vineyard.
2. "Good cowboys are *scarce*," the rancher said. "I'm glad I found Gus and Bob to work for me."
3. Rainfall was *scarce*, so the creeks dried up and the hills were brown all year.
4. The astronaut turned on his air tanks because oxygen was *scarce* on the blue planet.

and Verbalize...

_____

_____

_____

scissors: a tool made of two blades joined so that they can cut paper or cloth

Visualize...

1. Small children can use blunt *scissors* to cut paper safely.
2. The secret to a good haircut is a pair of very sharp *scissors*.
3. Don't use sewing *scissors* to cut paper—it will make the blades dull.
4. *Scissors* are helpful when you're cooking, to snip open packets of food or trim leaves from vegetables.

and Verbalize...

_____

_____

_____

scoop: a small or large tool like a shovel used for digging or lifting; a rounded amount

Visualize...

1. The *scoop* attached to the steam shovel digs into the ground, picks up the dirt, and dumps it into the truck.
2. A silver *scoop* for measuring out candy was tied to the candy bin.
3. "One *scoop*, two *scoops*, three *scoops*?" asked the man at the ice cream counter.
4. The man behind the counter put a *scoop* of hot popcorn into a paper bag and Flo gave him a quarter.

and Verbalize...

_____

_____

_____

scrape: to scratch or rub in a rough way

Visualize...

1. Billy fell off his bike and *scraped* his elbow, then ran into the house to get a band-aid.
2. The sailors had to *scrape* the rust off the old ship before they could paint it.
3. "*Scrape* the bottoms of of your shoes on the door mat," Lucy's mother called. "I just mopped the floor."
4. The students moaned and covered their ears when the mean teacher *scraped* her fingernails across the blackboard.

and Verbalize...

_____

_____

_____

sculptor: an artist who creates figures from stone, wood, clay, or other materials

Visualize...

1. The *sculptor* used a hammer and chisel to carve a statue from the block of stone.
2. From the mound of clay the *sculptor* formed the figure of a running horse.
3. Which *sculptor* carved the life-sized bear out of the huge tree trunk?
4. "I've got to run," the famous general explained. "The *sculptor* is coming and I've got to pose for my statue."

and Verbalize...

_____

_____

_____

scuttle: to move with quick, short steps; to make holes in the hull of a ship to sink it; to get rid of

Visualize...

1. Crabs and lobsters don't run or gallop—they *scuttle* when they want to get somewhere fast.
2. Each night Mary could hear something *scuttling* back and forth in the basement.
3. The pirates *scuttled* the stolen ship and watched it sink as they escaped in a lifeboat.
4. "Let's *scuttle* this plan," Mr. Smith said, erasing the blackboard in the meeting room. "Does anyone else have a better idea?"

and Verbalize...

_____

_____

_____

sensation: the experience of seeing, hearing, smelling, tasting, or touching; an impression produced by the senses; an exciting thing or person or a state of excitement

Visualize...

1. Smoking cigarettes dulls the *sensation* of taste.
2. Children spin around so they can feel the *sensation* of being dizzy.
3. Hula hoops were a big *sensation* back in the 1950's.
4. Madonna creates a *sensation* wherever she goes, no matter what she wears.

and Verbalize...

_____

_____

_____

sequence: an arrangement in which one thing follows another in a particular order

Visualize...

1. "A, B, C, D" is the *sequence* of the first four letters of the alphabet.
2. The *sequence* of events leading up to the 20-car accident was unknown.
3. The acrobat's routine unfolded in a *sequence* that began with back flips, moved to somersaults, and ended with handstands.
4. "My notes for the recipe are all out of *sequence*," Agnes complained. "'Put the cake in the oven' comes before 'Mix the flour, eggs, and sugar.'"

and Verbalize...

_____

_____

_____

serpent: a large snake

Visualize...

1. At the circus Della watched the "Snake Man" wrap a *serpent* around his neck.
2. That rattlesnake is a deadly *serpent*!
3. The python is a *serpent* which can grow to be almost 30 feet long.
4. "The Loch Ness Monster is a 'sea *serpent*,' a make-believe animal," Professor Lopez told Beth.

and Verbalize...

_____

_____

_____

session: a single period of time for learning and practice; a meeting of a group or a series of such meetings

Visualize...

1. After three *sessions* with his teacher, Jerome could play 'Mary Had a Little Lamb' on the trombone.
2. Dan's hardest basketball practice was a *session* on Friday, the day before the big game.
3. Professor Lopez attended four *sessions* of the scientific conference.
4. "This *session* of Congress achieved almost nothing," the disgusted senator complained.

and Verbalize...

_____

_____

_____

shanty: a roughly-built, run-down shack

Visualize...

1. The old pirate lived alone with his parrot in a *shanty* along the beach.
2. Tarzan and Jane built a *shanty* out of tree branches and vines beside a secret lake.
3. We used to live on the outskirts of town, in a *shanty* without electricity or running water.
4. The hills above the seaport were covered with thousands of *shanties*.

and Verbalize...

_____

_____

_____

shin: the front part of the leg between the knee and the ankle

Visualize...

1. Ted lifted his pants leg to show his mother the bruises on his *shin*.
2. The thrown bat hit Tom between his ankle and knee, right on his *shin*.
3. Bob pulled his socks high on his *shins* and slipped his pants legs down.
4. Some golfers wear "knickers," baggy pants which reach down only to the *shins*.

and Verbalize...

_____

_____

_____

shoreline: the place where shore and water meet

Visualize...

1. The three-story cabin on the *shoreline* of the lake has its own boat dock.
2. Pam likes to walk along the *shoreline* and pick up shells that the waves have brought in.
3. The *Shoreline* Cafe has a dining room built out over the waters of the bay.
4. The *shoreline* of the tropical island was a long, smooth beach bordered by groves of coconut palms.

and Verbalize...

_____

_____

_____

shortcut: a way that is quicker or shorter

Visualize...

1. Did Rex go the long way around, or take the *shortcut* through the empty lot?
2. There's no *shortcut* to learning—you just have to study.
3. "I can see a *shortcut* that will save us 50 miles," Mary said, looking at the road map.
4. The Panama Canal is a *shortcut* between the Caribbean and the Pacific Ocean.

and Verbalize...

_____

_____

_____

shriek: to scream or make a loud shrill sound

Visualize...

1. The first time I heard a peacock *shriek*, I thought someone was being attacked.
2. The monkeys at the zoo jump from swing to swing, *shrieking* at one another and the people who watch them.
3. "What are you doing in my closet?" *shrieked* Agnes when she saw Martha trying on her new dress.
4. The horses reared and galloped across the pasture when they heard the train whistle *shriek*.

and Verbalize...

_____

_____

_____

S

sift: to pass through a sieve; to sort through

Visualize...

1. We *sifted* the flour through the sieve—a tin cup with a screen for a bottom—so the batter for the cake wouldn't have any lumps.
2. The miners looked for gold nuggets by *sifting* the river sand through a wire mesh.
3. Rex *sifted* through the grass cuttings, trying to find his contact lens.
4. "Would you *sift* through that big stack of photographs?" Della asked Ron. "See if you can find a picture of Lucy."

and Verbalize...

_____

_____

_____

significant: important, notable, large; having special meaning

Visualize...

1. The young movie star had a *significant* part in the movie about invaders from Mars.
2. Wanda did a *significant* amount of work in setting up the meeting: she wrote letters, made phone calls, and picked people up at the airport.
3. June 10th is a *significant* date for my parents because that is the day they first met.
4. The white rose Stan left for Della was a *significant* gift. It meant he wanted to be her friend.

and Verbalize...

_____

_____

_____

silhouette: an outline drawing filled in with black or another solid color; a dark outline of something against a lighter background

Visualize...

1. A portrait done in *silhouette* usually shows the profile—the side view—of a person's face.
2. For Valentine's Day Mary cut *silhouettes* of a boy's face and a girl's face out of red paper and pasted them on a white paper heart.
3. The dog's shadow on the white wall was a perfect *silhouette*—Beth could see his nose, his tongue hanging out, his ears, and the dog license hanging from his collar.
4. On the closed window shade, the detective saw a shadow—the *silhouette* of a man holding a gun.

and Verbalize...

_____

_____

_____

silt: fine particles of sand, clay, dirt, and other material carried by flowing water

Visualize...

1. The farmer was glad when the river flooded and left behind a layer of *silt* that would make his land richer.
2. The stream was brown with *silt* the recent rains had washed from the hills.
3. Tons of *silt* washed down from the mountains and clogged the entrance to the river.
4. "If this *silt* gets any worse, I'll have to put my boat on a truck and drive it up the river!" the old tugboat captain exclaimed.

and Verbalize...

_____

_____

_____

simple: easy to understand or do; without anything added, plain

Visualize...

1. Adding 465 + 334 in your head is hard, but adding 3 + 2 is *simple*.
2. The book was *simple* to read, with easy words and short sentences.
3. Ruby wore a fancy dress with pearl buttons and lace cuffs, but Della was dressed in a *simple* cotton blouse and a pair of jeans.
4. Bill's room was *simple*—a bed, a chair, and an old chest of drawers for his clothes.

and Verbalize...

_____

_____

_____

situation: circumstance; problem that needs to be handled

Visualize...

1. Flo's living *situation* was perfect—she had her own bedroom and bath and a refrigerator for cold drinks.
2. At the dance there were eight girls and one boy, a *situation* that Stan liked.
3. Ten strangers showed up for dinner, but Mr. Wong handled the *situation* by cooking two extra turkeys.
4. "The *situation* is this," the teacher told Mrs. Green. "Your daughter comes to class late every day."

and Verbalize...

_____

_____

_____

S

skeleton: the framework of bones that supports and gives shape to an animal's body

Visualize...

1. The doctor held the x-ray up to the light and looked at the picture of Mr. Smith's *skeleton.*
2. Dr. Gray used a white plastic *skeleton* to show me which bone I had broken.
3. Mary made a Halloween costume by painting a white *skeleton* on a large black cloth.
4. The scientist spent many months fitting together all the bones of the dinosaur's *skeleton.*

and Verbalize...

_____

_____

_____

skim: to remove something that floats on the surface of a liquid; to move quickly and lightly along the surface of something; to look at written material very quickly

Visualize...

1. The farmer's wife *skimmed* the cream off the top of the bucket of fresh milk.
2. Rex *skimmed* the shiny layer of fat off the top of the stew with a big spoon.
3. The hockey puck *skimmed* across the slippery ice.
4. "I didn't really read the book," Tim told his teacher. "I just *skimmed* it, skipping here and there."

and Verbalize...

_____

_____

_____

skin: the outer covering of a human or animal body; the outer surface layer of something

Visualize...

1. Beth is pretty because she has dark eyes and smooth brown *skin.*
2. Too much sun can hurt your *skin,* even if you don't get sunburned.
3. The *skin* of an orange or lemon is called the "rind."
4. The baby tried to eat a banana without peeling its *skin.*

and Verbalize...

_____

_____

_____

skull: the bony framework of the head

Visualize...

1. Did Mike fracture his *skull* when he fell off his bike and hit his head?
2. "The *skull* on the label means that bottle is full of poison," June said.
3. The white *skull* and crossbones on the black flag told Dan it was a pirate ship sailing toward him.
4. The two scientists helped each other lift the dinosaur's giant *skull*.

and Verbalize...

_____

_____

_____

skyline: an outline, especially of buildings, against the sky; the horizon

Visualize...

1. New York City has a famous *skyline* with well-known skyscrapers like the Empire State Building and the World Trade Center.
4. The peaks of the Rocky Mountains make an impressive *skyline* behind Denver, Colorado.
2. The overcast sky was the same gray as the sea, so it was difficult to see the *skyline*.
3. The planet Venus suddenly appeared when the sun dropped below the *skyline*.

and Verbalize...

_____

_____

_____

skyscraper: a very tall city building

Visualize...

1. The Empire State Building used to be the tallest *skyscraper* in New York City.
2. The Sears Tower in Chicago is a *skyscraper* with 110 stories.
3. Some *skyscrapers* have offices, apartments, restaurants, shops, gyms, and even indoor parks.
4. "I'm sorry I'm late," Mr. Wong said. "I decided to climb the stairs in this *skyscraper* instead of taking the elevator."

and Verbalize...

_____

_____

_____

slogan: a word or group of words that is easy to remember and is used to get people to pay attention

Visualize...

1. "We're going to need a catchy *slogan* to sell this toothpaste," said the manager of the advertising agency.
2. "Speed Kills" is a *slogan* used to remind people to slow down when they drive.
3. "Just Say No" is the *slogan* for the fight against drugs.
4. "A mind is a terrible thing to waste" is a well-known *slogan* about the importance of learning.

and Verbalize...

_____

_____

_____

slope: to go up or down at an angle or slant

Visualize...

1. The green hills *sloped* down gently to the white sand and blue sea.
2. Our roof *slopes* steeply so the snow will slide off and not stick to the shingles.
3. The path *sloped* upward, and the hikers began to get tired.
4. Pam stopped pedaling her bike and began to coast when the road *sloped* down toward the lake.

and Verbalize...

_____

_____

_____

slosh: to move clumsily through mud or water; to shake a liquid or something in a liquid

Visualize...

1. The soldiers *sloshed* through the mud in their heavy boots.
2. Phil had to *slosh* through the rain in his good shoes when his car broke down.
3. The hiker *sloshed* the water around in his canteen to feel how much was left.
4. "*Slosh* those dishes around in the water and then let them soak," Beth called to Hortense.

and Verbalize...

_____

_____

_____

slot: a narrow, straight opening, usually metal

Visualize...

1. The mailman pushed some letters through the mail *slot* in our front door.
2. Della likes to drop pennies through the *slot* in her piggy bank and listen to them clink as they hit the other coins inside.
3. After we voted we folded up our ballots and slipped them through the *slot* in the ballot box.
4. Ruby put a couple of quarters in the stamp machine's *slot*, but nothing happened—the machine kept the coins and gave no stamps.

and Verbalize...

_____

_____

_____

slush: partly melted snow or ice

Visualize...

1. After the sun came out, the ice and snow began to turn into dirty *slush*.
2. Tom's boots got soaked when he had to wade through the *slush* in the barnyard.
3. "Did you go skating?" Wanda asked. "No," Ruby said, "the ice was like *slush*."
4. In the summer you can buy "*slushes*," cups of crushed ice mixed with fruit juice.

and Verbalize...

_____

_____

_____

smock: a long, loose shirt worn to protect clothes

Visualize...

1. The artist put a *smock* on over her dress before she began mixing her paints.
2. Della wears her father's old flannel shirt as a *smock* when she works in her garden.
3. "Put on a *smock* if you're going to spray-paint your dollhouse!" Mary's mother called.
4. Dr. Gray wears goggles and a long blue "motoring *smock*" when she drives her antique car.

and Verbalize...

_____

_____

_____

smother: to kill or die by stopping breathing; to conceal or be concealed; to cover or be covered thickly

Visualize...

1. I nearly *smothered* when my pullover sweater got stuck on my head and I couldn't get any air.
2. "The mother pig could *smother* her babies if she rolled over on top of them," Mr. Finch told Mark.
3. The heavy snow *smothered* all noise, and everything was smooth and white and still.
4. The delicious chopped steak was *smothered* with mushrooms.

and Verbalize...

_____

_____

_____

snarl: to growl; to speak in an angry way

Visualize...

1. Our dog doesn't bark at strangers, but if they come too close he curls his lips and *snarls*.
2. The tiger crept along the floor of the jungle, *snarling* and lashing its tail.
3. "Don't *snarl* at me!" Mrs. Jones said to her grouchy husband.
4. "I don't care where you're going," I *snarled* at my sister. "I don't want you wearing my red dress without asking me first!"

and Verbalize...

_____

_____

_____

soak: to keep in water or other liquid for a long time

Visualize...

1. June likes to *soak* dirty dishes overnight, but her mother thinks they should be washed and dried right after dinner.
2. Beth got the mustard stain out of her white blouse by *soaking* it in bleach.
3. The heavy rain *soaked* the fields and made the river overflow.
4. Susan's father likes to *soak* in a hot bath with a book and his yellow rubber duck.

and Verbalize...

_____

_____

_____

solar: operated by the sun's energy; having to do with or coming from the sun

Visualize...

1. The *solar* panels on Ed's roof use the sunlight to heat water for bathing and washing clothes.
2. Scientists are working on *solar* cars, so we won't have to depend on gasoline.
3. "Sunspots" are *solar* storms on the sun's surface which affect the Earth's climate.
4. Ancient Egyptians had a *solar* religion: they worshipped the sun.

and Verbalize...

_____

_____

_____

solitary: single or isolated

Visualize...

1. A *solitary* white cloud floated across the clear blue sky.
2. The *solitary* pine tree grew at a distance from the grove of pines.
3. Beth heard the roar of many engines but when she looked up she could see only a *solitary* plane.
4. Rex used to lead a *solitary* life, but now he's always surrounded by people.

and Verbalize...

_____

_____

_____

soul: the spiritual part of a human being—the deepest source of thought, feeling, and action

Visualize...

1. Most religions teach that each human being has a *soul* that survives the death of the body.
2. The great leader touched the *souls* of the people and they were ready to follow him anywhere.
3. "I believe that animals have *souls* too," Ruby said as she petted her cat.
4. "In my heart—deep in my *soul*—I know I should return the stolen money," Tom said.

and Verbalize...

_____

_____

_____

souvenir: something given or kept to remember something by—keepsake, memento

Visualize...

1. Mrs. Jones is bringing back a silver bracelet as a *souvenir* of her trip to Mexico.
2. The tourists bought little models of the Eiffel Tower for *souvenirs*.
3. Airports always have shops that sell hats and T-shirts and other *souvenirs*.
4. Jerome kept his movie ticket stub as a *souvenir* of his date with Della.

and Verbalize...

_____

_____

_____

spacecraft: rocket or other vehicle used for flying in outer space

Visualize...

1. It has been many years since a *spacecraft* from Earth landed on the moon.
2. The space shuttle is a *spacecraft*.
3. The "Enterprise" is the most famous *spacecraft* on T.V.
4. Many people think U.F.O.'s are *spacecraft* from other planets.

and Verbalize...

_____

_____

spar: to box, especially using light blows; to argue

Visualize...

1. The two boxers *sparred* with each other for a while, then left the ring and went to the showers.
2. We were just *sparring*, so I was surprised when Dan hit me as hard as he could.
3. Lucy and Wanda argued, *sparring* with each other over who would get to cut the birthday cake.
4. "I don't like *sparring* with people, but *sparring* with words is better than *sparring* with your fists," Mr. Finch said.

and Verbalize...

_____

_____

_____

sparkle: to shine by giving off flashes of light

Visualize...

1. The stars *sparkled* brightly in the clear night sky.
2. The drops of water caught in the spider web *sparkled* like jewels in the morning sun.
3. Pearls shine but diamonds *sparkle*.
4. In the moonlight I could see the fish *sparkle* as they darted through the dark water of the pond.

and Verbalize...

_____

_____

_____

specialize: to concentrate on a special thing or area

Visualize...

1. Peking Pizza is a restaurant which *specializes* in Chinese food but also serves Italian dishes.
2. Bob's uncle sells all kinds of used cars, but he *specializes* in American cars from the 50's.
3. In medical school Dr. Gray *specialized* in family medicine.
4. "Do you plan to *specialize* in American or British history?" Professor Lopez asked his student.

and Verbalize...

_____

_____

_____

species: a group of plants or animals that have certain common features

Visualize...

1. There are nearly one million different *species* of insects.
2. A zebra and a horse look alike but they don't belong to the same *species*.
3. All men and women and children on Earth belong to the same *species*: we are all human beings.
4. The admiral, monarch, and swallowtail are different *species* of butterfly.

and Verbalize...

_____

_____

_____

S

spectacle: an impressive sight; a big public show or display

Visualize...

1. Stan trembled at the *spectacle* of 100 smokestacks spewing black smoke into the air.
2. The Grand Canyon is a natural *spectacle* no one should miss seeing.
3. The three marching bands, the 50 majorettes, and the real tigers and lions on leashes made the halftime show quite a *spectacle*.
4. Jeff and Ted made a *spectacle* of themselves when they jumped up on the stage and began to sing with the band.

and Verbalize...

_____

_____

_____

spectacular: very impressive

Visualize...

1. "Aaaahhh," said the crowd as they watched the *spectacular* fireworks display.
2. The football fans jumped to their feet and shouted as the halfback made a *spectacular* play.
3. The night sky glowed orange as lava shot into the air during the *spectacular* volcanic eruption.
4. White smoke billowed a mile into the air after the *spectacular* explosion.

and Verbalize...

_____

_____

_____

spectator: a person who watches something

Visualize...

1. There were 50,000 *spectators* at the football game.
2. A crowd of *spectators* stood in the street and watched the old building burn down.
3. "I didn't fight—I was only a *spectator*," Harry told the policeman.
4. "Are you going to help or are you just a *spectator*?" Mary's father asked her as he raked the leaves.

and Verbalize...

_____

_____

_____

spike: a very large nail; a pointed piece of metal

Visualize...

1. Mr. Finch drove the *spike* into the tree with a heavy hammer.
2. "That's a railroad *spike*," Mr. Mendoza said when his son showed him the thick, 8-inch nail.
3. The golfer never slipped on wet grass because his shoes had *spikes* on the bottoms.
4. The logger wore boots with *spikes* so he could balance on the spinning log.

and Verbalize...

_____

_____

_____

spiritual: religious, having to do with the spirit or soul

Visualize...

1. The earth and air and water are holy, according to the *spiritual* teachings of the American Indians.
2. For Agnes, singing in the church choir was a *spiritual* experience.
3. "It's possible to be very *spiritual* and never go to church," Tom said. "Not in our religion," Susan said.
4. The rich man gave all his money to the poor because he cared about *spiritual* and not worldly things.

and Verbalize...

_____

_____

_____

sponsor: to pay for or to support

Visualize...

1. Is your father *sponsoring* your trip to Colorado or are you paying for it yourself?
2. The car company stopped *sponsoring* the two T.V. shows when their ratings began to fall.
3. The Writer's Club *sponsored* a series of lectures by famous poets.
4. No one would have known about the dance if the local paper hadn't *sponsored* it.

and Verbalize...

_____

_____

_____

squall: a sudden, strong windstorm that often brings rain or snow

Visualize...

1. The dangerous *squall* brought rain and 80-mile-an-hour winds.
2. The *squall* ended as fast as it began, leaving broken branches and puddles of water in the street.
3. The weatherman warned about *squalls*, but the foolish men set sail for the island.
4. "Those dark clouds mean a *squall* is coming," Phil said. "Let's head for shore."

and Verbalize...

_____

_____

_____

stadium: an enclosed area used for sporting and other events

Visualize...

1. The bleachers in our football *stadium* can hold 60,000 fans.
2. Ed and Rob had tickets to go see the big soccer match at the *stadium*.
3. On the 4th of July, Greg and Hortense went to the *stadium* to watch the fireworks display.
4. From her front porch Martha can see the tall lights of the *stadium* and hear the roar of the crowd.

and Verbalize...

_____

_____

_____

stake: a sharp stick or post

Visualize...

1. Tex drove a wooden *stake* into the ground, then tied the horses to it so they wouldn't run away.
2. Rex tied each corner of the tent to a *stake* he had pounded into the ground.
3. A line of *stakes* with red flags marked the path of the new highway.
4. Lucy tied the tomato plants to tall *stakes* so the plants wouldn't fall over.

and Verbalize...

_____

_____

_____

234

stare: to look at something for a long time without moving your eyes

Visualize...

1. The hungry gray cat *stared* at the robin in the apple tree.
2. Susan couldn't stop *staring* at the handsome new boy in class.
3. Flo had to stop and *stare* when the old man zoomed by on his skateboard.
4. The lion in the cage *stared* at June with its big yellow eyes.

and Verbalize...

_____

_____

_____

stilts: a pair of long poles you can stand on to walk above the ground; posts supporting a building over land or water

Visualize...

1. Mark was eight feet tall and took yard-long steps when he got up on *stilts*.
2. The clown at the circus walked on *stilts* 20 feet tall, so his head was higher than the elephant's back.
3. Some houses in India are built on *stilts* to keep flood waters out.
4. Part of Mr. Smith's house is on *stilts* because it's built on a steep hill.

and Verbalize...

_____

_____

_____

stool: a chair that has no back

Visualize...

1. Mr. Finch sits on a three-legged *stool* when he milks his cow.
2. Martha has to stand on a kitchen *stool* if she wants to reach the highest shelf.
3. Rex sat on a *stool* while his mother gave him a haircut.
4. Mr. Wong sat back in his armchair, put his feet up on a *stool*, and closed his eyes to take a little nap.

and Verbalize...

_____

_____

_____

S

storage: a space for keeping things until they are needed

Visualize...

1. Wanda had to put some of her furniture in *storage* because it wouldn't fit in her new apartment.
2. Every June we get our lawn chairs out of *storage* and put them out in the yard.
3. Mrs. Smith wants to park the car in the garage, but she never can—Mr. Smith uses it all for *storage*.
4. "There's so much stuff in this house we need to buy another house just for *storage*," growled Mr. Mendoza.

and Verbalize...

_____

_____

_____

store: to save something for later use

Visualize...

1. Rex *stored* his skis in the garage during the summer.
2. The bear *stored* up fat so he could sleep all winter and never have to eat.
3. Mrs. Jones *stored* her Christmas decorations in a big trunk.
4. "Shall I *store* the barbecue grill, or are we going to be using it?" Beth asked her mother.

and Verbalize...

_____

_____

_____

strenuous: requiring great effort

Visualize...

1. The P.E. class was *strenuous*—the kids had to run around the track three times and then do 100 sit-ups.
2. At the end of the *strenuous* race only three runners out of 200 were left.
3. "Football is just too *strenuous* for me," Greg said. "Let's play cards instead. "
4. Mrs. Jones is always exhausted because her job is so *strenuous*.

and Verbalize...

_____

_____

_____

stubble: a short, rough growth

Visualize...

1. Fred mowed the tall weeds close to the ground until only *stubble* was left.
2. After the harvest, fields of golden *stubble* were all that remained of the tall, waving wheat.
3. Two days after Jerome shaved his head he began to feel the first *stubble* growing back.
4. Dark and scratchy *stubble* grows on my father's face when he forgets to shave.

and Verbalize...

_____

_____

_____

studio: a place where movies or radio and T.V. programs are filmed, broadcast, or recorded; a place where an artist or craftsperson works

Visualize...

1. Madonna was tired after working at the movie *studio* all day.
2. Flo's father is a cameraman at the T.V. *studio* downtown.
3. A painter's *studio* must have lots of light and plenty of room to mix paints and stretch canvases.
4. The floor of the sculptor's *studio* was littered with chips of rock.

and Verbalize...

_____

_____

_____

submarine: a boat (usually military) that travels underwater

Visualize...

1. The *submarine* finally surfaced after 60 days underwater.
2. *Submarines* used torpedoes to sink many surface ships during World War II.
3. The captain of the *submarine* used a long periscope to look for enemy ships.
4. The incredible *submarine* in the book 20,000 Leagues Under the Sea is called "The Nautilus."

and Verbalize...

_____

_____

_____

S

subterranean: underground

Visualize...

1. A subway is a *subterranean* railway. The trains run through tunnels under the ground.
2. Prairie dogs live in *subterranean* houses or "dens."
3. The electric pump drew water from a *subterranean* water supply.
4. In <u>Journey to the Center of the Earth</u>, Jules Verne writes about a *subterranean* sea.

and Verbalize...

---

successful: having reached a goal; rich or famous

Visualize...

1. One reason Ruby is a *successful* student is because she always does her homework.
2. Flo's party was *successful*—everyone had a wonderful time.
3. The *successful* businessman owned three stores and had a million dollars in the bank.
4. "Everybody wants to be *successful*," Mr. Wong told Ted, "but money and fame don't matter if you don't have real friends."

and Verbalize...

---

summit: the top

Visualize...

1. Jerome didn't make it to the *summit* of the mountain—he had to stop 300 yards from the top because of the strong winds.
2. After we left the *summit*, all our walking was downhill.
3. A *summit* conference is a meeting of the world's top leaders.
4. Becoming president of the United States was the *summit* of Mr. Bush's political career.

and Verbalize...

---

sunrise: when the sun rises in the morning

Visualize...

1. At *sunrise* the sun comes up in the east, and at sunset it goes down in the west.
2. The old rooster always stands on the mailbox and crows at *sunrise*.
3. Mr. Finch gets up when it's still dark and finishes milking the cows before *sunrise*.
4. Hortense tossed and turned until *sunrise*, when the long night finally ended.

and Verbalize...

_____

_____

_____

sunset: when the sun goes down in the evening

Visualize...

1. The western sky turns purple, red, and pink at *sunset.*
2. After *sunset* the sky turns dark blue and the stars come out.
3. The jet plane left a long pink trail as it crossed the sky at *sunset.*
4. At *sunset* the birds flew toward the grove of trees where they would roost for the night.

and Verbalize...

_____

_____

_____

superb: excellent

Visualize...

1. The master chef cooked a *superb* dinner: lean slices of beef, tender pasta, and fresh asparagus.
2. Bill is a *superb* pitcher—everyone agrees he might play in the major leagues someday.
3. Wanda is a terrible cook, an average poet, a good dancer, an a *superb* sculptress.
4. Lars is a good singer but not a *superb* one.

and Verbalize...

_____

_____

_____

S

supplies: things that are needed

Visualize...

1. Rex bought enough *supplies* for a four-day camping trip.
2. I began to worry when our *supplies* got low—we had only one apple and a can of grape juice left.
3. The hiker's pack was full of *supplies*—dried fruit, powdered milk, and packages of instant soup.
4. The airplane used parachutes to drop *supplies* to the survivors.

and Verbalize...

_____

_____

_____

supply: to provide needed things

Visualize...

1. The river *supplied* the grizzly bear with all the fish he needed.
2. The delivery man keeps the grocery store *supplied* with bread.
3. The volunteers *supplied* the hospital with blood for its blood bank.
4. Flo *supplied* the sandwiches and Rex *supplied* the drinks and potato chips for the picnic.

and Verbalize...

_____

_____

_____

support: to hold up; to provide for

Visualize...

1. The walls of a house *support* the roof.
2. Mr. Finch used a thick pole to *support* the bending branch of the apple tree.
3. Dr. Gray *supports* her family by working as a doctor at the hospital.
4. My mother's regular salary isn't enough to *support* us, so she has to work a second job.

and Verbalize...

_____

_____

_____

supreme: highest

Visualize...

1. The job training program was of *supreme* importance—the future of the nation depended on it.
2. The President is often called the *supreme* commander of the armed forces.
3. A good education is of *supreme* importance when you begin looking for a job.
4. Endurance is not of minor but of *supreme* importance to a long-distance runner.

and Verbalize...

_____

_____

_____

surface: the outside of something

Visualize...

1. The long-legged fly landed on the *surface* of the pond.
2. How many miles is it from the *surface* of the Earth to its center?
3. The new kitchen tile has a slick *surface*, and I almost slipped and fell when I ran across it.
4. Rex liked to hold the river stones in his hand and feel their smooth *surfaces*.

and Verbalize...

_____

_____

_____

surname: a last name or family name

Visualize...

1. John Smith's *surname* is "Smith."
2. Most applications ask for your first name, your *surname*, and your middle initial.
3. "Jones" is an English *surname*, and "Lopez" is a Spanish surname.
4. Miss Green took her husband's *surname* when she got married, so she became "Mrs. Mendoza."

and Verbalize...

_____

_____

_____

S

suspend: to hang or be hung from something fastened above; to stop or be stopped temporarily

Visualize...

1. Beth used little wires to *suspend* the Christmas ornaments from the tree's branches.
2. The injured man was *suspended* by a safety line from the bottom of the helicopter.
3. The man's license was *suspended* after he ran the stoplight and hit the other car.
4. Mr. Wong had to *suspend* his daily exercise program when he got sick.

and Verbalize...

_____

_____

_____

sustain: to keep up or keep going; to endure; to nourish

Visualize...

1. Bob couldn't *sustain* his pace any longer—he began to run more slowly and finally had to stop.
2. The boxer *sustained* blow after blow until he finally became dizzy and fell to the canvas.
3. "We can't *sustain* another year like this without going broke," Mr. Green told his business partner.
4. The apples *sustained* us on our long hike through the woods.

and Verbalize...

_____

_____

_____

swell: an unbroken wave (n)

Visualize...

1. An ocean wave that is about to break is called a "*swell*."
2. The little rowboat bobbed up and down on the gentle *swells* of the lake.
3. The surfer paddled and then stood up as the *swell* broke into a crashing wave.
4. Jeff got sick when the big *swells* rocked the boat back and forth.

and Verbalize...

_____

_____

_____

swell: to grow or cause to grow in size (v)

Visualize...

1. Greg put some ice on his sprained ankle so it wouldn't *swell*.
2. The red balloon began to *swell* as I blew more and more air into it—and then it popped!
3. The crowd in the auditorium began to *swell* as more and more people arrived.
4. The plums began to *swell* and turn dark blue as they got ripe.

and Verbalize...

_____

_____

_____

sympathy: the sharing and understanding of another person's feelings

Visualize...

1. Flo had a lot of *sympathy* for Gus when he broke his leg because she broke hers last year.
2. "You have my *sympathy*," Wanda said when she saw Jerome had a bad cold.
3. Rex showed his *sympathy* for Ruby by giving her a hug and telling her he was sorry her dog had run away.
4. "I was out of work once," Phil said. "I have *sympathy* for anybody who can't find a job."

and Verbalize...

_____

_____

_____

Chapter 19

The T's

tackle: fishing gear; the act of grabbing someone and throwing him to the ground (n)

Visualize...

1. The fisherman kept his *tackle*—hooks, lines, and floats—in a special box.
2. "I have my pole and my *tackle*," Phil said as he left to go fishing. "Now all I need is a little luck."
3. The linebacker made a *tackle* on the quick, shifty halfback.
4. The left defensive end led the team in *tackles* and recovered fumbles.

and Verbalize...

_____

_____

_____

tackle: to grab someone and throw him to the ground; to try to do something (v)

Visualize...

1. Agnes and Martha *tackled* the robber as he ran out of the store and sat on him until the police arrived.
2. You are not allowed to *tackle* anyone in basketball.
3. The roof is leaking, but we can't *tackle* the job of fixing it until it stops raining.
4. After June learned to swim, she decided to *tackle* diving.

and Verbalize...

_____

_____

_____

talent: a natural ability or skill

Visualize...

1. Ruby has a lot of *talent*—she sings, she dances, and she is always the star in school plays.
2. Lars has a *talent* for writing: everyone loves to hear him read his stories.
3. Beth and Agnes are good friends: Beth has a *talent* for cooking and Agnes has a *talent* for eating.
4. Mrs. Jones seems to have a *talent* for making people angry.

and Verbalize...

---

tassel: a hanging bunch of threads tied together at one end

Visualize...

1. The edges of the fancy white tablecloth were decorated with shiny white *tassels* .
2. A white *tassel* hung from one corner of my brother's graduation cap.
3. The bishop's robe was white, with gold silk *tassels* sewn across the front.
4. Long pink *tassels* decorated the border of the baby's pretty blanket.

and Verbalize...

---

technician: a person having detailed knowledge of a certain job, especially someone skilled at using special machinery

Visualize...

1. The lab *technician* in the white coat looked through the microscope.
2. An optical *technician* knows how to grind lenses for eyeglasses.
3. A good metal sculptor is both an artist and a skilled *technician.*
4. Computer *technicians* know how to program and fix computer systems.

and Verbalize...

technique: a way to do something

Visualize...

1. To be a good painter you must learn the *technique* of mixing colors.
2. My sister has an interesting *technique* for washing her socks: she wears them in the shower.
3. Lucy's *technique* of peeling potatoes is to boil them first and then pull the skins off with a fork.
4. My cat's *technique* for waking me up is to jump on my bed, climb on my chest, and rub her face against mine.

and Verbalize...

_____

_____

_____

technology: the use of science in industry or business; methods, machines, and materials used in a science or profession

Visualize...

1. Computer design is one of our fastest-growing *technologies*.
2. "If we have the *technology* to give all people good medical care, why aren't we doing it?" asked Phil.
3. Mr. Mendoza uses solar energy *technology* to warm his house: he has three solar panels on the roof.
4. Mr. Finch knows everything about the *technology* of tomato-picking machines.

and Verbalize...

_____

_____

_____

tedious: long and tiring, boring

Visualize...

1. Last weekend Mom gave us the *tedious* job of weeding the backyard.
2. The math problems weren't difficult, just *tedious*.
3. Picking grapes looks pretty in pictures, but in real life it is hot and *tedious* work.
4. Uncle Rollo likes to tell *tedious* stories about when he was in the Army.

and Verbalize...

_____

_____

_____

tempest: a violent storm with high winds; any noisy disturbance

Visualize...

1. "The *tempest* has begun!" shouted the pirate as the ship began to lurch on the stormy ocean.
2. "The *Tempest*" is a play by William Shakespeare about a storm which shipwrecks people on a magical island.
3. A big fuss about something unimportant is called "a *tempest* in a teapot."
4. The *tempest* began when Flo accused June of flirting with Beth's boyfriend.

and Verbalize...

_____

_____

_____

temporary: not long-lasting; used for the time being

Visualize...

1. My summer job with the Forest Service was *temporary*—it ended the week before school started.
2. A *temporary* power loss left our street dark for a few hours..
3. Your baby teeth are *temporary*—they fall out when your permanent teeth start to come in.
4. "This is just my *temporary* car," Martha told Agnes, waving her hand at the old Pinto. "I'm waiting for my new Jeep."

and Verbalize...

_____

_____

_____

terrain: a certain area of land, especially its physical appearance

Visualize...

1. The *terrain* in the Mojave Desert is flat, flat, flat, and dry, dry, dry.
2. The green hills and rocky cliffs of California's central coast make up some of the most beautiful *terrain* in the world.
3. We traveled by horse over rough *terrain*, and by boat across rivers and lakes.
4. The *terrain* near Pismo Beach includes sand dunes.

and Verbalize...

_____

_____

_____

terrify: to be very scared or to scare greatly

Visualize...

1. The hikers were *terrified* when the huge grizzly bear stood in the middle of the trail.
2. Greg was *terrified* when the airplane started roaring down the runway, but after we were in the air he felt better.
3. The movie "Aliens" *terrified* me, but it made my father laugh.
4. "My little brother is strange," Flo said. "He likes roller coasters, but merry-go-rounds *terrify* him."

and Verbalize...

_____

_____

_____

theme: the main idea; a short piece of writing; a melody that identifies a show or musical group

Visualize...

1. One of the *themes* of the movie "The Wizard of Oz" is "There's no place like home."
2. The *theme* of the mayor's speech was that we all need to help one another.
3. We had to write a 600-word *theme* on Shakespeare's "Hamlet" for our English class.
4. The *theme* for the T.V. show "Twilight Zone" sounds like, "DOO doo doo doo, DOO doo doo doo, DOO doo doo doo."

and Verbalize...

_____

_____

_____

thrash: to give a beating to; to toss about wildly; to give a full discussion of

Visualize...

1. Godzilla could *thrash* Alf very easily.
2. Our football team *thrashed* our opponents in the game last night.
3. Dan *thrashed* around in the water, waving his arms and yelling "Help!" because he didn't know how to swim.
4. "We need to *thrash* this problem out," Martha said to her friend. "I'll get us some hot chocolate and we'll talk it over."

and Verbalize...

_____

_____

_____

T

thread: a very thin cord used for sewing; the ridge or groove that winds around the outside of a screw or bolt, or around the inside of a nut

Visualize...

1. Fred used the green *thread* to mend the hole in his green shirt.
2. Beth bought two spools of *thread*, a needle, a thimble, and some blue cloth.
3. The plumber twisted the nut tightly onto the bolt's *thread*.
4. The *threads* on a screw or bolt are "stripped" when they are rubbed smooth and won't work anymore.

and Verbalize...

_____

_____

_____

threat: a sign of danger; a statement of something that will be done to hurt or punish

Visualize...

1. Because of all the rain, there was a *threat* that the river would rise and flood the surrounding land.
2. Rod knew there was a *threat* of explosion when he smelled the gas leak and saw the open flame.
3. The newspaper editor received *threats* in the mail after he wrote the unpopular article.
4. "Do your homework or you can't watch TV for two weeks," Mrs. Mendoza said to José. "And that's a promise, not a *threat*."

and Verbalize...

_____

_____

_____

tighten: to make tighter or become tighter

Visualize...

1. Lucy put the saddle on her horse's back and *tightened* the cinch under his belly.
2. The wheel began to come off the car because Ed didn't *tighten* all the lug nuts that held it on.
3. Mary *tightened* her grip on Spot's leash when the black cat walked by.
4. "I know I'm gaining weight when I feel my clothes *tightening*," sighed Martha.

and Verbalize...

_____

_____

_____

T

tomb: a grave for the dead

Visualize...

1. The *Tomb* of the Unknown Soldier in Washington, D.C. is a memorial for all unidentified American soldiers who died in war.
2. A small building used as a *tomb* is called a "mausoleum."
3. In scary movies Dracula's *tomb* is always a cold, dark room full of spider webs.
4. "I get nervous when I go to the library," Jerome said. "It's always as quiet as a *tomb*."

and Verbalize...

_____

_____

tower: a building or part of a building that is very tall and narrow

Visualize...

1. The old stone castle had a steep roof, small windows, and high *towers*.
2. We looked up at the church *tower* when the bells began to ring.
3. The forest ranger climbed the lookout *tower* to look for smoke from a forest fire.
4. The Eiffel *Tower* is the world-famous *tower* in Paris, France.

and Verbalize...

_____

_____

trade: work that calls for skill, usually with your hands (n)

Visualize...

1. After high school, Tim's brother decided to learn a *trade* instead of going to college.
2. Carpentry is a good *trade* for anyone who likes to work with wood.
3. My grandmother was a tailor and she worked at her *trade* for 60 years.
4. Plumbing is a *trade* which requires you to cut and thread steel pipe.

and Verbalize...

_____

_____

251

trade: to exchange one thing for another (v)

Visualize...

1. At lunch today, Gus *traded* his tuna sandwich for Rod's egg salad sandwich.
2. Sometimes you can *trade* in your old car as a down payment on a new one.
3. Mr. Wong and Mr. Finch like to sit together at parties, *trading* stories about "the good old days."
4. *Trading* things instead of using money is called "bartering."

and Verbalize...

_____

_____

_____

transform: to change or be changed in shape or nature

Visualize...

1. When water freezes, it is *transformed* into ice.
2. After weeks of painting and carpentry, we *transformed* the old house into a beautiful home.
3. "All these caterpillars will be *transformed* into beautiful butterflies," the forest ranger told Pam and Ed.
4. Falling in love *transformed* the grouchy woman into a lovely lady.

and Verbalize...

_____

_____

_____

treacherous: dangerous or untrustworthy

Visualize...

1. Icy roads and heavy snow make driving *treacherous*.
2. "Walking on thin ice" means you are in a *treacherous* situation.
3. Beth's "friend" was *treacherous*—he smiled to her face and talked about her behind her back.
4. Politics is a *treacherous* profession—you never know who you can trust.

and Verbalize...

_____

_____

_____

treasury: the government department in charge of money; a place where money or valuable things are stored

Visualize...

1. The U.S. *Treasury* prints all our paper money.
2. The *Treasury* Department is in charge of our country's finances.
3. The queen kept her crown and other jewels locked away in her *treasury*.
4. Your town library is a *treasury* of information.

and Verbalize...

_____

_____

_____

tremble: to shake

Visualize...

1. The mayor's voice was calm during his speech, but the paper in his hands was *trembling*.
2. Ron's voice *trembled* nervously as he asked Lucy to go to the dance with him.
3. The water was so cold my legs *trembled* and my teeth began to chatter.
4. The old dog *trembled* with excitement when he saw the orange cat walk by slowly.

and Verbalize...

_____

_____

_____

trench: a long, deep ditch

Visualize...

1. Never play near a construction *trench*—the loose sand might slide and trap you.
2. The plumber buried the water pipe in a deep *trench.*
3. Mr. Finch dug a small *trench* from the creek to the meadow to bring water for his cows.
4. The soldiers dug a *trench* and then climbed inside as the enemy approached.

and Verbalize...

_____

_____

_____

triangle: a flat shape with three sides that all touch one another; a musical instrument that is a steel rod bent in the shape of a triangle

Visualize...

1. A *triangle* looks like a flat pyramid.
2. How would you divide a square into two *triangles*?
3. A musical *triangle* is played by hitting it with a thin metal rod.
4. The orchestra conductor waved his baton and Jeff hit the *triangle* three times.

and Verbalize...

_____

_____

_____

tribe: a group of people who live together and follow the same customs

Visualize...

1. The Indian *tribes* who lived along the Pacific coast used seashells for jewelry.
2. The Navajo people are a *tribe* of Native Americans who live in Arizona and New Mexico.
3. There are *tribes* of Indians who live deep in the rain forests of the Amazon.
4. Some Arabic *tribes* travel back and forth across the desert with their tents, horses, and camels.

and Verbalize...

_____

_____

_____

tribute: forced payment, tax; something given or done to show respect

Visualize...

1. All the people in the kingdom had to pay the evil king a *tribute* of silver coins.
2. The pirates demanded *tribute* from each ship that entered the bay.
3. Our class gave Mrs. Smith a watch as a *tribute* to her patience.
4. "This toast is a *tribute* to the bride and groom!" Mr. Wong said, raising his glass.

and Verbalize...

_____

_____

_____

triumphant: victorious, successful; showing excitement because of victory

Visualize...

1. Last night our baseball team was *triumphant*—we won 5 to 2.
2. In a war no one is completely *triumphant*—people are hurt on the winner's side too.
3. "I won the spelling bee!" June said in a *triumphant* voice.
4. The band played a *triumphant* march as it paraded down the street.

and Verbalize...

_____

_____

_____

twilight: the time between sunset and darkness

Visualize...

1. *Twilight* is the time just before dark when the light is a soft and hazy blue.
2. At *twilight* Agnes walked around the house turning on lamps.
3. Mr. Martinez always drives carefully at *twilight* because it's hard to see cars and pedestrians in the dim light.
4. "*Twilight* is an in-between time," Ruby said. "It's not daytime anymore, but it's still not nighttime."

and Verbalize...

_____

_____

_____

Chapter 20

The U's

understand: to get the meaning of; to know how someone else feels or thinks

Visualize...

1. Seeing pictures in your mind when you read helps you *understand* the words.
2. "I have trouble *understanding* math," Lucy told Mrs. Smith, "but spelling is easy for me."
3. Rex feels lonely because he believes that no one *understands* him.
4. "I *understand* your excitement," Mr. White told Flo. "Not every girl gets to join the circus."

and Verbalize...

_____

_____

_____

unexpected: not expected, surprising

Visualize...

1. A cow sitting in the middle of your lawn is an *unexpected* sight.
2. A letter from a long-lost friend is *unexpected*, but welcome.
3. "This is an *unexpected* pleasure," Professor Lopez said, bowing to Mr. Finch. "I didn't know you were coming to this meeting."
4. The *unexpected* knocking on his door made Bill jump.

and Verbalize...

_____

_____

_____

U

unity: the state of being a whole; feeling of cooperation or togetherness

Visualize...

1. "This silly story doesn't have any *unity*," Pam said. "It has a beginning and an end, but no middle!"
2. Using the same colors for different things in a room can give the room a feeling of *unity*.
3. There's no real *unity* in Ted's family—someone is always arguing with someone else.
4. The team won the game because of their *unity*—they all helped one another.

and Verbalize...

_____

_____

_____

upward: toward a higher place

Visualize...

1. Our plane flew *upward* into the blue sky and bright clouds.
2. The explorer in the deep cavern began to climb *upward* toward the light.
3. The elevator began to move *upward*, then stopped with a jerk. "Oh no, " Frank said, "somebody has pushed the DOWN button!"
4. Tim came downward, then rose *upward* again, as the seesaw rocked back and forth.

and Verbalize...

_____

_____

_____

urge: a strong desire (n)

Visualize...

1. "I have a strange *urge* to jump," Flo said, looking down from the tower, "but of course I won't."
2. Late at night Agnes often has the *urge* to go out and buy some chocolate chip ice cream.
3. "I always feel the *urge* to sing in the shower," Mr. Mendoza told his wife. "Fight it," she said.
4. Do you have any *urge* to drive a race car? I don't.

and Verbalize...

_____

_____

_____

urge: to try to persuade; to drive or force on (v)

Visualize...

1. Dr. Gray always *urges* everyone to take long walks and drink plenty of water.
2. "'Roger Rabbit' is a great movie," Gus said to Beth. "I *urge* you to go see it."
3. The army captain shouted and waved his gun as he *urged* his men up the hill.
4. The cowboy *urged* his horse on with his spurs, but the horse reared up suddenly and threw him from his saddle.

and Verbalize...

_____

_____

_____

utensil: a useful tool or container

Visualize...

1. The only *utensil* Flo's baby sister can manage is a spoon.
2. Pens, pencils, and markers are all writing *utensils*.
3. Basic cooking *utensils* include mixing bowls, eggbeaters, rolling pins, and baking pans.
4. A good *utensil* for draining spaghetti is a colander (a metal bowl full of holes).

and Verbalize...

_____

_____

_____

Chapter 21

The V's

vague: not clear or definite

Visualize...

1. At our house dinnertime is usually *vague*—we just know it's sometime between twilight and bedtime.
2. We saw *vague* shapes in the fog, but couldn't tell if they were people or bushes.
3. Mr. Grey's instructions were so *vague* that Rex didn't know which of the three trees to trim.
4. Greg had only a *vague* idea of how to put the lawnmower's motor back together.

and Verbalize...

_____

_____

_____

variety: many different kinds; change or difference

Visualize...

1. Phil has worked at a *variety* of jobs: shoe clerk, teacher, fisherman, carpenter.
2. Our grocery store has a wide *variety* of breakfast cereals: 15 hot kinds and 22 cold kinds.
3. Just for *variety*, Della's family likes to eat dinner on the patio now and then.
4. "*Variety* is the spice of life" is a saying which means that change makes life interesting.

and Verbalize...

_____

_____

_____

V

vast: very great in size

Visualize...

1. The Grand Canyon is impressive because it is such a *vast* and beautiful gorge.
2. Driving across the United States makes you realize how *vast* a country it really is.
3. The little boy's ignorance was *vast*—he didn't even know that milk came from cows.
4. "This is a *vast* improvement," Mrs. Smith said to Tim. "Your history grade has gone from a 'D' to a 'B'!"

and Verbalize...

_____

_____

_____

vault: a room for keeping valuable things safe; a burial chamber (n)

Visualize...

1. The bank keeps its money in a locked metal *vault* that has a steel door three feet thick.
2. Martha kept her ruby ring in a safe-deposit box in the bank's *vault*.
3. A secret *vault* inside the pyramid held the pharaoh's mummy.
4. The archeologist found the Persian king and queen together in a gold-lined *vault*.

and Verbalize...

_____

_____

_____

vault: to jump in the air or over something, especially by using your hands or a pole to lift yourself up (v)

Visualize...

1. The fat clown jumped on one end of the seesaw and the thin clown *vaulted* into the air.
2. When Mr. Mendoza saw his new car rolling down the hill, he *vaulted* over his front gate and ran after it.
3. Athletes are using new, light, fiberglass poles to *vault* higher than ever before in the pole vault.
4. The track star ran down the track, pushed his pole into the ground, and *vaulted* over the bar at 17 feet.

and Verbalize...

_____

_____

_____

veer: to change direction sharply

Visualize...

1. "*Veer* to the right when you get to the Y in the road," the farmer told the traveling salesman.
2. A flock of geese flew overhead, then *veered* to the south when the hunter shot at them.
3. The speedboat *veered* suddenly when its driver saw the rocks ahead.
4. Agnes is not a very good driver—she tends to *veer* all over the road.

and Verbalize...

_____

_____

_____

version: an account or description given from a particular point of view; a translation; a form or variation of something

Visualize...

1. We never really knew what happened at the party because Mary gave us one *version* of it and Hortense gave another.
2. Mark's *version* of the sad movie made us laugh instead of cry.
3. The Spanish *version* of the book The Adventures of Tom Sawyer is called Las Aventuras de Tomas Sawyer.
4. Many songs have both long and short *versions*.

and Verbalize...

_____

_____

_____

vertical: straight up and down

Visualize...

1. Telephone wires are horizontal, but telephone poles are *vertical*.
2. The famous Tower of Pisa was originally *vertical* before it began to lean.
3. Helicopters can fly straight up in a *vertical* line.
4. "Try to stay *vertical*," Mr. Wong joked as he began teaching Fred how to ice skate.

and Verbalize...

_____

_____

_____

victim: a person or animal that is harmed or killed

Visualize...

1. The *victim* of the car accident was put on a stretcher and taken to the hospital in an ambulance.
2. The bear with the burned paw was a *victim* of the forest fire.
3. The child who was hurt in the robbery was an innocent *victim*.
4. "Mr. X is a *victim* of foul play," the detective said as he looked at the body.

and Verbalize...

_____

_____

_____

victory: success; the defeat of an enemy

Visualize...

1. It was a real *victory* for Mr. Finch when he was able to quit smoking.
2. If you are shy, it's a *victory* just to say hello to a stranger.
3. In the Civil War, the First Battle of Bull Run was a *victory* for the South and a defeat for the North.
4. We celebrated our football team's *victory* with a dance in the gym.

and Verbalize...

_____

_____

_____

villain: a wicked or evil person

Visualize...

1. One of the worst *villains* in history was Adolf Hitler.
2. In old Westerns the hero always wears a white hat and the *villain* wears a black one.
3. In the Roadrunner cartoons, it's hard to tell if Wily Coyote is the *villain* or the victim.
4. Sometimes a *villain* is a woman, like the witch in "Sleeping Beauty."

and Verbalize...

_____

_____

_____

visible: able to be seen

Visualize...

1. The first "star" *visible* at twilight is the planet Venus.
2. The stars are not *visible* during daylight but the moon often is.
3. Dark lines under your eyes can be a *visible* sign that you are tired or sick.
4. Bacteria are small animals *visible* only under a microscope.

and Verbalize...

_____

_____

_____

visor: an eyeshade

Visualize...

1. The man dealing the cards wore a green *visor* to protect his eyes from the bright lamp.
2. Beth wears a blue plastic *visor* to the beach so her face won't get sunburned.
3. A baseball cap has a long *visor* called a "bill" which shades the player's eyes.
4. Flo's father lowered the car's *visor* when the sun shone too brightly through the windshield.

and Verbalize...

_____

_____

_____

visual: having to do with seeing

Visualize...

1. Sometimes children have trouble learning because of *visual* problems—they can't see the blackboard or the words on the page.
2. Being near-sighted and far-sighted are *visual* problems that can be corrected with glasses.
3. Even newborn babies are *visual*—they love bright colors and moving shapes.
4. Good writing is always *visual*—it makes you see pictures as you read.

and Verbalize...

_____

_____

_____

vitality: energy

Visualize...

1. At the age of 84 my grandmother still has a lot of *vitality*: she cooks, she sews, she takes piano lessons, and she goes dancing once a week.
2. It's hard to have any *vitality* when you're feeling low—just getting up in the morning and putting your socks on is a victory.
3. Zorba the Greek was a man of great *vitality*. He loved to sing and dance and talk for hours with his friends.
4. The artist's *vitality* was visible in his paintings—the bright colors gave a sense of energy and movement.

and Verbalize...

_____

_____

_____

vivid: very bright and colorful

Visualize...

1. The colors in our kitchen are *vivid*: the walls are yellow, the rug is red, the pots are bright blue, and the table is green.
2. South American parrots have feathers that are *vivid* green, blue, and red.
3. The images on our new color T.V. are so *vivid* they look real.
4. Emma is a *vivid* woman—she wears her red hair tied up in a purple scarf and leaves a ring of orange lipstick on your cheek when she kisses you goodbye.

and Verbalize...

_____

_____

_____

volume: amount that something holds; level of sound; a book

Visualize...

1. This big glass pitcher holds the same *volume* of tomato juice as that half-gallon can does.
2. The *volume* of this swimming pool is 800 gallons.
3. "Turn down the *volume* on that radio!" my sister said to me. "I can't study with all that noise."
4. The city library has over 500 *volumes* of children's stories.

and Verbalize...

_____

_____

_____

Chapter 22

The W's

waist: the part of the body between the chest and the hips

Visualize...

1. "I love this dress," Martha said, looking at herself in the mirror, "but the belt is too small for my *waist*."
2. A vest is a sleeveless jacket that stops at your *waist*.
3. Mr. and Mrs. Smith began to waltz across the floor, her hand on his shoulder and his arm around her *waist*.
4. Mrs. Mendoza tied the apron around Mr. Mendoza's *waist*. "Your turn to cook dinner," she said.

and Verbalize...

_____

_____

_____

wallet: a thin, flat case used for carrying money and small cards

Visualize...

1. My father keeps paper money in his *wallet* and coins in his pocket.
2. My mother has 12 credit cards in her *wallet* but she won't let me borrow any.
3. The woman wrote a check and opened her *wallet* to show the clerk her driver's license.
4. A robber who steals people's *wallets* is called a "pickpocket."

and Verbalize...

_____

_____

_____

walrus: a large seal-like animal that lives in the cold waters of the North

Visualize...

1. A *walrus* looks like a very big seal with long, straight white tusks.
2. The name "*walrus*" comes from the Dutch words for "whale" and "horse."
3. The *walrus* spends a lot of time sunning itself on the rocks.
4. In the book <u>Alice</u> <u>in</u> <u>Wonderland</u>, a make-believe *walrus* and a carpenter take a walk on the beach together to "speak of many things."

and Verbalize...

_____

_____

_____

warning: sign or notice of approaching danger

Visualize...

1. I stopped when I heard the bell and saw the flashing lights—a *warning* that a train was coming.
2. The alley cat hissed a *warning* when we tried to pet him.
3. Not being able to sleep might be a *warning* that something is bothering you.
4. The policeman gave the speeding driver a *warning* and told her that next time she would get a ticket.

and Verbalize...

_____

_____

_____

weary: very tired

Visualize...

1. After hiking all day we got back to camp *weary* and hungry.
2. By Friday evening Greg has worked all week and sometimes feels too *weary* to go out.
3. At the party, Mrs. Jones talked to me until I was *weary*.
4. Flo is so *weary* of bad news that she has stopped reading the newspaper.

and Verbalize...

_____

_____

_____

welfare: well-being (health and happiness)

Visualize...

1. "I make you eat bran cereal for your own *welfare*," my mother tells me.
2. Exercise and rest are both important for your physical and mental *welfare*.
3. A leader's job is to protect the *welfare* of his people.
4. National parks are important to the *welfare* of wild animals.

and Verbalize...

_____

_____

_____

whale: a large, air-breathing sea animal shaped like a fish

Visualize...

1. *Whales* look like giant fish, but they're really mammals who live in the sea.
2. Blue *whales*, gray *whales*, and humpbacked *whales* are three different kinds of *whales*.
3. Orca is a black-and-white "killer *whale*" that performs at Sea World.
4. Some kinds of *whales* communicate by making sounds scientists call "songs."

and Verbalize...

_____

_____

_____

whirlpool: water that is moving rapidly in a circle

Visualize...

1. The powerful *whirlpool* spun the ship in a circle, then pulled it under the waves.
2. Rex pulled the bathtub plug and watched the soapy water go down the drain in a spinning *whirlpool*.
3. Some people have tubs called "spas" which give massages with *whirlpools* of warm water.
4. Hospitals use baths with gentle *whirlpools* to help patients who have sore muscles and joints.

and Verbalize...

_____

_____

_____

wield: to use skillfully

Visualize...

1. The pirates leaped aboard the ship, shouting and *wielding* swords.
2. *Wielding* a large knife, the butcher quickly cut the meat into chops.
3. Julia Child is a cook who can *wield* a cooking spoon to make wonderful soups.
4. A writer is someone who *wields* a pen—or a typewriter—to put ideas on paper.

and Verbalize...

_____

_____

_____

wilderness: a wild place

Visualize...

1. Two hundred years ago much of America was *wilderness* where only Indian tribes lived.
2. Many national forests and parks have special *wilderness* areas with no roads or buildings.
3. Rex got tired of the city, so he went to live with the animals in the *wilderness*.
4. People from the country sometimes think that a big city is like a *wilderness*.

and Verbalize...

_____

_____

_____

wizard: a person who can do magic; a person who is very clever and skillful

Visualize...

1. The most famous *wizard* ever was Merlin, King Arthur's teacher and friend.
2. The *wizard* who pretended to rule the Land of Oz by magic was really just a man from Kansas.
3. Flo is a *wizard* at making spaghetti sauce.
4. Computer *wizards* are people who know everything about computers.

and Verbalize...

_____

_____

_____

worship: to pray to; show respect and honor for

Visualize...

1. Some people *worship* together in church, and some *worship* alone in the wilderness.
2. The ancient Egyptians *worshipped* a sun god.
3. We all *worshipped* my grandfather because he was a kind and good man.
4. Some people *worship* Elvis Presley and Marilyn Monroe.

and Verbalize...

_____

_____

_____

wreck: what is left of something broken or destroyed; the crashing of a car, plane, ship, or train

Visualize...

1. The divers swam around the *wreck* of the pirate ship.
2. The old hay rake was just a rusty *wreck* in the barnyard.
3. The rescue team rushed to the scene of the plane *wreck*.
4. The dense fog caused a series of wrecks on the freeway.

and Verbalize...

_____

_____

_____

wrench: a tool for turning nuts and bolts or pipes (n)

Visualize...

1. A pipe *wrench* is a heavy metal tool for screwing and unscrewing pipes.
2. A monkey *wrench* is another name for a pipe *wrench*.
3. Greg used a crescent *wrench* to tighten the bolts on the toy tractor.
4. A socket *wrench* has an open cylinder at one end which fits over a nut or bolt.

and Verbalize...

_____

_____

_____

wrench: to twist or pull sharply (v)

Visualize...

1. The ship's mast was *wrenched* apart during the storm.
2. Ed used a claw hammer to *wrench* the old boards from the wall.
3. Mr. White *wrenched* his back when he tried to lift the heavy box alone.
4. Mary *wrenched* the bag of money from the robber's hand while Beth sat on his chest.

and Verbalize...

_____

_____

_____

wrestle: to force or try to force an opponent to the ground; to struggle

Visualize...

1. Hulk Hogan *wrestled* "The Destroyer" to the mat as the audience clapped and cheered.
2. Texas Slim *wrestled* the calf to the ground in record time at the Blue River Rodeo.
3. My father stayed up until late an night *wrestling* with our bills.
4. "After *wrestling* with the problem for a week, I've decided to let Spot sleep inside at night," Flo's mother announced.

and Verbalize...

_____

_____

_____

writhe: to twist or turn with physical pain; to suffer mental upset

Visualize...

1. Dr. Gray gave Jake a painkiller when he began to *writhe* from side to side after he awoke from the operation.
2. Greg *writhed* on the ground when he fell from the ladder and hurt his knee.
3. The children began to *writhe* with impatience as they saw the castle towers of Disneyland in the distance.
4. Beth *writhed* with embarrassment when she looked in the mirror and saw her bad haircut.

and Verbalize...

_____

_____

_____

Chapter 23

The X's, Y's & Z's

Xerox: an office copying machine; the photographic copy made by a Xerox

Visualize...

1. The office workers were relieved when the new *Xerox* machine was delivered and the old mimeograph machine was taken away.
2. Lee used the *Xerox* to make 500 copies of the new business manual.
3. Rod made a *Xerox* of his history paper because he likes to have a copy of all the papers he turns in.
4. "Is a *Xerox* acceptable, or do you want the original document?" the lawyer asked the judge.

and Verbalize...

_____

_____

_____

yacht: a boat for pleasure trips or for racing

Visualize...

1. Fred looked through the telescope at the millionaire's white *yacht* at anchor in the harbor.
2. The bank president sailed his *yacht* to Hawaii.
3. The two *yachts* with tremendously tall sails raced each other to win the America's Cup trophy.
4. Twenty *yachts* entered the race and sailed from Catalina Island to Los Angeles.

and Verbalize...

_____

_____

_____

X-Y-Z

yank: to jerk or pull suddenly

Visualize...

1. Lucy squealed when Lars *yanked* her pigtails.
2. Fred felt a big fish *yank* on his line just before the fishing rod flew from his hands.
3. "*Yank* those dirty sheets off the bed and put clean ones on," Flo's mother said.
4. "Don't *yank* the reins," the cowboy said. "My horse doesn't like that."

and Verbalize...

_____

_____

_____

yardstick: a ruler one yard (36 inches) long; any test or standard used in measuring or judging

Visualize...

1. A *yardstick* is as long as three one-foot rulers put together.
2. Susan had to measure a board two and a half feet long, so she used a *yardstick* instead of the one-foot ruler.
3. "How you play in practice is usually a good *yardstick* of how you'll play in a game," the coach said.
4. Beth's quick progress in math became a *yardstick* by which the other students were judged.

and Verbalize...

_____

_____

_____

yarn: a soft thick thread for knitting; a story

Visualize...

1. Agnes knitted the baby's sweater with beautiful Scottish *yarn* spun from lamb's wool.
2. Under its horsehide cover, a baseball has a cork-and-rubber center wrapped with *yarn*.
3. The old cowboy told the children *yarns* about the Old West.
4. When they were off duty, the sailors told each other *yarns* about the sea.

and Verbalize...

_____

_____

_____

yearn: to feel a longing or desire

Visualize...

1. The lovesick princess *yearned* for her prince who was always off fighting another dragon.
2. Rex's mother was from the coast of Maine, so she *yearned* for the sea when she lived in Iowa.
3. The retired jockey *yearned* to ride in a horse race again.
4. The homesick sailors *yearned* to return to their home port.

and Verbalize...

_____

_____

_____

yelp: to make a quick, sharp bark or cry

Visualize...

1. The black dog *yelped* when the alley cat scratched him on the nose.
2. The boys *yelped* with excitement when they saw the new pony in the stall.
3. Pam couldn't sleep when she heard the coyotes *yelping* to one another.
4. The dogs began to *yelp* and soon Greg heard the ambulance's siren.

and Verbalize...

_____

_____

_____

yen: a strong wish or desire; a Japanese unit of money

Visualize...

1. Beth had a sudden *yen* for ice cream and hurried downtown to the grocery store.
2. The old artist had a *yen* to see Paris again.
3. Everyone could see the prince and princess had a strong *yen* for one another.
4. At the airport in Tokyo, Ed exchanged his dollars for Japanese *yen.*

and Verbalize...

_____

_____

_____

X-Y-Z

yield: to produce; to give up

Visualize...

1. The cotton field *yielded* over 100 bales of cotton.
2. The new dining room *yielded* a tidy profit for the restaurant owner.
3. The white knight was brave and hardy and finally forced the black knight to *yield*.
4. The traffic accident occurred because the blue car failed to *yield* the right of way to the red car.

and Verbalize...

_____

_____

_____

yogurt: creamy food made from fermented milk

Visualize...

1. The frozen *yogurt* tasted just like ice cream but had less calories.
2. Unflavored *yogurt* tastes a little bit sour.
3. *Yogurt* is good with fresh fruit like strawberries, cherries, or blueberries.
4. "I'd like a cup of *yogurt* and a glass of orange juice for breakfast," Mrs. Smith told her daughter.

and Verbalize...

_____

_____

_____

yolk: the yellow part of an egg

Visualize...

1. The *yolk* of the boiled egg was hard and round and yellow.
2. Greg cracked the shell and carefully let the egg white run out, then put the *yolk* in a separate bowl.
3. One of the fried eggs looked perfect but the other one was runny and had a broken *yolk*.
4. The recipe called for egg whites, so Beth had to separate the whites from the *yolks*.

and Verbalize...

_____

_____

_____

youth: the time of being young; a young man

Visualize...

1. In his *youth* my dog could run up that mountain, but now he can't climb it at all.
2. The old man sometimes spoke of his *youth* with longing.
3. Five *youths* climbed the mulberry tree, picking and eating mulberries until their hands and faces were purple.
4. "I'm not a *youth* but a man," Rex protested when his mother told him he was too young to get married.

and Verbalize...

_____

_____

_____

yowl: to howl, to make a long, sad cry

Visualize...

1. The hound *yowled* and *yowled* at its master's door.
2. The injured cat hid under the house and *yowled* all night long.
3. The lion cub *yowled* like a kitten when it couldn't find its mother.
4. No one could sleep when the dogs began *yowling* at the moon.

and Verbalize...

_____

_____

_____

zany: clownish

Visualize...

1. The *zany* comedians had the audience roaring with laughter.
2. Lucille Ball was the *zany* actress who played the role of Lucy on "I Love Lucy."
3. Jerome expected a *zany* comedy, but the movie was a serious drama that brought tears to his eyes.
4. Soupy Sales' *zany* comedy routine featured lots of pie-throwing.

and Verbalize...

_____

_____

_____

X-Y-Z

zeal: eagerness, enthusiasm

Visualize...

1. The new traffic policeman was full of *zeal* and gave 100 tickets his first week on the job.
2. Tim lost his *zeal* for mountain climbing when his friend Tom fell and broke his leg.
3. The baseball player's *zeal* for the game carried him through the disappointing season.
4. Beth's *zeal* for learning led her to spend all her time at the library.

and Verbalize...

_____

_____

_____

zealous: eager, enthusiastic

Visualize...

1. The teacher made a *zealous* effort to teach every child to read.
2. Flo was a *zealous* student and almost always got all "A's."
3. The *zealous* leader urged his soldiers to sacrifice their lives for their country.
4. The judge was so *zealous* in putting criminals behind bars that he sometimes confused the innocent with the guilty.

and Verbalize...

_____

_____

_____

zenith: the point in the sky directly overhead; the highest point

Visualize...

1. At 12 noon the sun occupies the *zenith.*
2. At night the pole star occupies the *zenith.*
3. The famous actor reached the *zenith* of career when he played King Lear on the London stage.
4. "*Zenith*" is the highest point and "nadir" is the lowest point, so "*zenith*" and "nadir" are opposites.

and Verbalize...

_____

_____

_____

zest: sharp enjoyment; exciting quality or flavor

Visualize...

1. The thirsty football player drank the big glass of ice tea with *zest*.
2. "I have no *zest* for any more fighting," the wounded soldier said.
3. The lemon juice gave *zest* to the salad dressing.
4. The sudden arrival of the rock and roll band added *zest* to the party.

and Verbalize...

_____

_____

_____

zillion: a huge, indefinite number

Visualize...

1. Pam was upset because she had a *zillion* things to do and only three hours to do them in.
2. "I can give you a *zillion* reasons why you can't go to the movies," Mrs. Gray told her daughter.
3. There were a *zillion* grains of sand on the beach.
4. "Gosh, there must be a *zillion* stars in the sky," Frank said to Susan as their boat floated down the dark and quiet river.

and Verbalize...

_____

_____

_____

zodiac: a division of the sky into 12 sections or "signs" through which the sun moves on its yearly course—used in astrology

Visualize...

1. Tom was born on November 5, under Scorpio, the 8th sign of the *zodiac*.
2. July 21 to August 22 fall under the sign of Leo, the Lion, the fifth sign of the *zodiac*.
3. The astrologer asked me my birthday to find out what sign of the *zodiac* I was born under.
4. Some of the signs of the *zodiac* are represented by animals: the scorpion, lion, crab, bull, ram, fish, and goat.

and Verbalize...

_____

_____

_____

X-Y-Z

zone: area or region

Visualize...

1. The United States mainland is divided into four different time *zones*: Eastern, Central, Mountain, and Pacific.
2. Nevada, Arizona, and New Mexico have large *zones* of desert.
3. The Earth can be divided into four *zones* or hemispheres: northern, southern, eastern, and western.
4. "Can you give me a ride?" Tim asked. "My car was towed away when I parked it in a no parking *zone*."

and Verbalize...

_____

_____

_____

zoology: the study of animals

Visualize...

1. Greg wants to take a *zoology* class because he likes all kinds of animals.
2. The two main divisions of biology are *zoology* (the study of animals) and botany (the study of plants).
3. "If you want to work in a zoo," Mrs. Smith told her class, "you have to study *zoology*."
4. The artist drew a picture of an elephant for the new *zoology* textbook.

and Verbalize...

_____

_____

_____

Vocabulary Vignettes

with

Gunny and Ivan

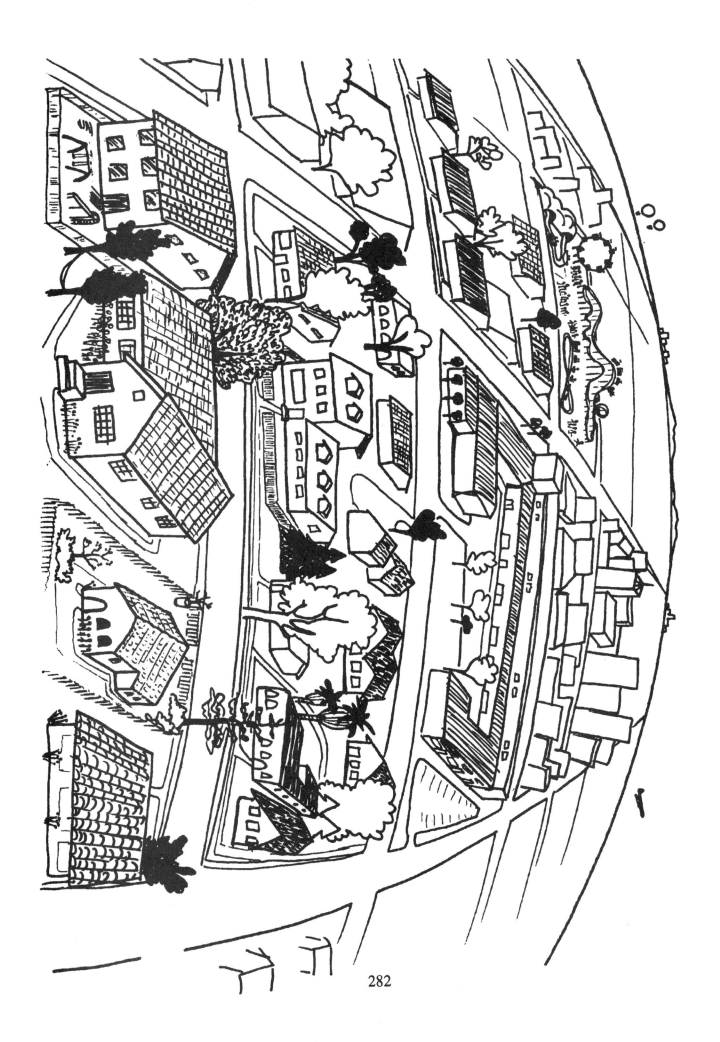

Gunny and Ivan

The Characters and the Background

The following description can be read to or read by the individual in order to set up the Gunny and Ivan imagery.

Gunny is over-middle-aged and sensitive about it, with a very large roundness in his middle section, commonly called a belly. He is round faced with no beard or mustache, has black eyebrows, little black eyes, and is balding on top with remnants of black hair around the sides. He is usually quite kind, and quite a character. He has little particular habits like fussing with his house plants and aquarium, sneaking food even though he lives alone, and snapping the suspenders over his belly. He talks aloud to himself at home and in his yard, and much to his embarrassment, is prone to fainting when alarmed.

Gunny is a retired military man with two grandsons. He enjoys it when they visit and enjoys it when they leave! He likes his life back to normal, habitual patterns. All in all, Gunny is quite a delight and considered a fatherly influence in his middle-class neighborhood.

Life for Gunny would be quiet and happy... except for Ivan.

Ivan is a cat. He is a very fat, very large tiger cat with a very mischievous personality. And, he seems to target Gunny for most of his mischief. He likes Gunny. Who else would pay so much attention to him? Gunny cares. Gunny reacts. Gunny has fish. Gunny is always home.

Ivan belongs to a 12 year old girl named Maya. Now, Maya is almost perfect. She has long brown hair, long brown eyelashes, large brown eyes, and is usually very pleasant, very witty, and very intelligent. She lives in the house next to Gunny. Not much separates the two homes—just a little picket fence—and she visits Gunny a lot. Since she is an only child and her mother works long hours, Ivan and Gunny are her closest friends.

Also in the neighborhood is Sam the Large Dog, Gertrude the unmarried older woman, and Puffy the little dog across the street. Ivan truly dislikes the dogs—especially Puffy. Gunny truly dislikes Gertrude—thin, narrow-faced Gertrude who considers him the neighborhood catch. But he is nice even to her...except that he often hides when he sees her coming to his door.

Ivan, on the other hand, hides from no one. He is king of the neighborhood...or thinks he is. Just watch.

The following pages are a sequential story of Gunny and Ivan, and their neighborhood. The Vanilla Vocabulary Dictionary words were purposely not italicized, nor was every word used. The illustrations, including the neighborhood map, were created to assist imagery rather than impede it.

We had fun with the vocabulary words and occasionally created a nonsense word just for imagery and a fragmented sentence just for effect. It's important that vocabulary be fun! Individuals need to lose their fear of words and enjoy them!

It wasn't always easy to use the vocabulary words in a story, but we hope we ended up with characters and a story to laugh with. (At least we've laughed!)

A

The Aerial Faint

It was finally fall and Gunny just had to go on an adventure. Ivan's antics had driven Gunny crazy all summer and then last week he (Ivan not Gunny) had gotten lost in the aquarium at the zoo and attacked the side of a fish tank, scaring the fish. Gunny's favorite fish! And, just a few days before that, Ivan had actually lunged into Gunny's aquarium. Plunged into it! Water went everywhere, fish were sent airborne, only to land on the floor gasping for air. Poor Gunny. He wasn't very agile, but somehow he managed to scramble like an acrobat and accumulate all the fish in his hands like a juggler. He assembled all his little fish and threw them back in the tank before Ivan could swallow even one.

The aquarium incident was the latest in a long line of terribly annoying stunts stretching as far back as Gunny could remember. No, not that far back, but Ivan had been bad, really bad, from the moment Maya brought him home as a kitten. Right now nothing was more important to Gunny than getting away from that cat! He had accumulated so much stress over the antics of Ivan that his head ached frequently, his plants were suffering, and sometimes he even forgot to feed his precious fish—not to mention that he had felt seriously faint when he heard Ivan sloshing in his fish tank. How embarrassing.

And then there was Gertrude. She'd called him every day this week. Every day.

All in all, Gunny was frazzled, "I *have* to arrange an adventure and get away for awhile. I'm under too much stress. Hmmm. It might even be an aerial adventure where I become airborne in a hot air balloon, or...wait, what an idea! What if I am able to accomplish two things at once?   Get rid of Ivan and have an adventure! Hmmm.

"What if I get Maya to bring Ivan on the adventure? She has the ability to get Ivan to do anything—even fly."   He knew he was accurate.   Ivan worshipped Maya and would surely do anything for her. "Here's the plan," thought Gunny.

"I'll get together an abundant amount of cat food and cookies, call Ivan and Maya over, and then start showing Maya pictures of flying in a hot air balloon.   I'll tell her about how animals really love to fly, especially cats...hmmm. How will I make her believe that?

"I know. I'll appeal to her intellect. I'll tell her that research from Sweden has proven that animals, especially cats, love to fly as high as possible as long as their master is with them. And, I'll make it appealing for Ivan by showing him lots of fish kept inside the hot air balloon basket...just for cats."

Snap went the suspender. SUH-NAP!

"What a great idea! I'll take advantage of Ivan's enormous appetite to achieve my goal! Serves him right! Now let's see. I'll have to be careful in arranging all this. I must somehow contrive an artificial picture of his ancestors—cats—flying in a hot air balloon. I'll take care of that this afternoon. Just think, when we get aloft at a low altitude, I'll be able to throw that active, appetite-laden, ache-in-my-head, over the edge. He'll land on his feet like always, but in another neighborhood, away from here. It's an ambitious plan, but it just might work."

Now, so you know, Gunny is really quite a nice fellow and didn't usually have any mean thoughts, except perhaps for Ivan. Ivan continually pestered Gunny. No one was sure, but he seemed to dislike Ivan so much that perhaps he actually *liked* him. Anyhow, Gunny's plan continued to take form.

Gunny acquired the cookies, cat food, balloon pictures (scissors, paste, and a couple of old magazines took care of that) and got Maya and Ivan over for a visit. While Ivan swallowed awesome bites of cat food, Maya looked over the hot air balloon pictures and began to get excited about the anticipated adventure. Gunny told her about the Swedish research, and suggested she let Ivan have access to the adventure of his life. He was very convincing, in a desperate sort of way. Finally Maya showed Ivan the picture with all the cats eating an enormous amount of fish. Ivan looked at the picture, turned his head, looked at Gunny casually, and then twitched his tail just a little. Sometimes he did seem very wise.

Soon after, Maya and Ivan headed for home anticipating the aerial adventure on Saturday morning. Meanwhile, Gunny was contemplating no more cats dropping on his back without warning, no more need to guard his aquarium...no more food stolen from the kitchen counter. Excited, he made all the preparations for the trip...and life after Ivan. Oh happy day!

However, when Saturday came, so did a problem. Maya was ready, Ivan appeared ready, but Gunny had a terribly upset stomach and felt woozie in the head. He thought it must be that third helping he had last night at dinner. By the time they all piled in his car and headed for the airfield, he was extremely sick. His head and upper lip were sweating, his stomach was churning, and he felt dizzy. The closer they got to the airfield, the more anxious he got. And by the time they were given access to the steps into the balloon, an anxiety attack was becoming unavoidable.

The momentum of the adventure was in full steam. Nothing could stop it now. So, they all stepped into the basket. Maya was happy and gay, Ivan appeared asleep in her arms, but Gunny's legs were so weak he could hardly climb over the edge of the basket. Finally he managed to roll clumsily in. He tottered weakly to the other side and leaned shakily against the wicker.

At last they were all in. The attendant to the balloon ride started the burner, hot air poured into the huge balloon above them, and after a strange pause, during which the burner roared dangerously but nothing else seemed to happen, they began to ascend. Maya was thrilled, Ivan still appeared asleep—though his eyes were open just a slit, with a hint of a smile—and Gunny was *paralyzed*. He couldn't look up or down! He just stared straight ahead, unable to look at the view at all. He was pale and wet from his head to his toes!

Up, up they floated. Gunny was catatonic. He just stood, holding tight to the rail and Maya's arm. She wasn't aware of him clutching her, she was too amazed at all she could see and how tiny it all was. Up they went. Everyone seemed to be having a good time and no one seemed to notice Gunny, except Ivan. Ivan opened his eyes a tiny bit wider to look at Gunny, and cat-smiled. Then he yawned and stretched, and jumped to the edge of the basket. He walked around the rim, balancing with his tail. His leap had rocked the balloon a little. Gunny whimpered. Ivan cat-smiled.

Finally, after what seemed like hours and hours, the silent attendant pulled a handle and down they started. Gunny stood like a popsicle in the sun, still frozen, but dripping messily on everything. He just stared straight ahead, all his plans gone. He was just holding on. Why had he forgotten how he hated to fly—to be airborne?

Ivan knew how Gunny was suffering and he struck on an idea, "Let's liven up this aviation adventure for poor old Gunny!" With that, he leapt to Gunny's back!

"YEOW!" screeched Gunny. He jumped so high and so quickly that he nearly tipped over the whole balloon basket. Maya jerked Gunny back just in time to help him avoid plunging over the edge. When the balloon finally stopped rocking back and forth, she looked around for him.

There was Gunny spread out flat (or what could be called flat for Gunny given his dimensions) on the bottom of the basket—in a dead faint.

Looking down at him, Maya said, "Poor Gunny. I wonder what made him screech like that? I guess he just doesn't like aerial adventures. But we sure enjoyed it, didn't we Ivan? Oh Ivan, how sweet of you to curl up on Gunny's tummy. We'll be down in a few minutes…then you and I can help get Gunny home. I'm sure he'll want to visit with us."

In the bottom of the basket, Gunny groaned.

Little Blimp™ Sausages and Brilliant Plans

Yet another day came and went in the neighborhood and Gunny stewed. His aerial plan had failed. There would be no burial (symbolic of course) of Ivan, no life of contentment.

Gunny sighed, "And to make matters worse, I fainted..."

As you may have guessed by now, Gunny couldn't have gone through with his plan to hurt Ivan, even if he hadn't had that terrible attack of anxiety. He probably wouldn't hurt anyone, even Ivan. However, he was still bound and determined to conjure up brilliant plans to bury Ivan.

"I have to get a serious plan *now*. Think how it would benefit the neighborhood. Ivan the Terrible—GONE. But, when will I break through and make one work? Last year I tried a barricade between my yard and Maya's yard. I stacked bricks, then wood on top of that, then a lot of wire. What happened? Ivan jumped right over the top. And the year before that I tried a different kind of barrier between our yards—the watering hole— and he bounded over that too. I've tried blotting him out of my mind by not paying any attention to him, only to have him leap on my back from a tree, or on my head from my grandfather's bust on the mantle! I've tried everything...everything!"

With that mournful, pitiful broadcast of his dismay, Gunny put on his bifocals and headed for the kitchen and a new recipe. He'd think about all this tomorrow. Tomorrow. He always had tomorrow. As he turned the corner into the kitchen he said, "I think I am on the brink of the perfect plan...hmmm. I'll just eat a few Little Blimp™ sausages while I think it through..."

The Carnival Caper

Gunny woke the next day still calculating because of yet another incident with Ivan. Unbelievably, just yesterday after Gunny had finished his package of Little Blimp™ sausages, Ivan had coaxed another cat into his house. The two of them concealed themselves behind the couch and then tried to conquer the aquarium again. If they weren't so clumsy they may have been capable of succeeding. But instead, in their greed and competition to get the most fish, they clumsily jostled and generally interfered with one another in such a fashion that they couldn't take even one fish captive.

Gunny just happened in on the final stages of the above scene. To think, that full from his sausage snack, he had considered the possibility that Ivan was tolerable. He'd almost convinced himself of it, so he was contemplating going to a concert in the park to celebrate. Then he came upon the two cats and saw his precious fish compressed to the sides of the tank in fear. Gunny's eyes got very big and then very small. The two cats hopped easily to an open window and disappeared outside.

Angry, he went to bed and resumed his concentration on yet a better plan. The challenge was upon him. He would have to create another plot. It worried him some that in the last few days he'd been making a career out of this creative planning. He thought about it the first thing in the morning and the last thing at night.

(But what about this possibility? Maybe Gunny didn't really have so much contempt for Ivan. Maybe Ivan gave Gunny purpose in life. Maybe Ivan was really a companion to Gunny, in a funny sort of way. After all, Gunny was retired and didn't appear to have any hobbies other than his fish and his food. Maybe he even liked Ivan...and vice-versa?)

Gunny thought and thought. What could he do? Where could he go to get rid of Ivan. Who could help him? Who had contempt for Ivan? Who would cooperate with him? Who was courageous enough to take on Ivan? Better yet, who was cunning enough to help him get rid of Ivan? Cunning. Cunning. Who did he know that was cunning?

Gunny's mind searched through his current friends and neighbors. Who was a candidate for this job? It had to be someone with the capacity to think creatively. That left out Gertrude! It had to be a cunning character who could comprehend the seriousness of this task! That left out Maya.

Gunny paced and snapped, paced and snapped. Thought and thought. Not one person came to his mind, until he thought about animals rather than people. It was then that Sam the Large Dog came catapulting into mind, into the picture, the big picture. Gunny did a little dance.

Sam! That was it. Sam the Large Dog could help him. Sam wasn't exactly cunning but he knew the seriousness of the task. Sam had clashed many times with Ivan and not come out the champion of the fight. Almost always Ivan was in command of the situation. And, although Sam proceeded in a climate of caution in all encounters with Ivan, things usually escalated into a terribly stormy climax. Ivan hissing and scratching, Sam barking and retreating. Naturally this was in sharp contrast to how Sam wanted these encounters to end. A completely crazed cat was quite a challenge even for a dog as large and cunning as Sam. But, it was really Ivan who was cunning. A fierce competitor who loved to compete, he intended to conquer! He intended to win!

Back to Gunny's plan. Gunny spotted Sam lying on his front step. Good old Sam! He might be the biggest dog Gunny had ever seen. Part Saint Bernard, he was white with brown spots, very large, with a huge head and short hair. When he was serious his tail went up in an arc. When he was happy his tail made a circular movement, kind of like a hairy jump rope. Sometimes he was comical and did funny antics like lying on his great back with all four legs straight in the air, *pretending* to be asleep. Sometimes he collapsed heavily on Gunny's front porch with a deep sigh and watched wearily for Ivan or Puffy. Both were a pain to him.

Gunny whistled for Sam. Raising his head, ears up, Sam looked to see who was calling him. Recognizing Gunny, he got up, stretched, taking his time, and finally trotted across the street to Gunny's. And Gunny, not taking his time, began talking his plan through out loud.

Sam heard his name mixed in with a lot of mush he couldn't understand.

He did think he heard Ivan's name several times. Trying to look intelligent, he stared at Gunny, ears up, tail wagging.

Gunny was saying, "Sam you *have* to help me get rid of Ivan. Here's the plan. There's a carnival in town, just a few blocks away. If we can get Maya to take Ivan over there, we might be able to lose him in one of the chambers on the Tunnel of Love ride. When we go into that big dark cavern, we could toss him out. You could jump out and chase him until he is completely lost."

Sam had no idea what Gunny was conjuring up, but he *thought* that it had something to do with Ivan. So he waited. Gunny went over to Maya's house and casually convinced her to go to the carnival with him, bringing along Ivan, of course.

As they all headed down the street, Ivan, safe in Maya's arms, appeared to be smiling. And he *was* smiling actually, for unlike Sam, *Ivan understood English.* And, it is rumored, several other languages. He practiced appearing uninterested, but really he connected to everything human. Everything. Plus, he had been hiding in his bush, listening to Gunny's plan. So he went along with it, and they arrived at the carnival later that afternoon. Maya talked gaily as they proceeded through the crowd. Sam followed along and Gunny spotted the Tunnel of Love ride far on the other side of the carnival.

They walked past the rocket ride with the space capsule. They walked past the caravan ride with the camels loaded with cargo, going around and around in a circle. They walked past the waterfall, cascading down the mountain made of plastic rocks. They walked past the kiddie train with the silent conductor in his striped overalls and hat. It was the "silent attendant" from the hot air balloon ride! Gunny was certain of it. But it couldn't be.

They walked past the "Guess Your Age and Weight" ceremony with a poor embarrassed contestant being made fun of in front of her friends. "That could be me," Gunny muttered. Horrified, he scooted by just as quickly as possible.

He forgot about Ivan. When they finally arrived at the Tunnel of Love, to Gunny's shock, Ivan was gone!

The Backyard Drama

When Gunny turned around, scanning for Ivan, he couldn't believe it. While he'd been "enjoying" the sights of the carnival, Ivan had disappeared!

"Just my luck, another opportunity lost." After much searching and much disgust, he and his headache decided not to worry anymore. Gunny treated Maya to a few rides, but no kiddie-train, no way. And they started for home.

Arriving back in the neighborhood, Gunny headed for his house, Maya searched for Ivan, and Sam slumped on his front porch, pouting.

Meanwhile, Gunny unlocked his door, went in, checked his fish, and padded over to the couch. He was tired! He lay on the couch, feeling just a little dizzy from all the excitement but not feeling faint—thank heavens. Then his thoughts returned to Ivan. He began to distrust his ability to get rid of that cat. "He's gone for now. But he'll be back. We both know it. He's playing with my mind."

"Maybe I'll just have to learn to defend myself against Ivan. He is cunning. Even though I've been determined and dedicated to getting rid of him, perhaps I'm going to have to just forget it for awhile. I don't seem to be able to win."

Taking a deep breath, Gunny settled back for a rest. "Oh well," he thought. "Maybe I'll draft up a plan tomorrow when I'm not as tired as I am today. I can't dwell on this Ivan problem daily. He makes me display such anger that sometimes people look at me like I'm the problem, not him! I guess

I'll just avoid him. Hmmm, I think I'll take a little nap and devote the entire afternoon to resting and digesting those four hamburgers. I can always start my diet tomorrow."

As Gunny drifted off to sleep and descended down to the depths of unconsciousness, he wasn't aware of the drama that was about to occur in his backyard.

It was Ivan, of course. He had not vanished. He had seen cages of big cats at the carnival, and gone for a closer look. The tiger was his favorite. It's claws were huge and sharp; its fangs looked deadly. "Like mine," he thought. "People and animals run screaming into the night when they see us. We are cats, he and I, and we attack at will." He stalked down the middle of the street, with fierce yellow eyes and a twitching tail. By now he was nearing his own house and yard, with high hopes of attacking one of the neighbors, human or animal. But, fortunately for them, no one was outside. The street, sidewalks, and yards were deserted.

Scrambling up a big tree, he settled high on a branch. His eyes surveyed his neighborhood looking for prey. "That trip to the carnival was boring. I'm determined to have some fun this afternoon. I am a tiger, hunting. I'll leave Gunny alone. Today I'm not after humans—I'm after dogs. What do I care if Gunny's in there resting. He needs his sleep, and besides, Sam deserves a lesson."

Ivan felt Sam had been bothering him lately, in fact more than ever. "Sam has been barking too much, too often, and he even came in my yard the other day, sort of prancing like he could scare me if he wanted. Anyhow, I'm bored and can use a little excitement."

Dazzled by the depths of his cunning mind, Ivan devised a plan. He knew Sam would probably come sniffing around, looking for him this afternoon...or looking for food to devour to fuel that big body. Ivan was sure that somehow Sam would find his way to Ivan's backyard. He was dependable, you know. You could always count on Sam. Just a whiff of food would bring him in an instant.

Down from the tree he came, claws digging into the bark. He retrieved the chicken bone he'd hidden in his sticker bush and cunningly placed it in the perfect spot in his backyard. And he waited. Very patiently. He waited and waited. Perfectly hidden.

Sure enough, here came Sam. Strutting diagonally across the backyard, he approached with his tail turned up in that half circle that so irritated Ivan. His nose twitched along the ground. Now, as you might have guessed, Ivan was strategically hidden near the bone, right behind some debris—a pile of junk.

Sam came closer to the chicken bone—and Ivan—still with his nose to the ground. Suddenly sensing some unseen danger, he raised his head and looked around. But the yard looked desolate. There was no one in sight. He stood till for a moment with his front foot raised. He finally relaxed, put his head down and proceeded to track that smell.

And Ivan waited. Very patiently. He waited for just the right moment to leap on Sam.

Gunny slept.

Sam came closer. Ivan crouched, tail slightly twitching, eyes intently focused. Using immense discipline, he timed his attack perfectly. When Sam was just about to the bone, Ivan's hind legs began a rhythmic back and forth motion. Steady. Lock and load, baby. Missile primed and ready for launch. Ready. So ready. KA-POW!!

But, just as Ivan released his energy and hurled himself into midair, another neighborhood player came onto the scene. It was Puffy, the disgusting little dog from across the street. He'd seen Sam nosing around, and with arrogant determination had decided to try an attack of his own. Being a little white dog with a very large ego, and not many brains, he considered himself a dynamo of unmatched ability. So, he started a wild yipping and landed in the middle of the Ivan-Attack!

Everyone was startled! Ivan thought he was making a surprise attack on Sam. Sam thought he was sneakily getting a morsel of food from Ivan's yard, and Puffy thought he was courageously attacking that very large spotted dog. Fur was flying everywhere! For a second, the three were a grey, brown and white blur, then they sprung apart.

Ivan stood for a moment, hissed until out of breath, and then darted off across the yard. Sam, dumfounded by the confusion, stood his ground in a distinguished manner for a moment, then pretended to chase Ivan. And Puffy, considering himself the winner, departed cockily for home.

Gunny slept, delighted by a dream that his grandchildren came to visit...and only stayed a few hours.

No Excuses!

When Gunny awoke from his nap, the backyard drama was over and the neighborhood seemed quiet and peaceful. He was not aware of Ivan's elaborate plan to get even with Sam. Nor was he aware that Ivan had come up empty-handed and was therefore pouting in his yard.

Gunny headed for the kitchen. As usual, he had an enormous hunger, which was evident by the size of his very round belly! Food was very important to him. In fact, even *thinking* about food was an integral part of his existence. What did he care if he expanded his size? Yes, his belly extended over the top of his pants, but who cared?

Gunny efficiently created an elaborate plate of food and emerged from the kitchen for the living room and the TV. He grabbed his precious remote control, clicked it on, sat down on the couch and began eating, and waited to be entertained by the television. His enthusiasm for it soon dwindled, however, when all he could find were news shows discussing the crisis in the economy, the crisis in education, the crisis in the environment, the inequality of this or that, the epidemic at the equator, etc.

"It is always something negative," mused Gunny. "Can't they ever report anything positive? It is always the evil of this or that, the erosion of the environment, the eruption of a volcano, the terrible state of the economy in this era, the extinction of some wonderful species, the evaporation of the ozone layer, or something. I'm exhausted by the negatives. Can't we ever hear about positive events? Like an expedition in Alaska by a courageous explorer or. . ."

With that the phone rang. Gunny got up, went to the desk, and tentatively picked up the phone. He didn't really want to be bothered, unless it was his son or daughter. He wanted to finish his food.

"Hello?" he said cautiously. Instantly, his worst fears were realized. It was Gertrude.

"Gunny," she screeched into the phone. "Gunny are you home?"

With a deep sign, Gunny breathed, "Yes, Gertrude, I'm home."

"Oh, that's good," she screeched, completely unaware of his mood, "I'm coming over for a visit."

Gunny felt a faint feeling of nausea wash over him. Covering the phone with his hand, he started pacing and talking aloud to himself. "Oh no. A perfect afternoon ruined. Can I endure this? Gertrude's shrill eerie voice has such an awful effect on me. How can I endure another of her endless visits? Oh please, please, please...let something interfere with this."

Just as Gunny was pausing and pacing, there was a knock at the door.

"Uh...Just a minute, Gertrude, there's someone at the door."

Excited, Gunny hurriedly padded over to his front door, peered out and saw his son, Chuck, and his two grandsons. "This is one of those times I really am glad to see the boys," sighed Gunny. He whipped open the door and encircled them all with a giant hug.

The perfect excuse to enable him to get out of Gertrude's visit. (He knew it was essential that he have a real excuse, since she watched his house nearly all day from her living room window.) This family visit was direct evidence that he couldn't visit with her. He had established the perfect excuse!

Exhilarated, with the snap of a suspender, Gunny headed back to the phone.

"Gertrude, I'm *really* sorry, but my family just arrived." Smiling contentedly, he waited for her reply.

"Oh, that's OK Gunny, I don't mind if your family visits with us too," she shrilled.

Gunny fell back on the couch, exhausted again. It would take some encouragement to get him up.

Here's Gertrude...and "the boys!"

Poor Gunny. He began to feel a serious attack of fatigue—both Gertrude and the boys were going to be *in his house*. But, there was no way to flee the scene. He ran over to the window and sure enough Gertrude was already on her way over. He turned back for the couch and spotted the boys looking at the aquarium. Chuck was heading for the kitchen—like father, like son.

Gertrude was over middle age, just like Gunny, but she hadn't faired as well as he. Her figure was stick-like with bony legs, bony arms, bony hands, bony neck, and even a fairly bony head. She had very thin gray hair, that she futilely tried to keep back in a tight bun at the back of her neck. Her face was long, bony of course, and thin, with little eyes, no eyebrows, and thin lips pinched over discolored teeth. In fact, she was so thin and bony that she looked fragile enough to blow away in a strong wind. But it wasn't her looks that factored into Gunny's dislike. It was her personality.

Gertrude was a nosy pest. She watched everybody in the neighborhood, especially Gunny. She had a thing for him. She often appeared to froth at the mouth at just the mention of his name—white, round dots at the corner of her mouth, causing Gunny to feel stomach-sick and almost faint. Her voice was very loud and shrill, like a bandsaw cutting tin. And, she never stopped talking and never paid attention to what anyone else thought or said. She drove Gunny crazy!

Now that you can picture Gertrude, you'll understand what happened that day at the hands of Gunny's grandson's—Rodney and Kirk. Rodney, eight years old, had curly blond hair, a wiry active body, and a very active mind. Kirk, six, had straight brown hair, a plump little body, and an equally creative mind. Always ready to serve his brother, Kirk assisted in many *inventive* episodes.

It took "the boys" only a few moments to liven up the afternoon and run interference on Gertrude. She came over that afternoon all right, but she didn't stay long! As soon as she knocked on the door, fertile little imaginations went to work. Able to think of many ways to embarrass and irritate adults, the boys' eyes began to flicker with mischief.

"Boys," said Gunny, "This is Gertrude. She lives across the street."

"Oh, Gunny!" she screeched, heading in their direction with a hug on her face. "What adorable little boys. I've been wanting to meet them for a long time!"

"OH DEAR," thought Gunny, "there's something very fundamental she does not understand about these children. They *hate* two particular words: little and adorable. This could be enough to set them off, in which case they might be truly fearsome today."

Sure enough, as Gertrude got closer to them, it started. Rodney lunged at her, grabbed her arm and said, "What are those bumps on your hand?" Then Kirk lunged, until they both encircled her.

"Why do you have such big teeth? Why are you so skinny?" asked Kirk. The questions poured out of them. At first poor Gertrude tried to answer, and Gunny made a few futile attempts to bring them under control, but they continued to furnish themselves with fun at her expense.

Feeling fatigued, Gertrude mistakenly sat down on the couch. The boys considered this an invitation! Before anyone could stop them, Rodney jumped in her lap, feet first. Kirk flipped up her dress. Rodney, fascinated by her bun, tried to pull it. And the torture continued.

In amazed fascination, Gunny just stood and watched in one of his paralyzed states. He knew he should do something, but his eyes, feet, and mouth were not functioning. He was dumbstruck. He was fundamentally opposed to the boys harassing Gertrude, but he was powerless. (Something he'd been noticing about himself more and more lately.)

Finally Gertrude began to screech and wail just enough to make Gunny come to. Just as he was about to act, Chuck came in from the kitchen and took control of the situation. Gunny watched as Chuck grabbed the boys by their flexible little necks and hauled them past the aquarium, past the furnace. Quickly fading from the living room, out the back steps they marched on tippy-toe, ready to receive very fervent advice from their father. Each were held between a forefinger and a thumb, just below the ears.

Gunny turned back when he heard another screech. Gertrude had gotten herself up and was headed for the door, sputtering, when she stumbled on Rodney's skateboard. Gathering herself just before she hit the floor, she screeched again, grabbing for the door knob. Then she did the splits.

Gunny bit his hand real hard but a little sound still came out. "UK. UK. UK." Gertrude looked just like Olive Oil!

Gunny knew he should try to help her or stop her, but he just couldn't move. Out the door she went, huffing and puffing down the street. He watched her stride off and then turned back toward the kitchen. Slowly his mood began to change as he thought of food.

Snapping suspenders, suh-NAP, suh-NAP, he mumbled happily to himself. "Today I'll use my kitchen facility to prepare one of my fabulous, famous feasts. I'll figure out what to do about Gertrude, tomorrow. There's always tomorrow."

G

"He CAN Move!"

The feast was over. And Gunny was quite full.

"Oh, why did I eat so much? You'd think I could gauge how much I'm taking in and quit!" moaned Gunny, rubbing his gigantic tummy. "I'm so very full! I'll never gorge myself like that again! I think my swaller-gut has closed."

Now, no one has ever seemed to know what a swaller-gut is, but Gunny mentioned it often. He appeared to believe it was a flap in his throat.

Gunny was a very good grandparent. He tried to be attentive, pleasant, and kind...and glad to see the boys. Well, he generally was glad to see them, but after a few hours, he was also glad to see them leave. It wasn't that he didn't love them, it was just that he fatigued—much to his dismay. They just wore him out. Perhaps it was a generation gap. His generation usually liked to sit and listen to music or watch birds gracefully flying around in the park. The boys were a different generation. They were young and energetic. Sitting and watching graceful birds was out of the question.

Thinking of the boys, Gunny realized he hadn't heard them in awhile. "Where are they?" he pondered. "Things seem awfully quiet. Oh well, they're probably sitting and looking at books in the bedroom, or doing a puzzle. They really are good boys, they're just...ah...inventive."

Still rubbing his tummy, and seriously considering a nap, he shuffled from the kitchen to the living room. The couch looked so inviting. Just as he was positioning himself to gradually lower his body onto it's beckoning softness, he looked over at his aquarium...and gasped! Then shrieked!

There were the boys—and Ivan! All of them! At his aquarium! Rodney and Kirk had their little gritty hands in the water, Ivan was perched on the edge waiting to gain access, and the fish were stricken with fear. Their poor little gills were gyrating in and out while they frantically swam around and around trying to avoid the grimy hands. Oh those hands! Where hadn't they been? Sometimes they were absolutely *layered* with various filths.

Now, Ivan didn't actually want to be with the boys, and usually felt sorry for Gunny when he saw them burst out of the car as if from another galaxy. Besides, their growth terrified him. They were bad enough when they were toddlers, but now they were desperately dangerous. Usually just a glimpse of them in the yard had him heading for the nearest tree. But today was different. He'd heard them plotting about the fish tank and he just had to get in on the action! So there he was, perched on the edge, hoping for a chance.

Poor Gunny. Shrieking again, he struggled to get his very full body from the couch. Gasping and groaning, with the glands in his neck pulsating in and out—sort of like the gills on his precious guppies—he got up. With a wail, he headed for the aquarium. All his body in gear, he loomed larger than life at the three guilty perpetrators. With a burst of energy like a gust of wind, he sprang at the trio.

Shocked that old Gunny could move so fast, Rodney screamed, "Run Kirk! He CAN move!"

Gunny intended to get them. His face was purple and a little glossy with perspiration, and he looked MAD.

When he reached the aquarium, all three of them were scrambling just out of reach and heading out of the house. The boys' legs were moving like windmills in a storm, heads bent forward. Tail arched and ears flattened, Ivan was running for his life.

Gunny stopped and stood over his fish tank, wheezing for air. He carefully set to checking *every* fish. Meanwhile, Ivan flew into a tree and the boys flew to their father's side. They began asking him polite questions about the book he was reading. He wondered why they were out of breath and why they kept looking wildly back at the house. He noticed they had a mischievous glimmer in their eyes, but then they usually did.

The afternoon ended with the boys heading back home for their gymnastics class and Gunny heading for the kitchen. "Why on earth would anyone want *those two* to know more about gymnastics," he said to himself. He thought it was time to graze a little.

Padding happily into the kitchen, he talked to his fish as he went by, "I can't be too fat and too old, if I can move like that. I earned some food."

The Halloween Revenge Begins

It was a new day, and perhaps even a new era for Gunny. He couldn't stop thinking about how quickly he'd moved and how much he'd actually scared Ivan and the boys. Talking to himself as usual, he said, "I guess I wasn't a very good host! Hah! They had a hemorrhage! Ol' Lightning, that's me!"

He loved it. It had been a heroic, historic event...and, just the boost he needed. Gunny got up at the crack of dawn. "Ah. I'm a hardy lad. I'm up so early because I'm a light eater. Yeah. When it gets light I start eating. Har. Har. Har."

After another hearty meal of fruit and cereal, pancakes and potatoes, eggs and bacon, toast and jelly (and jam), he waddled outside to his hammock. "I shan't hibernate in the house all day," Gunny said as he rubbed his tummy and snapped a suspender. "Hmmm, I am a little husky this morning, that was a hoard of food. Oh well, I won't eat the rest of the day."

It was such a lovely morning in his backyard. He loved his homestead, even with Gertrude and Ivan in the neighborhood. The leaves were turning a bright orange and as the habitat got ready for winter, the air was brisk but the sun was warm. It was harvest time. Little families were heading for the pumpkin patch to pick out their perfect round, red-orange pumpkin. Halloween was tonight.

Getting horizontal was an effort, but Gunny finally settled into the hammock and pulled his hood over his balding head. Letting the sun warm his body, he said, "What a haven this backyard is to me. I feel safe here."

As you might suspect, all would not stay well for long. Ivan was irritated about yesterday's event at Gunny's aquarium. He was very irritated. Up to now he had considered Gunny just fun.

He'd been watching through the hedge as Gunny heaved his body into the hammock. He thought, "I can't let yesterday go unavenged. Hmmm. It's the time of year for haunting. Haunting. Hmmm."

While Gunny slept, Ivan conjured up an incredible Cat-Plan. After considering all avenues of revenge, he settled on a plan that Gunny would remember for a long, long time. Poor Gunny. He was going to need a sense of humor when this was over, for Ivan's plan would put him through some terrifying hoops. And loops and genuine barrel rolls.

I, J, and K.

The Imagination and the Trickster

Gunny rested in the sun, ate a little lunch (he'd already forgotten his morning vow of abstinence), went for a walk in the autumn afternoon, crunched some leaves under his feet, and checked out the Halloween decorations in the neighborhood.

Gunny had never been fond of Halloween. Things happened on Halloween.

His overly active imagination had plagued him all his life. When he was a little brown haired boy, he had been afraid of the dark. Throughout his childhood he had an image of a monster invading his bedroom. In fact, many times he thought he saw it. It was a *green light* inhabiting the corner of his room, perhaps even his closet. He called it the Green Ghost and had tried to tell his mother, but she just laughed at him. No amount of information he gave her concerning the antics of that monster in the interior of his room impressed her. So, for years he had slept with his large panda bear on top of him, protecting him from injury, insulating him from the scary dark. Actually it was quite a pitiful sight, but it helped a frightened, highly imaginative young boy get through years of terrifying nights.

When Gunny got older, he still sometimes dreamed of the Green Ghost and he still sometimes awoke in a panic. He knew it must have been an illusion, such as some weird play of light across his room, but his first instinct when he awoke was to check that corner and sometimes even check his closet. Now, as he prepared for yet another Halloween, he once again tried to convince himself that the Green Ghost had been in his imagination.

Muttering to himself, he said, "Now Gunny, you're an intelligent adult and you can't let this childhood fear influence you indefinitely. You must put this issue behind you."

Heading from the kitchen to the living room, he tried to put his afraid-of-the-dark fears aside and prepare for the Trick-or-Treaters. When the day ended, he had the candy set up, the porch light on, and his fears put to rest. Now, there was *one* thing he liked about Halloween. The candy, of course. He loved to go to the store and have an excuse to buy hordes of chocolate candy and brightly colored jelly beans. He always hoped the Trick-or-Treaters would ignore his house and then he'd have more treats left over.

Treats or no, the truth was that Halloween scared Gunny. So he always left his porch light on—and all the lights in the interior of his house too—until late into the night. Consequently, the ghosts, goblins, witches, pumpkin heads, pirates, fairies, and skeletons thought Gunny's lights were an indication of more treats, and they kept coming and coming. Tonight was no different. Waves of Trick-or-Treaters rang the bell. "TRICK-OR-TREAT," they squealed, and took his candy. Scary sight after scary sight appeared at his door. For instance, there was the 6 foot kangaroo, hopping up his steps, with boxing gloves, threatening to punch Gunny when he opened the door. There was the little squealing jockey, about 7 years old, screaming and pretending to be riding a wild race horse, threatening to whip Gunny when he opened the door. There was the jester, all dressed up in brightly colored tights, a black and white checkered top, and a cap with loud, ringing bells on the end, threatening to flip into Gunny as he grabbed the candy. Most fearful of all was the 200 pound Queen, jewelry piled high on her head, down her chest, on her wrists, who demanded Gunny kneel and kiss her hand (sticky knuckles and all) before filling her bag!

As it got later and later, Gunny's candy supply decreased and his fear increased. His fear had nothing to do with giving away all his candy. It had everything to do with going to bed on Halloween night. As usual it was very dark, with clouds covering the moon, and scary things about.

And just as Gunny feared, when the last of the treaters went into their homes for the night to gorge on their candy, *the real trickster of the neighborhood came to life.*

Ivan, isolated behind the juniper hedge, had patiently watched all the little monsters come and go, up and down the street, up and down the porch steps, in their incredibly ugly little costumes. How they disgusted him. The inventor of trickery, Ivan intensely detested the little monsters. Ingenious at tricks, knowledgeable in all aspects of terror, he despised such plainly inferior competition.

Finally, as it got quieter and quieter, Ivan inched out from his hedge. It was time to put his inspiration into action.

Gunny sat on his couch wondering if that had been the last of them. He turned the TV off and waited for awhile, listening to the wind begin to increase outside. Oh no. Here came that terrible shudder, illustrating his fears, so readily fueled by his imagination.

Outside, in the dark of the night, Ivan's intelligence was at work. Acting like an international spy, he crept silently over to investigate the landscape surrounding Gunny's. He was the instrument of fear as he silently slunk his way along. Inclined to believe in himself, he had no doubt what the outcome would be. Ivan the Terrible. Mister Insanity. There was no doubt about the outcome at all.

Turning off the lights in the living room, Gunny hurried down the hall to his bedroom.

"Why did I turn off all the lights?" he whispered. Reaching his hand inside the door, groping for the switch, he felt another shudder run through his body.

And here came Ivan. An individual cat, prepared to inject incredible fear into a slightly overweight, highly imaginative older man. The perfect prey.

L

The Green Ghost Returns

Gunny, frantically fighting to control his fear, found the light switch, and saw light pour into his room. Feeling his heart beating rapidly, hands clenching and unclenching, he walked across the room to his closet.

Whether it was Ivan's luck, or some cruel twist of fate, just as Gunny reached the closet door the power went out. All the lights in the neighborhood—and Gunny's house—went out. It was black everywhere.

Gasping, holding his chest, Gunny felt dizzy. And blind. The room was suddenly completely unfamiliar. Tentatively, he put out his hand, both to stop himself from falling in a heap and to make the room level again. But there was nothing. He could feel nothing in front of him, nothing behind him, and nothing to the side of him. There were no landmarks anywhere. There was NOTHING.

Paralyzed now, he felt the hair all over his body stand straight up! He couldn't move. He couldn't see. He could only hear. He heard loud labored breathing. He couldn't tell if it was his own or someone standing very, very close to him. There was the ticking of a clock somewhere in the darkness and throaty laughter somewhere in the distance. Perhaps across the street or perhaps in the hall, he couldn't tell which. His entire lifetime spread before his eyes. He was reaching his limit.

He began to lean and list to one side. The vision of the legendary Green Ghost surfaced in his imagination. He was sure he heard it—right outside in the hall. He also heard a calm, logical voice deep in his head saying, "You keep a lantern in your room for times just like this. It's under your bed...or in the closet."

He had to reach the lantern, somewhere in this unfamiliar place. He staggered and lurched forward. But there was still nothing. He lunged forward again and crashed into something unrecognizably large and soft. Arms frantically thrashing, Gunny wrapped the drapes around his neck like a leash. He lumbered backwards right onto the bed, where he fell in a heap of sweat and gasps.

He thought he heard more sounds in the hall. Or maybe it was his heartbeat. Just then, the hall noise got louder. In Gunny's terror, he thought he saw a figure looming at him. It resembled a giant lizard. No, a giant leopard. No, it had to be the Green Ghost.

All of a sudden Gunny was nine years old again. With loneliness surrounding him, he groped for the giant panda, imagination gone wild. Desperation setting in. And here came Ivan, outside, oozing around the corner of the house like molten lava, ready to launch his plan into action. Ready to give Gunny the "interrification" of his life.

M

The Mirror and a Dead Faint

In the pitch blackness, Ivan's eyes glowed in the dark as he jumped up on the window sill and peered into Gunny's room. Able to see anything and everything, he spotted Gunny flattened on his bed. He marveled at the moist, massive, mammoth figure shivering on the bed. There was Gunny, barely conscious, lying in a pool of quivering sweat.

Ivan contemplated, "I really do sort of like old Gunny, maybe I'd better not scramble his mind with mortal terror...," but then he recalled the last episode at the fish tank, and his resolve returned.

Maintaining his focus, Ivan continued to watch for a moment, noting the motion of Gunny's tummy rising and falling, rising and falling, almost in musical fashion. He scratched the window...just a little.

Scratch.

HAH!! Just as he hoped, Gunny's whole body bolted upward, eyes staring wildly at the hall. Unable now to detect the source of any sound, *Gunny suspected everything came from the hall.*

While Gunny sat fixated on the hall, Ivan in one perfect movement, leapt from the sill to the ground. Muscles rippling, he maneuvered through the mulch in the flower bed toward the hole in the basement window. Putting his paw through the mesh, he lifted up the screen and leapt down to the basement floor. He knew every moldy corner of this place, every leaky pipe covered in orange mineral deposits. He had used this method of entering Gunny's house many times!

Through the basement he came, up the laundry chute, into an air duct and on up to the attic. A shadow of silent motion, Ivan emerged from the air duct. He passed in front of it and stared across at the trap door above Gunny's hall. "Ah...perfect," he thought.

Outside, the darkness was broken by a tinge of moonlight as the clouds scattered overhead. And the longest night of Gunny's life continued.

Still perched on the edge of his bed, Gunny continued to stare. The moonlight relieved just enough darkness to enable him to see slightly down the hall. And then he heard it. A whisper.

HISSSSSSSS.

It was Ivan, of course. He hissed again into the air duct, using it like a microphone. HISSSSSSSS. HISSSSSSSS.

Gunny, certain it was the ghostly whisper of his name, couldn't move and couldn't speak. He tried to do both, but nothing happened. Forced to just sit and stare, he could do nothing but wait and watch.

HISSSSSSSS. HISSSSSSSS.

Gunny's heart pounded a frightening melody in his ears, his eyes bulged, and his limbs remained frozen—legs stuck out in front of him, arms slackened at his sides. And his mind began to play tricks on him again, manufacturing even worse events down the hall.

Muttering, he said, "It's a mammoth mummy covered with filthy material, migrating down the hall for me. No. It's a whole mob of mummies coming for me. No. It probably really is a mature Green Ghost, majestic in his terror, drawn to me like a magnet, only a few meters away."

Ivan filled with delight when he heard poor Gunny's lament. Now, he already knew about Gunny's fear of the dark and the Green Ghost, but the mummy mob really got him.

Once again, he had second thoughts about poor old Gunny. "Maybe I'd better not manipulate this old boy, he might have a major faint. Hmmm, I do sort of like this mammal."

But taken with his own powers, Ivan rapidly changed his mind. "Nope, no mercy tonight. I am the master of suspense and I have work to do. Now, to wait till midnight and then monitor and mold the situation just as I please."

Meanwhile, Gunny managed to turn his head slightly, caught sight of his own image in his mirror, and passed out in a dead faint.

Heading Toward Midnight

Gunny's house was deadly still as his faint moved into a sleep state and Ivan waited. He waited and waited. Oh so patiently he waited for midnight.

Much to his glee, the lights were still off in the whole neighborhood.

And since Gunny couldn't seem to walk, he hadn't even been able to get his lantern, or a candle or flashlight. Thus it was pitch black still, except for a little moonlight that now filtered in occasionally from outside.

While he waited for the witching hour, he relived the evening. So perfectly the network of events had unfolded. By day he had been a normal cat, snoozing on the porch. By night he was transformed into Ivan the Ghost Cat, an evil nomad, navigating unseen through the neighborhood in search of prey.

With nerves of steel he had frightened numerous children this evening. He loved to spin wildly in the dead leaves under his big bush right by the sidewalk, just as the hateful little mutants went by. They almost always screamed and ran, and sometimes they even dropped or spilled their candy. But nothing compared to what he was going to do to Gunny!

In the Bedroom...

Ivan continued to wait and Gunny continued to sleep, fitfully. Closer and closer it came to midnight. Tick-tock, closer and closer to Gunny's time of reckoning. His hour of doom. Ivan laughed wildly, for a cat. That is to say he twitched his whiskers softly. Twice on each side.

Finally, the clock on Gunny's mantle struck twelve times. Bong. Bong. Bong. Bong. Bong. Bong. Bong. Bong. Bong. Bong. Bong. Bong.

"Midnight!" thought Ivan, "Now for some fun. Thank heavens Gunny hasn't outgrown his childhood fears!"

With pupils dilated, Ivan strode to the trap door in the hall ceiling. He pushed it hard with a powerful paw and made it open. Because it had a spring on the hinge, it sprang open and then slammed back with a loud (rather outstanding) BANG!

Gunny bolted upright in his bed, foggily trying to remember where he was. Then as he faced the dark hall he remembered everything and was overcome with fear again.

Just then, Ivan made the trap door open and slam back again. BANG!

"Oh no," thought Gunny, "The origin of that sound was clearly the hall. This is not my imagination." This time his legs responded when he tried to move them and up he flew out of his bed, crashing to the floor. Scrambling to move, he heard an orchestra of sound pounding in his ears. His legs were going in every direction, nothing he did organized them enough to outrun anything. There he was, sort of spinning in one place, fearing he would be set upon by the faceless, nameless opponent in the hall.

Finally getting control of both legs, he orchestrated them into a forward movement and ran right into the closet. Unable to observe any signs of light or life, he had no idea where he was. Legs and arms flailing like an octopus, he spun around and headed blindly in the other direction. Just then, some moonlight filtered in through the window and he could see that he was right by the hall door. Worse than that was the sight of the trap door opening, and something dark and large dropping from it.

Poor Gunny, his head began to spin as if in orbit, and he once again began to feel faint and staggered backwards onto the bed.

But Gunny's ordeal wasn't over. *Ivan was now in the bedroom.*

P

"I am King and this is My Castle"

Not waiting for another moment to pass, Ivan decided not to permit Gunny to escape into a full faint. He wanted him to stay on a plateau of fear until the precise moment when Ivan chose to free him and be proclaimed the all time cunningest competitor. He wanted Gunny's fear to persist, but not to paralyze him. And besides, he figured that getting Gunny out of the bedroom in this prevailing predicament would produce more fun.

So he crept up on the bed and painstakingly leaned over Gunny's wet face and heaving chest—and licked his nose.

"YEOW!" With a high pitched scream—certain the Green Ghost had him—Gunny pivoted off the bed, and scrambled into the hall on his hands and knees with Ivan in hot pursuit.

Down the hall Gunny went, hands and knees, hands and knees, hands and knees, scrambling along as fast as he could. Not sure where he was or where he was going, he only knew he had to get out of there and find some light source. He couldn't stand the dark anymore. "Light, light, I have to have light," he wheezed.

But here came Ivan. Easily able to see in the blackness, he was loping down the hall, heading for the mantle where he would have a perfect view of his prey.

Groping wildly along, Gunny ran into a large object. Stunned and dazed, he felt it. To his great relief it was his couch. He heaved a grandiose sigh, "My couch. It's my couch."

Crawling up onto it, shivering with fear and sweat, he sunk into the cushions and began to collect his wits. Slowly, he started to prepare for battle. He wasn't just going to lie down and let the green Ghost get him. He'd fight. A faint recollection of his military days began to penetrate his consciousness.

Calming his heaving chest, he pondered his predicament. Here he was in the living room, on his couch, and if his visualization was accurate, his portable phone was right on the coffee table in front of him. Groping silently, he found the phone and turned it over. Yes! Thank heaven for lighted dials. He punched in Maya's number.

Barely breathing, waiting for the phone to ring, he thought he saw a dark form protruding from the mantle. The phone rang...once...twice. Getting progressively more terrified, he waited for someone, anyone to answer.

Finally, he heard Maya's sleepy voice say, "Hello?"

"The Green Ghost, the Green Ghost," he whispered into the phone. The trouble was that as soon as he heard his own whispering voice, it scared him. "The Green Ghost, the Green Ghost," he screeched.

"...Gunny?...Gunny? Is that you Gunny?" Maya said. She had heard his voice plenty of times, but never like this. "Gunny, is that you?"

"HELP!"

"I'll be there as soon as possible, Gunny. Hang on. What did you say? Something about a Ghost?"

"Yes. The Green Ghost. He's here. It's dark. It's so dark."

Ivan, perched on the mantle, prepared to prolong the process of terror with one last strike!

There in the dark, with only one of them able to see, Ivan sprang through the air, like an acrobatic performer, from the mantle to the piano. He soared. Heavily hitting the high keys—BLANGETY, BLANG, BLANG—Ivan heard Gunny explode to his feet just as he had predicted.

Tumbling over the fish tank, he was on the floor again, sliding on the water and flopping fish. He slid to a stop in front of the back door, just in time to hear Maya running up the back steps.

Still in his clothes, he sat there, wet all over and close to physical exhaustion. What a sight he was. Maya opened the door and shined her flashlight right on him.

"Oh Gunny!"

"I...I...I...I...," Gunny stuttered, pitifully.

"Gunny, why are your lights off? My lights came back on a little while ago." With that, she reached up and snapped on the kitchen light.

Stunned, Gunny looked around him. There was his fish tank under the kitchen table. There were his precious fish flopping all over the floor. There was the upturned coffee table. But, there was no Green Ghost.

"Gunny, are you Ok? Talk to me Gunny. Did you say something about a Green Ghost? I was positive you said something about a Green Ghost."

Sitting in water and sweat, heart pounding, ears ringing, Gunny finally began to collect his wits again. And he was becoming very embarrassed. Finding mobility, he turned and stared at the rest of the house, struggling to see in the living room and down the hall, checking out the piano. Nothing. Nothing to be seen. No Green Ghost.

"He must have gotten away," thought Gunny. "Uh-oh, nobody will believe me."

Trying to preserve his dignity in front of his neighborhood friend, Gunny stammered, "Green Ghost? No, I said...ah...Green Toast. Green Toast. I wanted you to come over so I could show you my new recipe for green toast. Yeah, that's it. Green Toast." His eyes frantically scanned the kitchen for likely ingredients.

Meanwhile, Ivan slithered in from the living room, unnoticed. Slinking through the kitchen, he was out the door and down the back steps.

Pompously strutting across Gunny's backyard, he said, "I am King. And, this...O Neighborhood, are you listening?...this is my castle and kingdom. Let it be known."

Is it Over...Yet?

Maya helped Gunny gather the fish into the aquarium and refill it with water, pondered his large quantity of strangely shaped fish, and gently mopped up Gunny and the floor. Then she said goodnight to her friend and headed for home.

Gunny stood in the kitchen, finally brightly bathed in electric light, and tried to think of the night's events. What had happened? Was it a dream? Was it really the Green Ghost?

He turned toward the living room, strained his neck, and looked down the hall. "It is so long and dark," he whispered to himself.

Moving tentatively, almost tiptoeing, he went into the living room. Standing in that silent room, he pondered. "Where is the quality of my life?"

Looking down the dark hall, into his dark room, he further lamented, "Was that all real? Do I qualify for the loony-bin?"

R

"Sergeant Gunfred Bustamante Reporting, Sir"

Refusing to give in and sleep on the couch, Gunny mustered up all his courage and reluctantly edged sideways toward the dark hall and his dark room...ready to face his raw fears.

At the head of the hall, he peered into the blackness and rigorously groped for the light switch. Finally light bathed the hall, and with a deep sigh Gunny robustly marched toward his bedroom. But the bedroom door was nearly shut and the room was very black, with a mere sliver of light from the hall revealing just an inch or two of his rug and bed.

Stopping momentarily in the hall, Gunny tried to regain his composure.

Unfortunately, while all the events of the night had been unfolding, a raging rainstorm had been brewing outside. Just as Gunny carefully opened the bedroom door, a loud clap of thunder hit the neighborhood. Gunny flew heavily onto the bed. And there he sat, trying to restrain the shivers and fears again beginning to ripple through his body.

Wildly reflecting on it all, he commanded, "I must think. One event at a time. I must recover."

Reviewing the evening meant going through each startling terror attack. So as Gunny went through his bedtime routine of putting on his pajama's, brushing his teeth, and doing *four* sit-ups, he recalled the entire travesty, bit by bit. And he came up with only one conclusion. There really was a Green Ghost and it really was *here.*

Climbing into bed, Gunny resolved to fight back. He tried to conjure up a plan. He had to be resourceful. He had to respond. "Please let me think of a plan, just a simple plan."

Meanwhile, while Gunny was meeting his fears, Ivan was receding into the night. Earlier he had chased an unlucky rodent hopping about for a little food, but now he was ready for a little nap and then perhaps another little attack on Gunny toward morning.

"Gunny is ridiculous," mused Ivan. "Afraid of the dark and the Green Ghost! He deserves another small attack. I didn't quite finish with him, you know. I'm the feared, fearless champion. I am King and this neighborhood is my castle. Yeah, the whole neighborhood." Rehearsing his attack in his mind, Ivan drifted off to sleep.

Rehearsing his defense for real, unable to sleep, Gunny was up and about in his room, searching for weapons. Revealing a cunning nature not often seen by others, Gunny now suddenly represented a threat to his enemy. He had located his old Army uniform, and become the renowned "Sergeant Gunfred Bustamante." Despite the fact that he could barely button the waist on his jacket, and the belt was on the last notch, he looked stunning. He would be ready to risk life and limb. He would be *dangerous*.

"In recognition of your courage and commitment, we recommend you to the rank of Sergeant," Gunny read the words on the plaque on his wall.

Looking at himself in the mirror with pride, he said, "And I won't let you down." Gunny stuffed one pillow under the covers on the bed to look like someone sleeping. Then he placed his bowling ball on the other pillow right where that someone's head would be. Gunny walked over to the chair near the window and sat down. Sitting very straight and very stiff, he waited. This time it was his turn. He would be the ruler of this night.

"Sergeant Gunfred Bustamante reporting, Sir."

The Final Halloween Session

The storm raged on outside for quite awhile, soaking the grass, almost a squall at times, and then the blackness turned to a quiet night. And still Gunny waited. Staring straight ahead. Alert. Ready. A solitary figure in the dark of his room. Ramrod straight. Ready for trouble.

Stretching, Ivan awakened. Since the rain had stopped, he decided to venture out. Feeling quite rested, superb and superior, he looked about and assessed the nighttime situation. Were there any other species awake? Was he the only supreme being able to see and successfully navigate in the dark? Why, yes. Naturally.

Sauntering along the wet surface of the sidewalk, then taking a shortcut across the grass and carefully traversing the muddy flowerbed filled with debris, Ivan made his way to Gunny's house. And his window. Leaping onto the sill, Ivan once again set out to be a spectator.

But this time there was something different. Gunny was waiting and ready. Next to his chair lay his weapons. He had collected everything and anything that could be thrown. All the souvenirs he had collected on his trips (hard rocks and pointed shells collected on his favorite shorelines), his box of garden supplies, the plastic models and toys left by his grandsons (the metal spacecraft, the small rubber satellite with spines, the King Kong skyscraper, one broken wooden stilt, a small metal slot machine, a large red plastic storage bin). He was ready.

Sitting very stiff and very straight, Gunny looked out the window. Hmmm. He saw a small dark figure coming across the yard. And he recognized it! IVAN. It was Ivan. What was he doing out at this time of night? What was he doing heading for Gunny's house? Gunny stiffened. He heard Ivan jump to the window ledge.

Sitting far enough back from the window, Gunny could see *out* of the dark but he couldn't be seen *in* the dark. At long last, Gunny could see a little better than Ivan. There sat Ivan a perfect silhouette against the night skyline. And the final Halloween session began.

Ivan patiently stared at Gunny's room, focused on the bed. Certain that Gunny was in it, Ivan watched and watched. Using the bowling ball was a stroke of genius on Gunny's part. For truly, the ball and Gunny's head were almost exactly the same size and shape. In the darkness they were one and the same. Finally, disturbed that it didn't move, Ivan decided to scratch the window pane and get a little action started. SCRATCH.

Nothing. No response from the bed.

Again. SCRATCH.

Still no response, except for the solitary figure sitting straight in the chair. On duty. He was responding. He was thinking! What was Ivan doing here? What was he doing scratching the window pane? Then a weird sensation began to come over him. A sensation of spectacular awareness. A sensation of incredible anger. A sensation of incredible relief. Could it have been? Gunny's eyes got very big. Then they got very, very, very small.

Gunny carefully watched Ivan through the sheer curtain, without moving anything but his little black eyes. He squinted in thought. Could it be? Could it have been?

Ivan, tiring of watching the bed, decided to enter the house. In he went through the basement window, scuttling along through the air ducts in the ceiling. Ever so quietly.

But this time there was something different. Gunny knew! Gunny was certain! Gunny was prepared!

When Ivan leapt off the sill, Gunny edged up to look out the window and saw Ivan scuttle toward the basement window. He couldn't believe his eyes when he saw Ivan enter through the hole. Sitting back in the chair, his mind continued to sift through the details of the night. He thought of the entire sequence of events. Yes. It *all* must have been Ivan's doing. He wanted to shriek with rage. Only military discipline and a single-minded desire for revenge prevented his doing so.

His careful planning and preparation suddenly became much more significant. He was ready for action, but his plan would need a few changes.

"Tonight," Gunny said to himself, "I will make Ivan feel what I felt...I will take him where he has never been... to the summit of fear. I will sustain his fear as long as I can." Angered beyond belief, he continued to fantasize extreme possibilities. "By sunrise he will be a gleaming white skeleton, all the fat melted off of him from being so afraid for so long. He will feel the icy stake of terror in his heart as I did. He will learn from this...deep in his soul he will know it's not funny to scare someone. He will wish he had never dared to spar with Sergeant Gunfred Bustamante."

Gunny knew that by now Ivan would be getting into the attic. And then dropping out of the trap door into the hall. He knew he would have to act fast, but he hadn't planned this part. He pictured himself standing in the shadows...holding something scary to menace Ivan with. He looked at the supply of weapons, previously assembled beside his chair in preparation for the Green Ghost. He needed a skull... or a rubber serpent...or some sort of big hairy animal skin. Hmmm. He didn't have any of those things. He would need something more simple. His eyes rested on the gleaming silver scissors in his weapon pile.

In one move he scooped up the scissors and shot from his chair. To give Ivan something to wonder about, he scraped his fingernails along the wall as he skimmed toward the door. His fingers caught on something large and soft. "My gardening smock," he whispered. "This will be perfect."

In his haste he failed to notice the wooden footstool in his path until his shin cracked against it. But he was a military man with a mission to complete. Pain would not interfere. Smothering a yell and actually emitting a conveniently scary hiss in the process, he swept the three legged stool into his arms and crept into the shadows of the hallway.

Time was becoming short. The transformed Cunning Gunny knew Ivan could see so well in the dark he would recognize Gunny immediately. So, like a sculptor, he began to transform himself into something Ivan couldn't recognize. Fingers working quickly and a thin smile forming on his lips, he put the seat of the stool against his back, and used the sash of the smock to tie it there like a saddle. The legs stuck up from his back like spines on a dinosaur. He draped the smock over himself and lay down on his belly. He held the scissors out in front of him and opened and shut them twice. Snip, snip. It sounded good and scary there in the dark. (But then everything sounded scary in the dark to Gunny.)

Then Gunny decided to test one loud, raspy, growly SNARL. Perhaps a tactical blunder to do so before the enemy was in sight, but he couldn't resist.

In the attic, Ivan was poised at the trap door. His tail twitched wildly and his pupils were huge and black. Every bit of him was tight and ready for the hunt. Then Sergeant Gunny's attack began.

"SNARL."

Ivan leaped straight into the air, bumping his head on the overhead rafter. With a loud thump he landed, legs spread and claws out. His ears twitched and his eyes narrowed. What was that? It didn't sound like a noise Gunny would make in his sleep. Where *was* Gunny? Was there *something* down there?

Frizzed, Ivan decided to gingerly sniff about, listening cautiously. Creeping close to the floor, very slowly, Ivan edged up to the opening of the trap door. Carefully, and oh-so-slowly, he stuck his nose over the side of the opening and tried to look down in the hall. Slowly, slowly he moved. Nose twitching.

Gunny spotted Ivan's oh-so-careful movements. The time was nearing. His attack was readying. Just a little more. How did that saying go? Something about curiosity killing the cat. Hah! "Just a little more, Ivan dear. Just a little more. Get curious enough to jump into the hall," Gunny thought.

Ivan peered slowly around in the dark. Nothing. He saw nothing. He heard nothing. He smelled nothing. Uh-oh! What was that? A slight movement near the floor at Gunny's bedroom door. A rodent? A leaf? A paw? What was it? Where did it go?

Oh! There it was again. A slight movement, back and forth, back and forth. Stopping for a split second. Then, back and forth, back and forth. *Forgetting all*, Ivan knew he had to know what it was. He leaped down to the hall floor. A mistake.

Gunny's face betrayed just a hint of a thin steely smile. With immense satisfaction, Gunny thought, "Here he comes...here he comes. I'll move my finger just a little bit more, then I'll stop it in plain sight and he won't be able to stand it. He'll have to attack."

Ivan saw that rodent or paw or whatever it was starting to move again.

Back and forth. Back and forth. Ivan was as still as a stone. Watching. Watching.

Suddenly, it stopped. Ivan stared. It didn't move. Ivan stared some more. It still didn't move. Unable to stand it, instinctively Ivan's hind legs started making those quick little back and forth movements, his eyes dilated, every part of his body focused. And, he pounced. A long, high, leaping pounce.

Just as Ivan was ready to land, Gunny jumped up, arms over his head, back bowed, smock flapping, lungs bellowing. "SNARL" in the loudest, growliest voice he could get out!

Ivan twisted in midair and went straight to the ceiling. Stiff as a board, all four appendages straight out, claws bared, fur standing straight up! He seemed suspended in air. When he hit the floor, his feet scrambled in one spot as he tried to get traction on Gunny's slippery wood floor.

"SNARL," Gunny bellowed again, spread out like a giant bat.

Ivan scrambled and scrambled, tail looped, fur frizzed, until he finally got through the living room and slightly dazed, jumped right at the kitchen window. Knocking himself almost unconscious, he fell back in the sink, controlled himself, and slipped-flopped to the floor where he landed with a grunt. Something he had never done before. Looking wildly for an exit, he heard loud footsteps coming down the hall.

Here came Gunny. Around the corner of the kitchen he bounced. Costume swirling around him. "SNARL." He jumped at Ivan.

Ivan, with nowhere to go and completely terrified, swelled up, tail-fur straight out, back arched, gave off his fiercest HISS.

Completely delighted with himself, Gunny forgot to disguise himself. "HA. HA. HAAH. HA. HA. HAAH." he laughed.

Eyes staring and then moving slowly from side to side, Ivan sniffed a rat. A very large rat. "That...is...Gunny," grimaced Ivan.

And there the Halloween session ended—Gunny and Ivan facing each other in the kitchen. Only this time it was Sergeant Gunfred Bustamante that won. Completely delighted with himself, Gunny opened the back door. "Out you go, Ivan dear," he chuckled. Ivan, miffed, with ears slightly flattened, arrogantly descended Gunny's back steps. Sauntering down the first few steps, he took off like a shot for the young sapling in the yard.

As Gunny opened the door for Ivan to exit, he noticed it was almost sunrise. Standing in the doorway, he watched Ivan rocket across the yard. And he felt the slightest tinge of sympathy for him. "Hmmm. Poor Ivan," thought Gunny. "Perhaps I was a bit too much for him. Really, I must remember, he's *just* a cat."

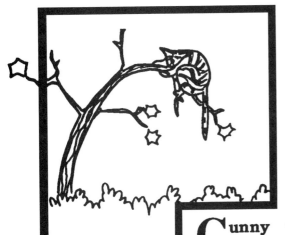

T

Pouting...Humiliated

Gunny was exhausted. Ivan was furious... mortified...and temporarily insane. He would end this game, triumphant.

The next day came and almost went, and Ivan never left the sapling. Bowed from his weight, it nevertheless held him up throughout the day while he pouted. He didn't—rather couldn't—eat. He couldn't sleep. He couldn't stop thinking about last night.

All day he sat on that branch. All day he stared straight ahead. All day he thought. And his thoughts were not happy, they were treacherous. Trembling with anger, often threatening suicide, he studied the terrain below.

Gunny had transformed from a pleasant aging human-pushover to a mortal enemy. Ivan might choose to get even or he might choose to never acknowledge Gunny's presence again. Either theme was equally appealing. If he chose to get even his thoughts were endless. He might tackle him on the back. No, not good enough. He had done that many times before. He might trip him into a trench. No, he couldn't remember but he thought that he'd done that too. He might entice a tribe of wild children to attack him. No. Too much like the grandchildren visiting. He might shoot him from a tower. No. He didn't believe in using guns. He might fancy up a tomb somehow and bury Gunny. No. How could he ever do that? He was a talented genius, but even he had limitations. How about a hanging? He could get Maya to put a rope in the tree, tighten the noose around Gunny's thick neck and...No. Perhaps the ignoring technique was better. *Never, ever* look at Gunny again. *Never ever* notice him or hear him. No matter what. *Never.*

Just then Maya came out the back door calling for him again. "Ivan. Here kitty, kitty. Ivan. Come here, Ivan. Where are you? What's wrong with you?"

Head on paws, eyes closed, faking sleep, Ivan thought, "How I wish she wouldn't blast my predicament to the whole neighborhood. She's been doing that all day. Ivan...Ivan...here kitty, kitty. What a pain she can be. Why can't she leave me alone? Why can't everyone just...leave...me... alone?"

Slowly opening one eye very nonchalantly, he saw Maya go back inside. But he feared she'd be back. It was then that the whole day deteriorated with a frightful climax. A strong wind suddenly arose. Forgetting that he was tediously sitting on a tender branch of a young sapling, Ivan mistakenly moved forward to a triangle of smaller branches. And by the time he realized the branch he was on was the size of thick thread, it was too late. With a crack, the now twig-sized branch split and broke down the middle.

Ivan hung on as best he could, swinging from his claws, his face contorted with a chagrinned grimace. Then, the last straw. The branch snapped completely off, sending Ivan thrashing a whole two feet into the sticker-bush below. He saw clearly that here he belonged and here he would remain.

It was twilight and Ivan still sat under the bush. Never to come out again.

"Ivan. Here Ivan. Here kitty, kitty. Ivan, where are you? I have some news for you. We're going to have a visitor."

U and V

Puffy's Mistake

"**A** visitor? What could that mean? A visitor. Like I want to see anyone. Or have anyone see me. Oh sure, come see King Ivan in his castle of thorns."

Then another Maya interruption. "Ivan, here Ivan. Kitty. Kitty. Where are you, Ivan? Here kitty, kitty. Here kitty, kitty. Come on Ivan."

Still under the bush, pouting but beginning to feel the initial stages of serious hunger, Ivan's mood continued. "Sometimes Maya really bugs me. Sometimes she just doesn't understand anything. Like, she always thinks Gunny's unexpected "accidents" are actual accidents. Really, you'd think she would get it by now. It's that constant chipperness that finally gets to you...always cheerful, always helpful...hmmm always ready with food. There is *that*...food."

Feeling the increased urge for food, Ivan contemplated, "Perhaps *it is* time to go in. Poor Maya. I shouldn't punish her any longer. She probably can't think of anything else but me. In fact, I've probably ruined her day. She needs me, you know."

Ivan stood up and stretched, long and slow. Forward he leaned, one back leg stretching way out and then the other. He'd take his time responding to Maya's call. "Yawn. She'll come out and call me again. Hmmm, I am getting pretty hungry. But doggone it, a cat's a cat. With a cat's protocol and a cat's modus operandi."

While Ivan played his I'M-HARD-TO-GET cat-game, things changed. Maya came out of the house as expected, walked part way into the yard as expected, looked around expectantly as expected, and then made a sudden right hand turn, got in the car with her parents and was gone!

Shocked, Ivan stood up. Looking upward to the sky, Ivan saw big, dark clouds. He looked at the house. No signs of life. No lights. And it was getting dark. And it was getting windier. He had been left! Abandoned! Used, abused, and cast aside like common garbage!

The picture of disgust, visibly upset, Ivan felt once again like a "Cat-Victim." The wind blew the hair on his back as he stood still as a stone, just staring, in disbelief. He had been left. Left. Finally, ears back, he retreated to his bush, hunger intensifying.

Meanwhile, Puffy had once again escaped from his house. He was one of those little dogs who could be seen staring out the window, begging to be let out. But now he was free and he intended to take advantage of it. Visor in place, he strutted across the street, heading for Ivan's yard.

A vast variety of trash was blowing everywhere, the result of a previous escapade of Sam's. Puffy's little feet were a blur beneath him as he flew across the street like a wind-up toy. More aware than usual of his surroundings, he dodged the debris. He veered out of the way of the vivid pink plastic bottle, vaulted (somewhat) over the latest version of Tidy-Diapers, and ran pell-mell into a vertical volume of decaying stench. That returned him to his usual semi-confused state, and he spun in several quick circles. Finally, victorious, he leapt up the vertical curb.

Strutting along, feet firmly beneath him, Puffy in his dizzy semi-conscious state, entered Ivan's yard. It was then that The King, the villain of villains, sighted the intruder.

Up sat Ivan. Eyes narrowing. A vague sense of power returning. Ivan's hunger for food was all but forgotten. Replaced by a much more ravenous hunger. A hunger for conquest.

W, X, Y, and Z

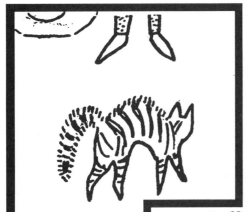

Who or What is Mordred?

In Puffy trotted, without thought or concern for his own welfare, proceeding across the driveway, through the grass, to Ivan's favorite bush. He started to raise his pitiful little leg.

Ivan couldn't believe it. This dog was so stupid it wasn't funny. What was he, an idiot? Didn't he know he was a little, puny dog, able to be done in by any of the neighborhood animals. With a warning yowl, Ivan sprang into action.

Bearing down on Puffy like a run-away train, Ivan flew across the yard, yearning to vent his anger on this wretched fidgety fluff. Ivan hit Puffy from behind and like a churning whirlpool rolled him around and around on the ground. Yelping miserably, Puffy couldn't shake his attacker. In a zealous furor, Ivan kept it up. He wasn't really hurting Puffy, but he had no intention of letting him go either.

Puffy, his pitiful little legs flailing in the air, yelped over and over. "YIP, YIP, YIIIP, YIP, YIIP,"

It was to no avail. Ivan kept it up. He was power hungry and mad. He wrenched and Puffy writhed as they wrestled on the ground. Finally weary, standing over him for just a long moment to prove his point, Ivan let Puffy up.

Puffy, with his tail between his flying little legs, ran through the grass, across the drive-way, and out to the street. Not even yielding to cars, he went straight through the garbage, up the curb on his side of the street, and off into the wilderness of his yard. He wasn't hurt, but he was a wreck.

Ivan, hair frizzed, tail looped, with no yen to follow, watched him go. "Hah. I am KING and this is my castle."

A few hours later, wind howling and rain threatening, Maya and her family returned. Ivan heard the car coming down the street and decided to greet them. He would forgive them for locking him out if they had had enough sense to bring him just the right left-overs. This would be the zenith of his return. With unparalleled zeal and zest, he would cover Maya with a zillion rubs on her leg. Perhaps even the rarely seen figure-eight-a-la-Ivan around both ankles. He was the best cat in the zodiac where leftovers were concerned. No more zany antics, he would behave.

"Please, please, please, let there be leftovers," he thought.

He saw Maya get out but she had a plastic bag of groceries, not leftovers. "Yogurt—YUK. And eggs—YUK. Those slithery egg yolks make me gag. Look what else...red and blue yarn, a wooden yardstick, a toy yacht for a snotty youth, and no leftovers. Well, maybe there's more."

Striding out stiff-legged from under his bush, ready to be worshipped, Ivan came toward the car. Stopping, he stared suspiciously. What was that in the back seat? Standing very still and staring very intently, the hair on Ivan's back began to stand up. Could it be?

Just then, the back door of the car flew open and Ivan spotted his most dreaded visitor. Mordred.

Maya crooned, "Ivan. There you are kitty. Where have you been? Look who is going to be visiting us for awhile."

Meanwhile, having been in the kitchen for one last snack, Gunny heard the car and peered out his window. Spotting Mordred he grimaced, "Even Ivan doesn't deserve this. Especially now, right after getting his much deserved comeuppance from yours truly!"

Then a strange thing happened. Watching from the window, Gunny saw Ivan wheel on his hind feet and head for *Gunny's*. He watched Ivan rocket up the back steps and explode through the back door. "Even Gunny is better than this," Ivan thought, catching his breath. "I AM KING...*and King I shall stay. But just for now, I think I'll stay with Gunny.*"

> P.S. *Find out who or what Mordred is in the next episode of Gunny and Ivan. Any Guesses?*

Glossary

ability: the power to do something, 1
abundant: a lot, 1
accompany: to go along with, 2
accomplish: to do or complete, 2
accurate: correct, 3
ache: a dull or constant pain (n), 3; to hurt with a dull or constant pain (v), 4
achieve: to gain through effort or work, 4
achievement: something that has been gained or accomplished through great effort, 4
acrobat: a person who can do hard tricks like tumbling and balancing, 5
active: moving around or doing something a lot, 5
adore: to love very much, 5
advantage: a better position from which to get something, 6
adventure: an exciting or unusual experience, 6
advertise: to call attention to a product with the intention of selling it, 6
advice: an idea you give someone about how to act or how to solve a problem, 7
aerial: of or in the air, 7
agile: able to move and react quickly and easily, 7
agriculture: the science of growing food and raising animals, 8
aide: a helper, 8
airborne: off the ground, 8
album: a book with blank pages for photos or stamps, 9
algae: tiny water plants, 9
alien: someone who isn't a citizen of the country he or she lives in, 9
aloft: up in the air, 10
alternative: a choice between two or more things, 10
altitude: how high something is, 10
ambitious: having a strong desire to achieve something, 11
ancestor: a family member who lived a long time ago, 11
anticipate: to look forward to, 11
appeal: to ask strongly for something, 12
appetite: the wish for food, 12
applause: the clapping of hands to show approval, 12
approach: to come near, 13
arch: a curved shape, usually in a building or at the top of a door, 13
archeology: the study of people and things from long ago, especially through the discovery of buried ruins, 13
architecture: the art of designing buildings, 14
arrange: to put something in a certain position or order, 14
artifact: something made by people long ago, 14
artificial: not real or natural, 15
artistic: showing skill and a sense of beauty, 15
ascend: to climb or go up, to rise, 15
assemble: to put together, 16
assignment: a job to do, 16
assist: to help, 16
athlete: a person trained in a sport, exercise, or other physical skill, 17
attain: to get by hard work, to earn, 17
attempt: to try, 17
attendance: the act of being present, 18
attentive: paying careful attention to, 18
attitude: a way of feeling toward something or someone, 18
attract: to bring near, 19
attractive: pleasing, charming, pretty, 19
auditorium: a large room where people watch plays and concerts or hear lectures, 19
authority: the power to make decisions, to command, to act, or to control, 20
automatic: able to operate by itself, 20
average: the usual amount or kind, 20

aviation: the science of flying aircraft, 21

avoid: to keep away from, 21

awesome: causing wonder, fear, or amazement, 21

bail: to dip water out of a boat with a pail or other container, 23

barricade: a temporary wall or fence used for protection, defense, or as a means of preventing entry, 23

barrier: something that blocks the way, 24

beetle: a kind of insect with hard, shiny front wings and thin back wings, 24

benefit: to be helped by, 24

bifocal: a glass lens for seeing close up and far away, 25

bind: to fasten or tie, 25

bound: a limiting line or area (n), 25; to move in a jumping run (v), 26

bracelet: jewelry worn around the arm or wrist, 26

breakthrough: an important discovery that helps solve a problem, 26

brilliant: very bright or sparkling, 27

brink: the edge at the top of a steep place, 27

broadcast: to send out over television or radio, 27

burial: the placing of a dead body in a grave, 28

bury: to put something under the ground, 28

business: the buying and selling of things, 28

bust: a woman's breasts, 29

bustle: to move with a lot of energy, 29

calculate: to find out by using arithmetic, 31

candidate: a person who runs for or is considered for an office or award, 31

capable: skillful, 32

capacity: the amount that can be held in a space, 32

capsule: a small, thin case that encloses powdered medicine, 32

captive: a prisoner or anyone held by force, 33

caravan: a group of people traveling together, especially in the desert, 33

career: a person's long-term work, 33

cargo: goods carried by a ship, airplane, truck, or other vehicle, 34

carnival: a fair or festival that has games, rides, and other amusements, 34

cartilage: the body tissue that connects bones, 34

carve: to cut something into a shape, 35

cascade: to tumble down like a waterfall, 35

category: a group or class of things, 35

caution: great care, 36

cavern: a large cave, especially one underground, 36

ceremony: an act or set of acts for special events, 36

challenge: a call to take part in a contest or fight, 37; to ask to take part in a contest or fight (v), 37

chamber: a room in a house or other building, 37

champion: the first-place winner, 38

channel: the water between two land masses, 38

chant: to sing, say, or shout a short phrase over and over, 38

character: the way a person thinks, feels, or acts, 39

chasm: a deep canyon, crack, or opening in the Earth's surface, 39

circular: round, 39

civilization: the society and culture of a people, 40

clash: to fight or be in conflict, 40

cleft: a deep crack or opening, 40

climate: the main weather patterns of a place, 41

clumsy: awkward, 41

coax: to urge gently, 41

collapse: to fall in or fall down, 42

comic: funny, 42

command: an order to do something, 42

communicate: to exchange or pass along feelings, thoughts, or information, 43

compact: firmly or tightly packed or pressed together, 43

companion: someone who is with you, a friend, 43

compare: to see how two things are alike or different, 44

compete: to take part in a contest, 44

competition: a contest, 44

comprehend: to understand, 45

compress: to squeeze together into less space, 45

conceal: to hide, 45

concentrate: to pay close attention to, 46

concept: a general idea or thought, 46

concert: a musical show, 46

condition: the way that a person or thing is, 47

conductor: a person who directs a musical group, 47

connection: the place where two things are put together, 47

conquer: to overcome by force, 48

conquest: the act of taking over by force, 48

conservation: the protection of natural resources, 48

considerable: a lot, 49

construct: to build, 49

contempt: scorn, lack of respect, 49

contestant: a person in a contest, 50

continent: one of the seven large areas of land on the Earth, 50

contrast: a big difference between persons or things, 50

cooperate: to work together, 51

courageous: very brave, 51

create: to make, 51

creative: artistic or inventive, 52

crest: the highest part, 52

crevice: a narrow crack or split, 52

crew: a team of people who work together, 53

crust: the hard outside part or coating of something, 53

cunning: clever, sly, 53

current: air or water moving in one direction, 54; belonging to the present time (adj), 54

custom: something usually done by a group of people, 54

daily: happening every day, 55

dart: a small arrow (n), 55; to move quickly and suddenly (v), 56

data: facts, figures, and other items of information, 56

dazzle: to make almost blind by too much light, 56

debris: trash, 57

dedicate: to set apart for a special purpose or use, 57

dedicated: devoted, very interested and involved, 57

defend: to guard or protect, 58

delay: to put off till a later time, 58

delight: to make very happy, 58

delta: a triangle of land at the mouth of a river, 59

demonstrate: to explain, prove, or show clearly, 59

depart: to go away or leave, 59

dependable: able to be trusted, 60

deposit: to put money or valuable things in a bank or other safe place, 60

depth: the distance from top to bottom or from front to back, 60

descend: to move from a higher place to a lower one, 61

deserve: to have a right to, 61

desire: a strong wish or longing, 61

desolate: lonely and bleak, 62

desperate: reckless because of having no hope, 62

destination: the place where someone or something is going, 62

determination: great willpower to do something, 63

develop: to bring or come gradually into being, 63

device: something made for a special use, 63

devise: to think up, 64

devote: to give effort, attention, or time to some purpose, 64

devour: to eat greedily and completely, 64

diagonal: slanted, going up and down at an angle, 65

diameter: a straight line that cuts a circle in half, 65

diet: the foods a person or animal usually eats, 65

difficult: hard to do, 66

digest: to break down food in the stomach into usable forms, 66
director: a person who supervises and guides the work of others, 66
discipline: control of one's actions, behavior, and thoughts, 67
discover: to find, 67
display: a show or exhibit (n), 67; to show (v), 68
dissolve: to mix evenly with a liquid, 68
distinguish: to see the difference between certain things, 68
distrust: to not trust, 69
diver: a person who works or swims under water, 69
draft: a current of air, 69
drama: a story written for actors to perform, 70
dwell: to live somewhere, 70
dynamite: an explosive mixture, 70
dynamo: an electric generator, 71
economy: the management of the resources of a community, country, etc., 73
education: schooling, or the knowledge gained from a teacher, 73
eerie: strange and scary, 74
effect: impression or feeling, 74
efficient: working well, getting good results without wasted time or effort, 74
elaborate: complicated and fancy, 75
elder: an older person, 75
elevate: to raise to a higher level, 75
embed: to set firmly in something, 76
emerge: to come out, 76
employee: a person who works for someone else, 76
empty-handed: having nothing to show for your efforts, 77
enable: to allow, 77
encircle: to go around, 77
encouragement: something said or done to give hope and courage, 78
endure: to put up with, 78
enormous: huge, 78
entertain: to interest and amuse, 79
enthusiasm: a strong feeling of excitement and interest about something, 79
entry: the act of entering, 79
environment: the air, the water, the soil, and all the other things around a person, animal, or plant, 80
epidemic: a big outbreak of a disease, 80
equality: the quality or condition of being equal, 80
equator: an imaginary line around the middle of the Earth, 81
era: a period of history, 81
erosion: a wearing away, washing away, or eating away by wind, rain, or sand, 81
erupt: to explode, 82
essential: necessary, basic, 82
establish: to set up or begin, 82
evaporate: to change from a liquid to a gas, 83
event: happening, 83
evidence: proof, 83
evident: easy to tell, 84
evil: very bad, 84
exhaust: to make tired, 84
exhausting: very tiring, 85
exhibit: to show or display, 85
exhibition: a public display of objects or skills, 85
existence: being alive, real, present, or intact, 86
expand: to become larger, 86
expect: to look forward to something you think will probably happen, 86
expedition: a journey with a special purpose, 87
explorer: a person who travels to a place to discover new things, 87
extend: to make or become longer, 87
extension: something added on, 88
extinct: no longer found on the Earth, 88
fabulous: amazing, 89

facility: a building, room, or equipment that serves a special purpose, 89

factor: something that makes something else happen, 90

fade: to become less bright, 90

famous: known by many people, 90

fascination: a strong attraction to, or interest in, something, 91

fatigue: the condition of being tired, 91

fearsome: scary, 91

feast: a big meal made for a special event, 92

fertile: able to produce plants or young easily and plentifully, 92

fervent: having or showing deep feeling or being intensely devoted, 92

festival: a celebration, 93

figure: a symbol that stands for a number or word, 93; to compute, 93

flee: to run away, 94

flexible: able to bend and not break, not rigid, easily bent, 94

flicker: to grow bright and then dim and then bright in a shaky way, 94

founder: the person who starts or establishes something, 95

fragile: delicate, not strong, frail, 95

froth: a mass of bubbles, 95

function: purpose, 96; to work or to serve (v), 96

fundamental: basic, 96

furnace: a large enclosed metal box where heat is produced, 97

furnish: to provide, 97

futile: unsuccessful, useless, 97

gain: to get or add something as a result of your efforts, 99

galaxy: a very large group of stars, 99

gap: a hole or empty space, 100

gasp: a quick, short breath (n), 100; to take a quick, short breath (v), 100

gauge: an instrument for measuring, 101; to measure accurately, 101

gear: a wheel with teeth on the edge, 101

gem: a stone that is worth a lot of money, 102

generation: all the people born about the same time, 102

geology: the study of the earth's crust, 102

gigantic: very large, huge, 103

gill: the part of a fish or tadpole that lets it breathe underwater, 103

gland: a part of the body that makes needed fluids from materials in the blood, 103

glimmer: to give off a dim, unsteady light, 104

glimpse: a short, quick look, 104

glossy: shiny, 104

gorge: a deep, narrow canyon (n), 105; to stuff yourself with food (v), 105

graceful: beautiful or pleasing in design, movement, or style, 105

gradual: happening slowly, 106

grandparent: a grandfather or grandmother, 106

graze: to eat grass for food, 106

grit: small pieces of sand or stone, 107

growth: process of becoming larger as time passes, 107

guarantee: a promise to repair or replace something within a certain period of time, 107; to make sure, 108

gust: a quick, strong rush of wind, 108

gymnastics: physical exercises that require skill, balance, and strength, 108

habitat: the place where an animal or plant naturally lives and grows, 109

hammock: a kind of bed made of canvas or netting that is suspended by rope at both ends, 109

hardy: tough, able to put up with harsh conditions, 110

hare: an animal like a rabbit but a little larger, 110

harvest: the gathering in of a crop when it is ripe (n), 110; to gather crops (v), 111

haunting: strange and hard to forget, 111

haven: a place of safety or shelter, 111

heave: to lift, pull, push, or throw something heavy, 112

hedge: a row of bushes or low trees planted close together, 112

height: the distance from top to bottom, 112

hemorrhage: to bleed a great deal, 113

heroic: courageous, daring, or desperately energetic or resourceful, 113

hibernate: to spend the winter sleeping, 113

hire: payment for the use of a thing or the work of a person (n), 114; to pay for the use of a thing or the work or services of a person (v), 114

historic: very important and not likely to be forgotten, 114

hoard: to get and save carefully for future use, 115

holster: a leather case for holding a handgun, 115

home town: the town in which a person was born or grew up, 116

homesick: sad because of being away from one's home or family, 115

homestead: a house, sheds and barns, and the land around them, 116

hood: a head covering often fastened to the collar of a coat, 116

hoop: a strip of wood or metal formed into a ring or circle, 117

horizon: the line where the earth and the sky seem to meet, 117

horizontal: flat or level, parallel to the horizon, 117

horseshoe: a U-shaped metal plate that is nailed to a horse's hoof, 118

host: a person who entertains guests, 118

humor: the funny or amusing side of things (n), 118; to give in to the wishes of a person (v), 119

husky: big and strong, 119

hut: a small, roughly-made shelter, 119

icicle: a pointed, hanging stick of ice formed from dripping water, 121

igloo: an Eskimo's small, rounded house made of blocks of hard snow, 121

ignore: to pay no attention to, 122

illiterate: unable to read or write, 122

illusion: something that seems to be real but is not, 122

illustrate: to make clear or explain, 123

image: a picture or other likeness of a person or thing, 123

imaginary: existing only in the mind, 123

imagination: the act or power of forming pictures in the mind, especially of things that aren't present, 124

impress: to have a strong effect on someone's thoughts or feelings, 124

improvement: a change for the better, 124

inch: to move very slowly, 125

incline: a surface that slopes or slants, 125

increase: to grow in size, 125

incredible: unbelievable or astonishing, 126

indefinite: not clear or exact, vague, 126

indicate: to be a sign of, 126

individual: separate or single, 127

industry: any large-scale business, especially manufacturing, 127

influence: the power to produce an effect on others without using force or a command, 127

information: facts, 128

ingenious: clever, imaginative, and original, 128

inhabit: to live in or on, 128

inject: to put a liquid inside or into something by using a needle, 129

injury: harm or damage done to a person or thing, 129

inscription: words carved or written on something, 129

inspiration: a sudden flow of good ideas, 130

instruct: to teach, 130

instrument: a tool or mechanical device, 130

insulate: to keep from becoming too hot or too cold, 131

intelligence: the ability to think, learn, and understand, 131

intelligent: smart, 131

intense: very great or strong, extreme, 132

interior: the inside, 132

international: between or among different nations, 132

inventor: a person who thinks up new devices and machines, 133

investigate: to look into carefully in order to find the facts, 133

isolate: to separate or set apart from a group, 133

issue: a published magazine that is part of a series, 134; to come out, 134

jester: a person who told jokes to amuse the king or queen, 135

jewelry: decorations for the body; rings, bracelets, and necklaces, 135

jockey: a person who rides horses in races, 136

kangaroo: an animal of Australia with small front legs and large, powerful back legs for jumping, 136

kneel: to go down on one or both knees, 136

knowledge: information gained by study or experience, 137

knuckle: a place on a finger where two bones are joined, 137

label: a piece of paper or cloth that can be stuck or sewn to an object to tell something about it (n), 139; to mark an object to tell something about it (v), 139

labor: work, 140

lagoon: a small, shallow body of water usually connected to a larger body of water, 140

landmark: something which marks an historical place or event, 140

lantern: a lamp with a cover to protect the light from wind and rain, 141

laughter: sounds people make when they are happy or amused, 141

launch: to start, 141

lava: the burning melted rock that flows from a volcano, 142

lean: to stand at a slant instead of straight, 142; without fat (adj), 142

leash: a strap or chain fastened to a dog or other animal to keep it from straying, 143

legend: a story that may or may not be true that is passed down through the years, 143

legendary: not real, 143

leisure: time to rest or to do things you like, 144

leopard: a large wild cat covered with black spots that lives in Africa and Asia, 144

level: an instrument for showing whether a surface is horizontal (n), 145; having the same height everywhere, 145; height, 144; to scrape to the same height, 145

lifetime: the period of time that a person or thing is alive, 146

limit: the point or line where something ends, 146

lizard: an animal with a long body and tail, four legs, and scaly skin, 146

location: the place where something is, 147

loneliness: being alone and wanting to be with others, 147

loom: a frame or machine for weaving cloth (n), 147; to appear dimly or vaguely as a large, threatening shape (v), 148

lumber: to move along heavily (v), 148; wood that has been cut into boards (n), 148

lunge: to move forward suddenly, 149

lurch: a sudden rolling or swaying movement, 149

machinery: machines, 151

magnet: a piece of iron that draws other iron objects toward it, 151

maintain: to keep in good condition or repair, 152

majestic: grand or noble-looking, 152

major: largest, most important, 152

mammal: warm-blooded animal that has hair or fur—female mammals have glands that produce milk, 153

mammoth: an extinct large elephant with hairy skin and long curved tusks (n), 153; huge (adj), 153

maneuver: to move or manipulate skillfully, 154

manipulate: to handle or operate, 154

manufacture: to make things, especially by machine and in large numbers, 154

marvel: to feel wonder and astonishment, 155

massive: huge, 155

mast: a long pole that holds a ship's sails, 155

master: expert, 156

material: what a thing is made from or used for, 156

mature: having reached full growth or development, 156

melody: a series of musical notes that make up a tune, 157

merchandise: goods sold in stores, 157

mermaid: an imaginary woman with the tail of a fish who lives in the ocean, 157

mesh: an open space in a net, sieve, or screen, 158

meter: the basic unit of length in the metric system of measurement (a meter is just over 39 inches, 158

method: the way of doing something, 158

metric: a system of measurement based on the meter and the gram, 159

microphone: an instrument that turns sound into electrical signals and makes the sound louder, 159

midnight: twelve o'clock at night—the end of one day and the start of the next, 159

migration: a movement from one place to settle in another, 160

mineral: a material or substance that is dug out of the earth, 160

miniature: a very small copy or model, 160

mirror: a flat, silver-backed glass in which you can see yourself, 161

mitten: a covering for the hand, 161

mob: a crowd, especially one that is lawless and disorderly, 161

moist: slightly wet, damp, 162

moisture: a slight wetness, dampness, 162

mold: a furry fungus that grows on food and damp surfaces, 162; to make into a special shape (v), 163

molten: melted by heat, 163

monitor: a person with special duties, 163; to check or keep watch over (v), 164

moonlit: lighted by the moon, 164

mortal: unable to live forever, subject to death, 164

mosquito: a thin buzzing insect that leaves itchy bites, 165

motion: movement, 165; to signal or direct by making a gesture (v), 165

mountaintop: the top of a mountain, 166

mulch: leaves or straw spread on flowerbeds to help plants grow, 166

mummy: a body that is preserved after death by a special process the Egyptians used, which included the wrapping of the body with cloth, 166

muscle: the tissue in the bodies of people and animals that can be tightened or loosened to make the body move, 167

musical: a play or motion picture with songs, choruses, and dances (n), 167; able to make music, 167

nation: a country, 169

navigate: to sail, steer, or direct a ship or plane, 169

needle: a small, slender piece of steel used for sewing, 170

nerve: a bundle of fibers that carries signals between the brain and spine and other parts of the body, 170

network: an interconnected system of lines or wires, 170

nightfall: dusk, the time when night comes, 171

nomad: a person who belongs to a group of people who have no permanent home, but move from place to place, 171

nook: a cozy little corner, 171

normal: standard or usual, 172

numerous: many, 172

oar: a long paddle used to row a boat, 173

observe: to see, notice, watch, 173

obstacle: something that stands in the way or stops progress, 174

octopus: a sea animal with a soft body and eight long arms called tentacles., 174

opinion: a belief based upon what a person thinks or believes rather than what is proved or known to be true, 174

opponent: a person who is against another in a fight, contest, or discussion, 175

orbit: the path that a planet or other heavenly body follows as it moves in a circle around another heavenly body, 175

orchard: a piece of land on which many fruit trees are grown, 175

orchestra: a large group of musicians playing music together on various instruments, 176

ordeal: an experience that is painful or difficult, 176

organization: a group of people working together for a specific purpose, as in an agency, club, or business, 176

organize: to arrange or put together in an orderly way, 177

origin: beginning or starting point, 177

ostrich: a very large bird with a long neck, long legs, and tiny wings, 177

outgrow: to grow too large for, 178

outrun: to run faster or farther than, 178

outstanding: better than others, 178

overcome: to beat or conquer, 179

overflow: to fill up and run over, 179

overtake: to catch up with or pass, 179

painstaking: very careful or requiring great care, 181

paralyze: to lose or to take away the ability to move or feel in a part of the body, 181

partner: a person who joins another in a business, project, marriage, or dance, 182

patent: a government paper which gives a person or company the right to be the only one to make, use, or sell a new invention for a certain number of years, 182

pedal: a control you push with your foot to make a machine work, 182

performer: a person who entertains the public, 183

permit: to allow, 183

persist: to refuse to stop or give up, 183

personality: all of a person's individual characteristics and habits, 184

physical: having to do with the body or matter, 184

pirate: a person who robs ships at sea, 184

pitch: the lowness or highness of a sound in music, 185; to throw, 185

pivot: to turn quickly with few or no steps, 185

plateau: a high, flat piece of land, 186

pleasure: a feeling of enjoyment or happiness or something that gives enjoyment or happiness, 186

plenty: more than enough, 186

poison: a drug or other substance that harms or kills by chemical action, 187

pomp: splendid or showy display, 187

ponder: to think about carefully or deeply, 187

popular: liked or accepted by many people, 188

portable: capable of being easily carried, 188

positive: certain, 188

possible: capable of being done or happening, 189

poster: a large printed sign that often has a picture and can be put up on a wall, 189

precise: exact, perfectly accurate, 189

predicament: an unpleasant, difficult, or bad situation, 190

prediction: something a person claims will happen in the future, 190

prejudice: hatred or unfair treatment of a particular group, 190

prepare: to make, 191

preserve: to save or protect, 191

prevailing: in general use, common, 191

prey: an animal which another animal kills and eats (n), 192; to hunt and kill for food, 192

procedure: a way of doing something, usually by a series of steps, 192

process: a number of actions done in a certain order, 193

proclaim: to declare publicly and officially, 193

produce: to make or create something, 193

professional: trained to do a special job for pay, 194

progressive: moving forward in steps, 194

protrude: to stick or bulge out, 194

purify: to cleanse or filter, 195

pursuit: the act of following in order to catch up to or capture, 195

pyramid: an object with four triangular sides that meet in a point at the top, 195

qualify: to earn or win acceptance, 197

quality: a particular characteristic, 197

quarter: one of four equal parts, 198

rack: a wood or metal frame used for holding things, 199

raft: a kind of flat boat made by fastening logs or boards together, 199

raging: acting in a rough or angry way, 200

rainstorm: a storm with a lot of rain, 200

ramble: to talk or write too much about too many things, 200

rapids: fast-moving waters in a river, 201

raw: not cooked, 201

recede: to pull back or withdraw, 201

recognition: notice, 202

recommend: to advise or suggest, 202

recover: to get back, 202

reel: to be unable to walk straight, 203

reflect: to throw back light or heat, 203

refuge: a place that is safe from danger, 203

refuse: to say no to, 204

regain: to get back, 204

rehearse: to practice over and over, 204

reluctant: not wanting to do something, unwilling, 205

remote: far away in space or time, 205
renowned: very famous, 205
represent: to stand for, 206
research: studies to find out facts, 206
reservoir: a place where water is stored, 206
resolution: decision to do something, 207
resource: a supply of something useful, 207
respond: to react to something said or done, 207
restrain: to hold back, 208
retort: to answer sharply, 208
reveal: to show or display, 208
review: to study, 209
ridicule: to make fun of, 209
ridiculous: too silly or false to be believed, 209
rigorous: hard, difficult, 210
rim: the top edge, 210
ripple: a very small wave, 210
risk: the chance of danger or harm, 211
robot: a machine that can do simple kinds of human work, 211
robust: healthy and strong, 211
rodent: a type of mammal that gnaws with large front teeth—rats and mice are common rodents, 212
rotate: to turn in a circle, 212
routine: a set of movements done over and over in the same way, 212
rubber: a strong, elastic, waterproof substance that comes from the milky liquid in certain tropical trees and is used to make tires, balls, etc., 213
rudder: a flat piece of wood or metal fastened to the back end of a boat or airplane for steering, 213
rug: a floor covering made of wool or some other thick, heavy fabric—a carpet, 213
rugged: rough, uneven, 214
ruler: a straight strip of wood, plastic, or metal that is marked off in inches and used for measuring, 214
sacrifice: to give up for the sake of something or someone else, 215
saddle: a padded leather seat that the rider of a horse sits on, 215
sapling: a small young tree, 216
sash: a wide piece of cloth that is worn around the waist or over one shoulder, 216
satellite: a man-made object sent into space by rocket, 216
scarce: hard to find, 217
scissors: a tool made of two blades joined so that they can cut paper or cloth, 217
scoop: a small or large tool like a shovel used for digging or lifting, 217
scrape: to scratch or rub in a rough way, 218
sculptor: an artist who creates figures from stone, wood, clay, or other materials, 218
scuttle: to move with quick, short steps, 218
sensation: the experience of seeing, hearing, smelling, tasting, or touching, 219
sequence: an arrangement in which one thing follows another in a particular order, 219
serpent: a large snake, 219
session: a single period of time for learning and practice, 220
shanty: a roughly-built, run-down shack, 220
shin: the front part of the leg between the knee and the ankle, 220
shoreline: the place where shore and water meet, 221
shortcut: a way that is quicker or shorter, 221
shriek: to scream or make a loud shrill sound, 221
sift: to pass through a sieve, 222
significant: important, notable, large, 222
silhouette: an outline drawing filled in with black or another solid color, 222
silt: fine particles of sand, clay, dirt, and other material carried by flowing water, 223
simple: easy to understand or do, 223
situation: circumstance, 223
skeleton: the framework of bones that supports and gives shape to an animal's body, 224
skim: to remove something that floats on the surface of a liquid, 224
skin: the outer covering of a human or animal body, 224
skull: the bony framework of the head, 225

skyline: an outline, especially of buildings, against the sky, 225

skyscraper: a very tall city building , 225

slogan: a word or group of words that is easy to remember and is used to get people to pay attention, 226

slope: to go up or down at an angle or slant, 226

slosh: to move clumsily through mud or water, 226

slot: a narrow, straight opening, usually metal, 227

slush: partly melted snow or ice, 227

smock: a long, loose shirt worn to protect clothes, 227

smother: to kill or die by stopping breathing, 228

snarl: to growl, 228

soak: to keep in water or other liquid for a long time, 228

solar: operated by the sun's energy, 229

solitary: single or isolated, 229

soul: the spiritual part of a human being—the deepest source of thought, feeling, and action, 229

souvenir: something given or kept to remember something by—keepsake, memento, 230

spacecraft: rocket or other vehicle used for flying in outer space, 230

spar: to box, especially using light blows, 230

sparkle: to shine by giving off flashes of light, 231

specialize: to concentrate on a special thing or area, 231

species: a group of plants or animals that have certain common features, 231

spectacle: an impressive sight, 232

spectacular: very impressive, 232

spectator: a person who watches something, 232

spike: a very large nail, 233

spiritual: religious, having to do with the spirit or soul, 233

sponsor: to pay for or to support, 233

squall: a sudden, strong windstorm that often brings rain or snow, 234

stadium: an enclosed area used for sporting and other events, 234

stake: a sharp stick or post, 234

stare: to look at something for a long time without moving your eyes, 235

stilts: a pair of long poles you can stand on to walk above the ground, 235

stool: a chair that has no back, 235

storage: a space for keeping things until they are needed, 236

store: to save something for later use, 236

strenuous: requiring great effort, 236

stubble: a short, rough growth, 237

studio: a place where movies or radio and T.V. programs are filmed, broadcast, or recorded, 237

submarine: a boat (usually military) that travels underwater, 237

subterranean: underground, 238

successful: having reached a goal, 238

summit: the top, 238

sunrise: when the sun rises in the morning, 239

sunset: when the sun goes down in the evening, 239

superb: excellent, 239

supplies: things that are needed, 240

supply: to provide needed things, 240

support: to hold up, 240

supreme: highest, 241

surface: the outside of something, 241

surname: a last name or family name, 241

suspend: to hang or be hung from something fastened above, 242

sustain: to keep up or keep going, 242

swell: an unbroken wave (n), 242; to grow or cause to grow in size (v), 243

sympathy: the sharing and understanding of another person's feelings, 243

tackle: fishing gear, 245; to grab someone and throw him to the ground, 245

talent: a natural ability or skill, 246

tassel: a hanging bunch of threads tied together at one end, 246

technician: a person having detailed knowledge of a certain job, especially someone skilled at using special machinery, 246

technique: a way to do something, 247

technology: the use of science in industry or business, 247

tedious: long and tiring, boring, 247

tempest: a violent storm with high winds, 248

temporary: not long-lasting, 248

terrain: a certain area of land, especially its physical appearance, 248

terrify: to be very scared or to scare greatly, 249

theme: the main idea, 249

thrash: to give a beating to, 249

thread: a very thin cord used for sewing, 250

threat: a sign of danger, 250

tighten: to make tighter or become tighter, 250

tomb: a grave for the dead, 251

tower: a building or part of a building that is very tall and narrow, 251

trade: to exchange one thing for another (v), 252; work that calls for skill, usually with your hands (n), 251

transform: to change or be changed in shape or nature, 252

treacherous: dangerous or untrustworthy, 252

treasury: the government department in charge of money, 253

tremble: to shake, 253

trench: a long, deep ditch, 253

triangle: a flat shape with three sides that all touch one another, 254

tribe: a group of people who live together and follow the same customs, 254

tribute: forced payment, tax, 254

triumphant: victorious, successful, 255

twilight: the time between sunset and darkness, 255

understand: to get the meaning of, 257

unexpected: not expected, surprising, 257

unity: the state of being a whole, 258

upward: toward a higher place, 258

urge: a strong desire (n), 258; to try to persuade, 259

utensil: a useful tool or container, 259

vague: not clear or definite, 261

variety: many different kinds, 261

vast: very great in size, 262

vault: a room for keeping valuable things safe, 262; to jump in the air or over something, especially by using your hands or a pole to lift yourself up (v), 262

veer: to change direction sharply, 263

version: an account or description given from a particular point of view, 263

vertical: straight up and down, 263

victim: a person or animal that is harmed or killed, 264

victory: success, 264

villain: a wicked or evil person, 264

visible: able to be seen, 265

visor: an eyeshade, 265

visual: having to do with seeing, 265

vitality: energy, 266

vivid: very bright and colorful, 266

volume: amount that something holds, 266

waist: the part of the body between the chest and the hips, 267

wallet: a thin, flat case used for carrying money and small cards, 267

walrus: a large seal-like animal that lives in the cold waters of the North, 268

warning: sign or notice of approaching danger, 268

weary: very tired, 268

welfare: well-being (health and happiness), 269

whale: a large, air-breathing sea animal shaped like a fish, 269

whirlpool: water that is moving rapidly in a circle, 269

wield: to use skillfully, 270

wilderness: a wild place, 270

wizard: a person who can do magic, 270

worship: to pray to, 271

wreck: what is left of something broken or destroyed, 271

Bibliography

Bell, Nanci. <u>Visualizing and Verbalizing For Language Comprehension and Thinking</u>. Paso Robles, California: Academy of Reading Publications, 1991.

Briggs, John. <u>Fire in the Crucible, The Alchemy of Creative Genius</u>. New York: St. Martin's Press, 1988.

Fry, Edward B. <u>Vocabulary Drills</u>. Providence, Rhode Island: Jamestown Publishers, 1989.

<u>MacMillan Dictionary for Children</u>. New York: MacMillan Publishing Company, 1989.

<u>MacMillan First Dictionary</u>. New York: MacMillan Publishing Company, 1990.

Paivio, Allan. <u>Mental representations: A Dual Coding Approach</u>. New York: Oxford University Press, 1986.

Shostak, Jerome, and Alfred E. Chant. <u>Vocabulary Workshop</u>. New York: Sadlier-Oxford, 1980.

<u>The American Heritage School Dictionary</u>. Boston: Houghton Mifflin, 1977.

<u>Thorndike-Barnhart Children's Dictionary</u>. Glenview, Illinois: Scott, Foresman and Company, 1988.

Ulich, Robert. <u>Three Thousand Years of Educational Wisdom: Selections from Great Documents.</u> "Dewey." Cambridge: Harvard University Press, 1961

<u>Vocabulary Connections</u>. Austin, Texas: Steck-Vaughn Company.

<u>Vocabulary Development</u>. Evanston, Illinois: McDougal, Littell & Company.